The Art of

Unknowing

Among the three extensions, we must
include time, space, and silence.
Space is in time, silence is in space.
—Joseph Joubert, 1798

The Art of Unknowing

Dimensions of Openness in Analytic Therapy

Stephen Kurtz, C.S.W.

Jason Aronson Inc.
Northvale, New Jersey
London

Jacket photomontage: *Raleigh* (1983) by Mary J. Solimena. Reproduced by permission of the artist.

Library of Congress Cataloging-in-Publication Data

Kurtz, Stephen.
    The art of unknowing: Dimensions of openness in analytic therapy
    /Stephen Kurtz.
        p.   cm.
    Includes index.
    ISBN 0-87668-860-1
    1. Psychoanalysis. 2. Psychotherapy.   I. Title.
    [DNLM: 1. Psychoanalysis—methods.   2. Psychoanalytic Therapy—
methods.   WM 460.6 K96a]
RC504.K87   1989
616.89'17—dc19
DNLM/DLC
for Library of Congress   88-39471
                                                              CIP

Manufactured in the United States of America. Jason Aronson Inc. offers books and cassettes. For information and catalog write to Jason Aronson Inc., 230 Livingston Street, Northvale, New Jersey 07647.

To Mary and Tony

The author gratefully acknowledges the following sources for permission to reprint from their publications:

Excerpt from THE SEPARATE NOTEBOOKS copyright © 1984 Czeslaw Milosz. First published by The Ecco Press in 1984. Reprinted by permission.

Excerpts from "East Coker," "Burnt Norton," and "The Dry Salvages" in *Four Quartets*, copyright 1943 by T. S. Eliot, renewed 1971 by Esme Valerie Eliot, reprinted by permission of Harcourt Brace Jovanovich, Inc.

Excerpt from *The Family Reunion*, copyright 1939 by T. S. Eliot, renewed 1967 by Esme Valerie Eliot, reprinted by permission of Harcourt Brace Jovanovich, Inc.

Excerpts from "The Waste Land," "Gerontion," and "The Love Song of J. Alfred Prufrock" in *Collected Poems 1909-1962* by T. S. Eliot, copyright 1936 by Harcourt Brace Jovanovich, Inc., copyright © 1963, 1964 by T. S. Eliot, reprinted by permission of the publisher.

Excerpt from *The Cocktail Party*, copyright 1950 by T. S. Eliot, renewed 1978 by Esme Valerie Eliot, reprinted by permission of Harcourt Brace Jovanovich, Inc.

"On Silence" by Stephen Kurtz, copyright 1984, *The Psychoanalytic Review*. Reprinted by permission of The Guilford Press.

"The Analyst's Space" by Stephen Kurtz, copyright 1986, *The Psychoanalytic Review*. Reprinted by permission of The Guilford Press.

"In the Analytic Theater" by Stephen Kurtz, copyright 1986, published by Free Association Books. Reprinted by permission of the publisher.

"The Psychoanalysis of Time," by Stephen Kurtz. Copyright 1988, *Journal of the American Psychoanalytic Association* 36(4):985–1004. Reprinted by permission of International Universities Press.

Portions of "LOVE MINUS ZERO/NO LIMIT" by Bob Dylan, copyright © 1965 WARNER BROS. INC. All rights reserved. Used by permission.

"Silence" Parts I & II, by Stephen Kurtz. Copyright 1984, *Commonweal* CXI(5): 137–141. Reprinted by permission of the Commonweal Foundation.

Contents

Acknowledgments

Since only an arbitrary line divides the writing of this book from the years of living that preceded it, I am tempted to thank everyone who has ever sustained me. Since some limits must be found, however, I shall begin by thanking my wife, Mary, and my son, Tony, without whose presence, like the sun, my world would be dark and impossible. And equally my patients who so courageously opened their hearts and touched my own in the deepest ways.

When it comes to thanking friends and colleagues, I must single out Steven Day, a master clinician whose large and cultivated spirit so often bears mine with it. Among others, the banality of a list can hardly do justice to the uniqueness of each person's gift to me. I hope my gratitude is evident in more intimate ways. My appreciation and affection go to Fred Arensberg, Jean-Louis Bourgeois, Nahoma Clinton, Mike and Liz Dibb, Emery Gross, Chris Jaenicke, Stan Leavy, Ned O'Gorman, Pamela Oline, Tamar Opler, Carollee Pelos, Art Robbins, and Alan Stein.

I want especially to thank the Association for Psychoanalytic Self Psychology, which, through its conference and works-in-progress programs, gave me the opportunity to present several chapters in earlier versions and to benefit from its members' thoughtful commentaries. I was greatly helped too by the library of the Postgraduate Center for Mental Health—a unique institution for allowing nonmembers to join with full borrowing privileges. Without this arrangement, research would be nearly impossible for a working analyst.

Finally, I want to remember with affection the typist of most of the original manuscript, Gerald Barrett, a man of great kindness, patience and erudition, who died suddenly just before the work could be completed.

* * * *

Several chapters have been drawn, with slight alterations, from earlier papers, and I wish to acknowledge and thank my publishers:

(1984). Silence. *Commonweal* 111:137–141.

(1984). On silence. *Psychoanalytic Review* 71:227–245.

(1986). The analyst's space. *Psychoanalytic Review* 73: 41–55.

(1986). In the analytic theatre. *Free Associations* 6: 100–122.

(1988). The psychoanalysis of time. *Journal of the American Psychoanalytic Association* 36:985–1004.

PROLOGUE

1

The Languages of Analytic Therapy

The talking cure, as its name implies, began with the spoken word. And with each new relationship, indeed with each new session, it begins that way again. From the analyst's side, it is a word spoken with the intention of cure. His interpretations, constructions, interventions of all sorts are meant to make sense of the unconscious — carrying the unruly It into the realm of I. The patient's language, by contrast, has no such intention. To the extent that he follows the fundamental rule, he will speak a language closer to the unconscious—a language that, in conventional terms, does not make sense.

Two profoundly different speech-acts thus echo through the room, and a focal problem, as it has traditionally been framed, consists in relating the one to the other.

I want to redefine that problem. The analyst's task, though grounded in language, goes far beyond the need to comprehend. It is closer to that of the good mother who, in attuning herself to her developing child, manifests her love.

Against his conscious intention, an ego-centered notion of the analyst's work erects a barrier to cure. The compulsion to make sense will only hold attunement back, leaving the patient misunderstood, isolated, and unloved.

I have said "compulsion" rather than the more neutral "effort" since I believe that more than mere misguidedness is at work. To experience the patient's words openly, without passing them through a preformed cognitive screen, can occasion great anxiety. The defenses erected against this anxiety have found institutional expression in analytic theory and practice. In so doing, they are instances of a greater fear of unknowing that pervades the Western mind.

The languages of analysis fit themselves into two principal expressive categories—the spoken ones of therapy and the written ones of texts. In either mode, if the analyst's efforts are alive, he sets off into the jungle with only the sketchiest of maps: rumors of a lost city to the north, of a tribe at a bend in the river, or the plume of an unnamed bird. He must devise some structure to make the venture work, but his route and destination are unknown. When the work is dead, by contrast, the analyst's route is clear. Others have blazed these paths and their authority lights his way. No Cibola lies at the end, no bird without a name. He moves in labored steps from known to known.

When excitement or terror are expunged, all that remains is the minor pleasure of fixing "Q.E.D." after the proof.

Q.E.D., the old-fashioned sign that a Euclidean theorem has been solved, is not quite the right metaphor. The model for analytic practice has never been mathematical, after all; it is scientific. Although the status of psychoanalysis as science is very doubtful, belief in that model has produced a certain style of presentation, both in the consulting room and on the printed page. *Le style c'est l'homme même*," said Buffon. The style is the man himself. Yet the scientific style, with its ideolectic language and stance of objectivity, is held to be a nonstyle—an invisible cloak that helps escape Buffon's rule. But nothing does. Someone who strikes a scientific pose is rather like a child peeking through the fingers of his hand and saying "You can't see me." We humor the child through love, but ourselves through blindness or complicity.

Freud, no less captivated by science than his contemporaries, nevertheless wrote as an artist. Indeed, he was awarded the Goethe Prize in 1930 for the literary, rather than the scientific, merits of his work. If we attempt to isolate ideas from their manner of expression, style becomes trivialized as adornment— an effeminate refinement to be scorned by tougher minds. But we cannot make that separation. Joseph Joubert, expanding on Buffon's axiom, said, "*Le style est la pensée même.*" The style is the thought itself. It is a thought worth thinking about.

Because style cannot be translated, Freud's art is lost for those who have no German. In the original language, the weight of the thought and the quality of its expression are clearly inseparable. *Truth, after all, has an aesthetic dimension.*

"Beauty is truth, truth beauty"—Keats's famous line—can easily be dismissed as rapture. I want to take it seriously. Let me begin by distinguishing between those truths that affect us intimately and those that are merely true: not an academic distinction but a well-established one of ordinary life. It is the difference, for example, between knowledge of the human life-span drawn from insurance charts and the sudden awareness of mortality that can knife us in middle age. Or, in another sphere, it is the distinction between Pascal's wager and Paul's conversion. Most relevantly, it is the distinction between the truths achieved in analysis and those achieved in the laboratory. It was on the basis of this implied distinction, I believe, that Freud dismissed the findings of academic psychology even when they confirmed his own.

For the most part, the truths achieved through psychoanalysis will fail to meet scientific criteria. There are many reasons for this but, at very least, each pairing of analyst and patient is so unique, repeatability is impossible. But there is another, more profound reason: *these truths are too important*. There is a link here, because the very uniqueness that makes repeatability impossible is the one required for cure. In an age spellbound by science, we are accustomed to thinking of its discoveries, together with the necessary truths of logic, as the only ones that count. I want to assert the contrary: the generalizing truths of science are trivial; poetry is the only source of important truth. Poetry, the language of the particular. If, therefore, psychoanalysis has value, it is not for employing a scientific method but for being *inspired*.

Properly understood, the complementary rules regarding free association and evenly hovering attention are meant to promote inspiration, rather as a spiritual practice is meant to promote enlightenment. But the openness these practices imply is undone by knowledge. Knowledge screens the sounds the third ear hears, so we hear only what we know. *The analytic method—like the poetic one—proceeds through unknowing.*

The method is no different in writing. The rectangle of the

page becomes a frame for the free play of unknowing. "The page," here, stands for a bare scaffolding of chapters and paragraphs and also of subject matter that enable the play to proceed. These props parallel those of the analytic situation: the consulting room's couch and chairs, the time frame of the hour. If, as Donald Winnicott said, "Psychoanalysis has to do with two people playing together," what matters most is that the protagonists become absorbed in it—that the spirit of play prevails.

The spirit of play also animates art—an end in itself. But analysis and its literature have other ends in mind. How can we accomplish their purposes and transmit the content of our discoveries without recourse to a reasonable language?

In the sphere of its own literature, then, psychoanalysis presents a split. We are convinced that significant communication occurs only through rational discourse, yet that we achieve psychoanalytic knowledge only through immersion in the quite different discourse of free association—one that, in conventional terms, does not make sense.

The source of the conviction that only rational discourse can communicate psychoanalytic knowledge is, quite simply, a resistance.

It is not essentially different from the patient's resistance to free association or the analyst's to evenly hovering attention. *The compulsion to make sense is a resistance to unknowing*.

This resistance is strong in the history of Western culture, and increasingly so since the Enlightenment. Therefore, it enters the programmatic heart of psychoanalysis and lies there unexamined.

How can we overcome it?

I first faced this question, although in a relatively halting way, when treating the patient called Lydia whose case is discussed in Chapter 7, "Lost in Time." Lydia believed she'd lived for at least 500 years, and her conversation ranged freely through that enormous timespan, often using the languages of the places she'd occupied. Although even an extraordinarily long life can be reconstructed in principle, in Lydia's case, time's arrow split into multiple parts, taking flight in every direction. Memories were mixed with false memories, clairvoyant experiences, hallucinations, and inventions as if to make the very notion of biography absurd. And, indeed, Lydia declined to have her life figured out. As she put it, "God does not want to be understood; God wants to be loved." The profoundly derationalizing effects that experience had on me made the formulation of principles seem impossible. But then my apprenticeship to a second patient, whom I shall call A.N., reopened the question of a possible psychoanalytic discourse in a somewhat clearer way.

From the beginning the circumstances of treatment were highly irregular. A.N., a poet, came to see me only weeks before he was to begin a year's residence at San Isidro, an artists' retreat in the West. This unique and idyllic compound offered perfect privacy, mitigated by a common evening meal with the other artists gathered there—all of them immensely distinguished. The honor of an election had been too great to refuse, yet A.N. looked forward to going with dread.

There was no question of referring him to anyone else. San Isidro was nearly three hours' drive from any major city, and the quasi-monastic rules of the place forbade all but the briefest excursions. In any event, A.N. would not be referred: he had made his choice, and I was it. We proceeded, then, almost entirely by correspondence, punctuated only a few times by sessions on the phone. What follows is a brief extract from that correspondence, beginning with his sixty-seventh letter. I have eliminated only identifying information and left the inevitable ellipses of inkblots, coffee spills, and unintelligible words undisturbed.

July 17

Dear K—

No doubt, feeding on the stars of yesterday's half-digested interlude, you will want to spit the refuse into the hedgerows, alive now with roses and small birds. Never mind. They'll root anywhere, even in the marshes outside R_____ where the little blue marquise lost her . . . I want to ask, "Did she get it back?" With the loaves and the fishes you'll say. The dew glistened in her pubic hair like diamonds. Perhaps they were diamonds; that was the year for them. But this poor child would never set a fashion. If I loved her . . . after all, it's easy to love the dead. They caught him before long, or thought they did. The nuns of the Augustines were called—famous needlewomen. They threaded it through, passing the silk back and forth, back and forth. Oh how he screamed! One of them mopped his brow and their choir sang those beautiful *ténébreuses*. Do you know them? the ones based on Hebrew melodies? When they'd finished they chained him to a pillar and the court took their places. You can imagine the squabbles over precedence (one of the best bits in Saint-Simon). The horses were attached, M. Rameau raised his bow and . . . But that tiny orchestra couldn't possibly drown him out. The blood flowed, glasses were raised. In the lime-tree allées and the boxwood mazes the lovers found their way. The king himself, it is said, fathered two sons that afternoon.

I have no sons. Don't give me clichés about books and babies. Between the *robe* and the *épée* there's no real choice. Someone like La Rochefoucauld could afford to write. I can *only* write.

Otis on the gramophone all morning. "I've been lovin' yooou" (come on, Kurtz, sing along) "too-oo-oo lo-ong, to stop no-ow." Finally, "I love ya, baby, I'm down on my knees. Please don' make me stop. I love ya, I love ya." See how hard it is? What courage to sing that way! His whole being's in that song, abject and raw. And the way he draws out the words, like Monteverdi's "kingdom, kingdom . . . *non erit fi-ii-ii—iiinis.*" It's visceral knowledge of God; true knowledge. Or should we measure the decibels that give rise to that thrill, that make the nipples erect and the scrotum contract? Shove an electrode up your brain and to hell with the music. Everyone knows Freud had a tin ear, Kurtz, so if you even whisper "castration anxiety" I'll have yours stuffed and mounted like a moosehead.

Watch out, Kurtz. I'm a raptor flying on a column of air thin as cocaine.

                                                                    July 22
Dear A.N.—

Perhaps you know the last words of Marie Antoinette to her executioner? She said, "Forgive me, Sir," passing him on the stair, "Forgive me, I did not mean to do it." What could she have meant? Mean to do what? These words have always seemed to me mysterious, poignant, childish and, at the same time, majestic. Was she apologizing for the excesses of her reign? for her pug dog's mess? her ruthlessness? her styleless clothes? All this seemed a perfect cameo of the old world ending—perfect because ungraspable.

This morning I learned it was because she'd stepped accidentally on his foot! So, merely an "excuse me"; a conventional reflex. Isn't it a paradox that, just as a statement becomes explicit enough to acquire meaning, it becomes meaningless?

The mail arrived and I read your letter of the 17th. I read it several times through lunch and then had my usual nap. Of my first dreams, I have only a few fragments: first, a shimmer of blue, detached from any object; then the name of Lally-Tallendal, which has certain associations we've discussed; and finally this line from Borges, "*No volverá tu voz a lo que el persa dijo en su lengua de aves y de rosas . . .*" You will never recapture what the Persian said in his language of birds and roses. Afterwards I had the dream that follows, recorded more or less complete:

I have sliced through a layer of my penis with a razor so that two thick flaps of penis-shaped flesh hang down on either side . . . like banana skins. Although the operation was painless, even satisfying, I had not foreseen this consequence, this appearance. It so disturbs me that I cut off the flaps with scissors. This part, unlike the first, is indeed painful, or at least full of anxiety. Without losing this image or this feeling I move off to a great height so that, superimposed on it—this raw, erect penis—is a web of engraved lines, like an old bird's-eye view of a city. Paris, radiating from the Étoile.

July 27

Dear K—

I knew you wouldn't let me down. I'm staring down at my cock, bristling with black stitches and dried blood like a Bakongo fetish. It throbs like a heart. Forgive my handwriting but the pain is . . . I've no intention of killing it. At a certain point it becomes clear one can't solve the mind-body problem through thought experiments alone. We live simultaneously on two planes, searching for the point where they both can be said to meet. And now, here it is: my cock-in-pain, bound like a Coptic mummy inscribed with magic signs. The very point of entry into that OTHER WORLD. The hole opens wider, wider. Deep within, "The flower opens under a branch of the plum tree;" as Ikkyu says, "Delicately the narcissus revolves between thighs." "Narcissus" doesn't mean the same to the Japs, Kurtz. For them it's a kind of sexual superconductor.

Come enter that slit with me, traveling at a speed beyond any constant of the universe. Let us go and make our visit.

Here the past is an atmosphere, thicker or thinner according to unknowable laws and producing out of itself images of its time—just as matter, in some sense, manifests its space. In a corridor of dull gold and Venetian glass, two dancers out of Lancret, whirling . . . "Oh the dauncing, the dauncing . . ." the opening of Bach's third two-part invention. The precise four notes with which we shall be called from our graves. See them rising, rising, hands joining in that eternal corridor: Voltaire, pinch-faced and *méchant*, heroic Lally-Tallendal, the little diamond-decked marquise, you and me. Winding *en filade* through that infinite palace. There Landowska plays for Tolstoy, her harpsichord mounted on a sleigh, pulled through the snows towards Yasnaya Polyana. Two stone lovers leap across their path as lightly as gazelles. On her way to the sea, Queen Anne confronts a phallic menhir. Turning, she sees two children on the beach. Oh, the little boy is crying. She comforts him, reading to him from a big book. All of this reflected and re-reflected in the worn mirrors of the corridor to an infinite regression. And at its farthest point, forever receding yet supernaturally light, the Face, appearing white on black like an icon of the vernicle.

Oh shit, here comes that sculptress of the alabaster yonis. No doubt she's keen to have a look. Do you think she'll want to do me in chicken livers? Or, perhaps, in impermeable haliborite?

* * * *

The letter ends arbitrarily with this interruption. Even if A.N. had resumed, I believe the gap would warrant calling it a new beginning. But it ends not just arbitrarily but also incomprehensibly; the word "haliborite" does not appear in any dictionary.

What are we to make of this correspondence? If we define an analysis by the rules that frame it, this fragment clearly cannot qualify. The protagonists do not share a room for a set period of time, the analyst in his chair, the patient on the couch. Almost the entire relationship has been transposed to paper. Yet I am less concerned to establish that this was an analysis than to say what its salient features are.

Chief among them is the absence of interpretation. I had already learned from Lydia how alienating the effort to know can be and, therefore, how unproductive. So, when similar results began to appear in my work with A.N., I was more readily prepared to change course. As soon as I stopped trying to decode him and instead responded in kind, A.N. moved toward increasing openness and freedom of expression. The first necessity of the analytic relationship, after all, is the establishment of a bond. Not a "working alliance," which, after all, is a mere ego connection that can be forged between two even quite unsympathetic people. Rather, an empathic bond. The notion of empathy here must remain undefined. As with love, to which it is allied, we cannot prove that we feel it if we are challenged, nor can we adequately articulate what it is we do feel. Yet, only if we adopt a naive and impoverishing positivism will we therefore exclude such terms from our discourse. The youthful movement of the Vienna Circle, whose influence we still bear, may have been willing to do this. But wisdom accepts as fact many things it cannot explain. I take it as a fact then, that without the container of an empathic bond, the patient's universe cannot unfold.

To establish such a bond with A.N., to join with him in this deep way, I too had to become a poet.

I say "had to," but really it was a movement that seemed inevitable, a manifestation, if you like, of the counter-transference[1] but linked equally to my own deepest desires. In becoming a poet, I had to drop a conventionalized stance of intelligent discernment and become instead a true analyst, open to the unknown.

What is poetry? Given the distinction Saussure makes between *langue* and *parole*—the language of the community and the language of the individual—poetry clearly weighs itself on the side of *parole*. Not entirely, of course, otherwise we would have the glossolalia of certain enthusiasts or madmen—or, perhaps less pathologically, these words from Antonin Artaud:

---

[1]By "countertransference" here I mean a desire arising in the analyst out of an attunement to the patient's developmental needs.

o reche modo
to edire
di za
tau dari
do padera coco.

The more usual poet employs the language of the community but in highly individualized ways that preserve and enhance ambiguity. Layers of meaning are present, intended and unintended, to be heard *simultaneously*. Any explication, therefore, must betray that sense of simultaneity, to which a list of meanings laid out in a line can never approximate. To "get" a poem is quite different from the capacity to interpret it, involving different and incommensurable parts of the mind. It is a category mistake, therefore, to confuse them and to attempt to reduce the one to the other.

The patient also is a poet whose speech is closer to *parole* than to *langue*. For this reason, to translate the inherent ambiguity of his production into univocal propositions is false both to their nature and to our experience of them. It likewise reveals the analyst's own resistance to unknowing and may join its counterpart in the patient. The "cure" produced through this joining of resistances is a false cure—an achievement of closure rather than of further openness.

For analysis, properly understood, is the enemy of meaning—a relationship forged to keep meaning from congealing. Sustained by a certain bond, its voyagers can travel farther into the unknown—an interminable and playful unfolding that can end only arbitrarily. That, to my mind, is the goal of psychoanalysis and, if we must have one, not a bad definition of health. Its alternative is the creation of a culturally shared, fixed and bounded "reality"—the universe of the known, which is, in fact, a prison.

If the two protagonists in this drama are indeed poets,

mutually attuned through highly individualized languages, then their experience must be unique. It is an experience of high subjectivity offering little possibility for generalized rules and conclusions. And that, precisely, is its value: a level of particularity rarely possible anywhere else. And also, we may add, its morality. I believe it was Sartre who said, with Hitler's final solution in mind, that "evil is the systematic substitution of the abstract for the concrete." When it does not try to be a science and, abandoning an impossible objectivity, embraces the poetic non-sense of unknowing, psychoanalysis realizes its true nature . . . and its goodness.

How can this view of psychoanalysis be achieved in its literature?

To begin with, the field requires a genre that can express its own particular vision. And since its inception, psychoanalysis has had such a genre in the case history. In Freud's masterly hands, it became an art form of great distinction, balancing the imaginative values of the short story with the instructive ones of the scientific report. Since then, few writers have furthered the development of the form or even repeated Freud's successes.

The case history's proximity to fiction is unmistakable. First, there is the common practice of altering or omitting identifying information to protect the patient's privacy. More essentially, the aleatoric mess of actual experience is cleaned up by reflection so that what had been strange or unexpected now seems foreordained. To a great extent, the material had been screened by the analyst's ear even in the hearing. But as he writes, he screens it through an even finer mesh. The result is a series of preinterpreted "facts" marshaled in rhetoric that guides us down a single track. The false starts and digressions of true process—not to mention its mutuality—have been laundered out. Only in format, then, and in the superficialities of style, are case histories scientific. In fact, they are short stories.

If we were to drop the masquerade and accept their fiction status, what might be accomplished? For one thing, the subjectivity, the serendipitous slosh and roll of the real, could be shown and evoked in the reader—not just pointed out. Equally important, the form would become a vehicle for the writer's own movement—an opening into realms he does not know. In that there is the promise of revelation—of one's own self, to be sure, but also of the patient—one's partner in the play. Finally—and this is paramount—psychoanalysis would have a genre intrinsic to itself—one that developed according to the same internal principles as those of treatment. The split that now exists would be healed.

* * * *

Under the tutelage of A.N., as noted earlier, I too became a poet. And poets, at least since Plato, have been known for notorious liars. They may or may not lie in the service of a higher truth but, in common-sense terms, their words cannot be trusted. For all the reader knows, I may have entirely fabricated the preceding fragment of a case. And now, having implicated myself in a paradox—the famous paradox of the liar—I cannot get us out. If I should protest that the case is indeed true or, equally, if I should confess to having made it up, the paradox remains. Nor can we appeal, as Bertrand Russell hoped we could, to the ingenious notion of a metalanguage, since a metalanguage, we now know, is not a truly independent system but derives its meaning and existence entirely from the primary one. Since the paradox cannot be escaped, then, let us rather embrace it, accepting that fiction is truth and truth fiction, which is, perhaps, all we need to know. In one of his last letters, A.N. wrote to me: "You analysts walk around with your dicks in your ears, trying for endless aural orgasms and imagining you're communicating with the stars. Kurtz, my friend, you're no different, except that, more simplemindedly, you just enjoy getting off. For that, I shall always be grateful."

* * * *

The enjoyments of which A.N. speaks were not always so open to me. When I began this book, the demands of scholarly convention still carried weight, burdening the earlier chapters with excess pounds of references. Some have been excised, but their presence, like a palimpsest, continues to be felt. After all, style is a unity, so even skillful alterations can only partially succeed. The slavery revealed by too many quotes remains visible in other ways.

When I first set off on the journey of which this book is the record and the means, I could not travel light. The best I could do was to provide an itinerary so broad that almost anything might count as a visit. The great realms of space and time suited this plan well. Moving into them, I watched as themes emerged I could not have predicted. While I have not written autobiographically, these themes were all my own.

The one of narcissistic damage, opened especially through the lives of Freud (Chapter 2, "The Analyst's Space") and Eliot (Chapter 6, "Time and Death"), figured importantly among them. That it had been weakly developed in my own analysis is not surprising. Prior to Kohut's work, just beginning in the 1960s, no adequate theory of narcissistic growth and treatment had existed. Reading Kohut set off a movement in me with wide and shattering effects. Since a central part of my life during this time was lived in writing, the expression of these revelations inevitably found their place there. Have I written about Freud and Eliot, then, or have I written about myself? I cannot judge. But since I am concerned with the interpretation of a life, it is not even clear to me how this question could be answered.

In writing about Eliot the theme of death emerged as well.

I had just discovered it – the brutal reality of my own death – and this writing was one attempt to express and encompass it. Usually I am a driven writer; what others admire as discipline is to me a compulsion. But I put off work on that chapter as long as I could and, even having begun, put it away many times. When at last I finished, I thought I'd done with the theme itself. But not yet. It wasn't until months later when I dreamt of falling into the arms of Death – falling into its arms and resting my head on its shoulder – that I knew I'd reached firmer ground. With that dream came a sense of gratitude that I'd been shown the true, unthreatening nature of death.

But these writings had yet another function: they enabled an identification with two figures I greatly admired. Here were men, weak like me, yet great in accomplishment and courage. If I'd ignored their weaknesses, any identification would have been high and tottering, built on the card house of my own grandiosity. On the other hand, to ferret out their weaknesses for the purpose of devaluation would have left me without hope of their support. What I did, without knowing what I was doing, was to identify with them in their weakness, and yet preserve my admiration. This allowed me to pursue my own way, not in defiance or despair but on the model of their independence.

My own way led inexorably, it now seems, toward poetry – toward the particularity of its language and the wisdom of its irrationality. This thread begins in the chapters on silence (written first) and continues through the chapters on space and time in quotes from many poets and references to their lives. But it was only through my work with Lydia and the writing of "Lost in Time" (Chapter 7) that my own metamorphosis became visible to me. The more visible it became, the stronger the need to abandon the discursive voice – a voice that has no *existence*. In that sort of writing, knowledge is like the labor of living after the Fall – always tentative, always trying. Poetry, like play, doesn't try.

Similarly, analysis, conducted as living poetry, is not a labor. Winnicott's *aperçu* of the analytic process as play has been a liberation for me. Reversing his development, it has impelled me increasingly to work with children—work that is not merely instructive but full of delight. The leadership of the child, like that of the poet, opens the unknown.

A book of this sort is not given shape; it takes shape. Consequently, the Introduction, although presented first, can only be written last. To present the last as first is to play with time—a human prerogative. Our bodies age inexorably, but our minds operate otherwise. If this were not the case—if the child were not held in some corner of the soul, forever young—psychoanalysis would not be possible. Addled and in her nineties, my grandmother once said, "*Heute hab' ich mein Vater gesehen. Wir waren im Prater spazieren.*" ("Today I saw my father. We strolled together in the Prater.") In the language of her childhood, the distant past was present.

The door opened for some by senile decay requires a key in earlier life. In fear and yearning the child waits for the key to turn. Then, at the exact moment she yields up her distrust, the door swings open. There stands the analyst—a figure from the future admitted to the child's eternal now. And through that act of admitting him—of bringing him into her world—what had been unbearable can be sustained and transformed.

This saving act—like all acts of salvation—is beyond comprehension. It is not despite this incomprehensibility that it is effective, but because of it. Knowledge achieved rationally is fascinating—the illusion of power it offers is as addictive as cocaine. But it is also weak and superficial: when the high wears off, we see that nothing has changed. The art of unknowing consists in abandoning the mirrored casino of that kind of knowledge for the modest and transforming acknowledgment of mystery.

SPACE

2

The Analyst's Space

ORIGINS

The specific iconography of the analyst's consulting room begins in Vienna at Berggasse 19. But its prototype is the scholar's cell. In its essence, the cell is a space for self-contained absorption in intellectual reverie. Its image was perfected in the fifteenth century, especially in paintings of St. Jerome, where Netherlandish artists found an ideal subject to capture the values of enclosure. Each room in these paintings is a holding environment that sustains the man in his work by means of its walls, its furniture and books, its skull, crucifix, and little doglike lion. Even the view from the window serves only to return the scholar to his thoughts. This Jerome is an intellectual Crusoe; his island has shrunk to the size of his cell, which contains everything he might ever need.

The scholar's room is a world-for-one; the analyst's is manifestly for two. Yet, while constructed to be shared, it is made only by the analyst, who remains literally alone before and after his patient's visit—and in the solitude of his free-floating attention even during the hour itself.

Before he ever sees a patient, the analyst designs this room. Thus, it is a pure creative act that mobilizes and gives concrete, indeed institutional, expression to the most primitive elements in his personality. Since this truth can be obscured by the now timeworn conventions that guide him, it is instructive to examine their source at Freud's office in the Berggasse.

This room is preserved for us, not only in the memories of analysands, but in the photographs Edmund Engelman (1976) took just before Freud's flight to London in 1938. It impressed many (Recouly 1923), as it does the present writer, as a virtual museum. The walls were hung with framed photographs, lithographic reproductions, and engravings, as well as with sculptured reliefs and the mounted fragments of Pompeiian-style frescoes. Every table, cabinet, and shelf was laden with small-scale Greek, Roman, and Egyptian figures—so many objects that the surfaces eventually were unable to contain them, and some simply rested on the floor. Unseen, others were gathered, layer upon layer, in the drawers of cabinets. These objects were set against the room's dark walls or superimposed on the oriental carpets that draped parts of the floor, the tabletops, the couch and walls to produce a dense collage of pattern and color.

The room was a sensory *plenum*—a phenomenon only partially tied to late nineteenth-century taste and middle-class ideas of comfort. It must equally be understood as a manifestation of the same spirit that—in creating this space—created psychoanalysis.

Freud called his collecting mania "an addiction second in intensity only to his nicotine addiction" (Schur 1972). An addiction is hardly to be explained, as Peter Gay (1976) would do, entirely in terms of aesthetic gratification, escape from care, and a yearning for lands "*wo die Zitronen blühn*"—where the lemon trees blossom. These are "reasonable" explanations for behavior that is manifestly not reasonable. We meet with this kind of thinking again and again in accounts of Freud's behavior, as if it were intolerable to imagine his mental life to have been composed of anything but conscious ideas and nicely sublimated impulses.

The art museum, to which Freud's collection has been likened, is a quintessentially nineteenth-century institution. Although it developed out of eccentric cabinets of curiosities, it became in time a rationalized compendium in aesthetic terms of the history of civilization—graspable within the space of a single building. In self-psychological terms (but on a social scale) it is a product of disintegration and, at the same time, an Olympian effort to reproduce cohesion. Traditional societies are ahistorical, held together by unquestionable custom. In them the past is never lost, for one day it will again become the present. The dying out of this perspective—which reached a critical moment in the last century—unleashed seismic anxieties for both individuals and groups. One response to it was the formation of museums.

By means of the museum, the scattered shards of the unrecoverable and alien past are gathered, catalogued, and displayed, as if to assure curator and visitor alike that the past has not been lost. Curators always try to fill the gaps in their collections, offering didactic explanations. Narcissistically, the gaps are windows on reality that betray the illusory cohesiveness of the make-believe world they wish to sustain.

The museum has other functions in addition to compensating for narcissistic assault from the loss of the past. Besides its obvious exhibitionistic features, it is a monstrously omnipotent institution. By reducing history to an itemized collection of things, we become the very lords of time and, indeed, its owners. In this way, too, the museum can be seen as the temporal arm of an imperialistic civilization—appropriating the artifacts of alien past cultures as its political–military branch appropriates the artifacts of alien contemporary ones.

Kohut (1977) discusses Proust in related terms, noting that ". . . if the deeper source of our sense of abiding sameness dries up, then all our efforts to reunite the fragments of our self with the aid of a *Remembrance of Things Past* will fail" (p. 180). He analyzes Proust's novel as a monumental effort to produce cohesion that reveals, nevertheless, "evidence of his persisting fragmentation . . ." (p. 181). To the extent that Proust did achieve reconsolidation, the achievement rested on a "massive shift from himself as a living and interacting human being to the work of art he created" (p. 181). "The Proustian recovery of the past," Kohut continues, "is in the service of healing the discontinuity of the self. The achievement of such a cure is the result of intense psychological labors—whether in the analytic situation . . . or outside . . . as the result of the working through performed by an artistic genius" (p. 182). But the application of the historical point of view as a curative project will not compensate for the lack of a "firmly cohesive nuclear self" (p. 182).

Many of these remarks could be applied *passim* to Freud, who, in forming and arranging his collection of antiquities, in designing the environment of his office—indeed in setting up the psychoanalytic situation itself—attempted to recreate in compensatory form a past that was otherwise inaccessible. As Christopher Bollas (1978) remarks, "What Freud could not analyse in himself . . . was acted out in his choice of the ecology of psychoanalytic technique" (p. 108). This room embodies Freud's infantile relation to his mother.

More specifically, it embodies the symbiotic/narcissistic components of that relationship. The former are most apparent in the room's gestalt, which reveals a taste for overallness like that of a Schwitters *Merzbau* or of the extraordinary abbey church at Rottenbuch. The individual fragments of which such environments are composed submerge themselves in a patterned totality that comes to include the occupant himself. It is an aesthetic of symbiosis.

While the room may contain two people at once, it contains them both separately. Through the positioning of the couch and chair, each is alone, as Winnicott put it, in the presence of the other. For both participants, but especially for the patient, this positioning encourages immersion in an ambience of primitive merger. Then, through his involvement with the regressed patient to whom he gives his rapt attention, the analyst regains access to the empathic mother he either lost or never had.

By means of the room itself, and through the daily repetition of a special relationship with his patients, Freud enfolded himself in a mother's warmth over which he retained near-perfect control.

The issue of control—on a grandiose/omnipotent scale—permeates the analytic situation. It is the analyst, after all, who establishes the rules that govern behavior in this primal space.

However much these rules may be constructed to enable the patient's cure, the analyst is their maker and enforcer. Just because they are unvarying elements of his technique—the posts and lintels of his structure—their deepest meaning to him can go unnoticed. But in the innocence of Freud's collection, some part of their meaning is revealed. From his armchair in the corner, Freud surveyed a miniature Olympus of gods and goddesses ranged like toy soldiers on a counterpane battlefield. In this setting, Freud is the God of gods; a connoisseur of deities whose mysteries have been reduced to the elements of children's play.

But the outfitting of his office and the construction of his professional life responded to narcissistic needs beyond those of omnipotent control. Equally, they countered a tendency to a form of depression characterized by feelings of emptiness, isolation, and the anxiety of fragmentation. First, the visual and tactile plenum he created left no vacancy for the eye, no opening devoid of stimulus. Beyond the stimulation of the room, the demands of the role he created required highly focused attention to the stimuli provided by his patients. At least for the well-defined space of a session, the effort of work facilitated the coalescence of his dispersed self. Between hours, this task was accomplished principally through writing, and secondarily through the constant availability of his cigars, his dog, and his family attending in the rooms next door.

In this way, the narcissistic and psychotic (that is to say, symbiotic) layers of Freud's personality entered profoundly into his creation of the psychoanalytic situation and its manifestation in space. It is important to trace the origins of psychoanalysis to (among other things) these unanalyzed trends, because, to the extent that Freud's creation manifests them, it does so *in its structure*, far more than in its content.[1] Thus, every analyst to

---

[1] They are present in the content primarily through the conspicuous absence of a well-

some degree recreates that office in the Berggasse. And every analysand, walking into such a room, enters a dimension of Freud's (and of his analyst's) personality realized in space. In this connection, an analogy can be drawn with art in a way that it cannot be with science. Every new listener, for example, to the last contrapuncti in the *Art of the Fugue* can be said, in some sense, to find himself in Bach's presence. In the same way, however, every new observer of the classical experiments on Brownian movement cannot be said to find himself in the presence of Perrin.

Here I can only sketch the biographical evidence for these unanalyzed trends which we see — without knowing what it is that we see — when we look about Freud's room. Not that we can arrive at the truth of these matters in any definitive way. Freud was secretive about the facts of his early childhood (Jones 1955), and what memories he did record seem dappled by an idealizing light. It seems likely that he maintained this unblemished picture through some repeated censoring operation. Overtly, and on two occasions (first in 1885 and again in 1907), Freud burned his personal papers, saying (1885), "*I could not have matured* (italics mine) or died without worrying about who would get hold of these old papers . . ." (p. 141). Frank Sulloway (1979) imputes an intentional obfuscating effort to Freud, as if he were cultivating a media image for posterity. Although this interpretation is not unjustified, I think the issue is more subtle. These fires — rageful and purificatory — were schizoid rituals by means of which the past was cut off from the present, to enable the actor to get on with his life. Thus, a child's painfully dependent existence is disavowed in favor of a false and grandiose self-sufficiency, as if the arsonist had come into the world fully

---

developed theory of narcissistic development. As a result, the structure unwittingly invites very primitive, preoedipal processes, which, since the conscious theory does not take these issues adequately into account, are either lost or treated as resistances.

formed. From the destruction of his childhood, Freud set about fulfilling his own heroic persona. But from its irreducible ashes, he created the psychoanalytic situation.

What was it that had to be incinerated in such a violent and well-rationalized gesture? Nothing less than the intense and chronic emptiness of his early years. Freud's belief that he was his mother's well-beloved favorite and the real attentions she paid him left him with a lifelong confusion—intellectual as well as visceral—concerning the differences between narcissistic attachment and object love. Intellectually, the confusion appears in contrasting statements from the Leonardo essay (Freud 1910) and the *New Introductory Lectures* (Freud 1933). Viscerally, the confusion pervades his life. Freud's treatment by his mother as a wunderkind, and the repeated stories of heroic portents that attended his birth and appeared throughout his childhood (Sulloway 1979), have all the conventional earmarks of love. But they were not love. Amalie Freud's personal ambitions—which could be realized neither through her own efforts, nor vicariously through those of her ineffectual husband—were entrusted to her firstborn son (Abraham 1979). A child breathed beneath the heroic image in which she clothed him—but it was a child she never knew. Behind the mask his mother made for him, Freud spent his childhood alone.

The loneliness of the narcissistically cathected hero-child differs from that of an overtly rejected one precisely in this existential confusion. Bathed in gifts and affection, he cannot locate the source of his terrible emptiness. In order to earn his mother's "love" he must bury this truth and fulfill the destiny she has made for him, leaving him with a riddle far crueler than that of the Sphinx, namely: *Whose life am I really living?* [2]

---

[2]According to the Greek myth, the Sphinx dies when the riddle is solved. In the context of the Oedipus legend, this act of solution opens the way for Oedipus to marry Jocasta—not freedom, but a deeper enslavement. Removed from its setting in the Oedipus story, the Sphinx is seen to

To solve the riddle of his identity posed by a narcissistic mother requires a geometric intensification of the truth-seeking drives (Eigen 1981). Clearly, these drives had the greatest power in guiding Freud's discoveries, yet their outcome was only partially successful. His efforts and self-concept, cast in his mother's image, remained heroic—and his inner life remained painfully empty. To a great extent, the world has colluded in taking Freud's public image for the whole. But his office and the structure of his practice encode a condition that could not be incinerated with his papers. Here is the locus of an addiction to work of which he said, "I take no pleasure in anything else" (1910a). Without his work and the supplement of nicotine (Jones 1953), he fell prey to attacks of *Todesangst* (Jones 1953). The grandiose defense of constant achievement (work addiction) keeps the illusion of the self-object's availability alive. Death enters in the gaps where the illusion inevitably fails. Beneath this illusion lies an ever greater death-terror: merger through cannibalization. The Sphinx kills those who fail to solve her riddle.

When the self-object is unavailable, cohesion is lost; the self falls apart. Freud's collecting of ancient artifacts was an attempt to locate and bind the fragments into a whole—an impossible and therefore unending effort. It is because it is a substitute for a sense of cohesion that this kind of collecting is compulsive. The unconscious need it symbolizes is never satisfied.

Each item of the collection is a self fragment, but the totality is a constantly available mother who becomes stimulus or background in perfect synchroneity with one's present needs. Fittingly, Engelman could not photograph the view *from* Freud's chair, saving us the hubris of imagining we have his vision. Nevertheless, we know what he had directly in his view. It was a

be herself the confusing, engulfing mother. When the confusion she creates is dispelled, her son reclaims his own identity and her power is gone.

small group of Egyptian figures arranged hieratically on a carpet-covered table. Necessarily, their most idiosyncratic meanings must escape us, and we can only speculate, more or less informedly. No doubt we shall be drawn, as was Rita Ransohoff who captioned Engelman's (1976) prints, to the falcon-headed figure of Horus for the richness and pertinence of its associations. Horus the child-hero, the god of silence, conceived miraculously by a castrated father whose sundered body was literally pieced together and revived by his powerful and ingenious mother. Ransohoff relates this figure to the well-known dream in which Freud (1900) recorded, "I saw my beloved mother . . . being carried into the room by two (or three) people with birds' beaks and laid upon a bed" (p. 583). Freud knew these figures from Philippson's illustrated Bible, whose eight volumes were in the family's library. Not only did this book provide material for dreams and daydreams, but its figures populated the empty spaces of his childhood days; they were his companions. In those childhood reveries, filled with fantastic images, lie the origins of a talent for free association and the peculiar semi-isolation of the analyst's role. In *this* image the child is father to the man: the lonely little boy in a corner of the house, poring over his picture book. And the mature man in the corner of his office, attending raptly to his patients' words.

TRANSFORMATIONAL SPACE: THE ANALYST'S CORNER

Freud was unable to analyze these trends within himself and therefore, as Alice Miller (1981) has suggested, lived them out countertransferentially. Much more importantly, he lived them out in his invention of the analytic situation. That situation evokes the "transformational object"—an existentially (rather than cognitively) experienced process–object that evolves a metamorphosis of the self (Bollas 1978). In analogous or regressive states in adulthood, a situation that seems to offer transformation inspires reverence. In this way, the analytic room can become a sacred space.

Christopher Bollas suggests that, while the "culture" of the analytic space facilitates deep regressions of this sort, the analyst and the theory itself create blocks by treating them as resistances and by offering interpretations which the patient cannot hear. The greatest value an interpretation can have, heard from this deep place, is as the infinitely sustained hum of an angelic choir—"the song of the analyst's voice" (p. 102).

The analyst, sitting in his chair, himself seeks a transformational experience by immersing himself in the patient for whom—together with the total context he creates—he functions as transforming agent. Yet, because his yearning is unconscious and disallowed—a taboo institutionalized in his technique—he thwarts the patient and vicariously himself through his untimely demand for work.

Bollas speaks of narcissistic and schizoid patients as seeking to live "within a special ambience with the analyst" (p. 102), in which the content of interpretations is far less important than their holding value. But this is true of all patients in deep regression. At this stage, the analyst is not so much a person as a nest or burrow lined with moss—not the womb of primal experience but the hiding place of a lonely child. To *be* that hiding place requires an act of *entering into* the patient's experience—an empathic leap. The chief obstacle to this leap is the failure to recognize that the analyst has already hidden himself in a corner—the corner he has become for his patient. He has become that corner because, as Noël Arnaud (1950) writes in *L'état d'ébauche*, "*Je suis l'espace où je suis*" (p. 127). "I am the space where I am."

To understand the *patient*-in-the-analytic-situation we must, among other things, fill out a phenomenology of the couch. To understand the *analyst*-in-the-analytic-situation, we must develop a phenomenology of the corner. We have a basis for this project in the work of the French philosopher, Gaston Bachelard. In *The Poetics of Space* (1958), Bachelard turns to a novel, *L'Amoureuse initiation* by O. V. de Milosz (1910), whose protagonist frequently repairs to "that little dark corner between the fireplace and the oak chest" (p. 233) to daydream and reminisce. Safely tucked away in that cozy space, he thinks, "Here the meditative spider lives powerful and happy; . . . here the past can be rediscovered and yet remain hidden . . ." (p. 224). In the presence of his memories, he recalls, speaking to himself both now and then, that "already as a child, you loved the eaves of châteaux, and the corners of old libraries *à rossignols* [that is, full of books no one will ever read again] . . ." (p. 224). To recall such objects or, like Freud, to situate ourselves among them, is to remember our solitude. For, indeed, such objects are "memories of solitude . . . which are betrayed by the mere fact of having been forgotten, abandoned in a corner" (Bachelard, p. 142). These forlorn objects, part of a "vast museum of insignificant things" (Bachelard, p. 142), radiate kindness and sustain us. "Melancholy and despised, we confide in these things, offering them from the depths of our hearts those modest parts of ourselves no one knows about" (de Milosz, p. 226).

Through such evocations, we come to know Freud and ourselves as little children who, having sought the safety of a corner, confided our loneliness to the walls and the lamp. Is it then so surprising that we should later *become* that place—the corner to whom others confide?

The free-floating attention the analyst cultivates is an extension—a refinement—of his childhood corner reveries. As such, it keeps the creative freshness of its origins only through the analyst's openness to the reality of the moment. In his openness, he abandons formulaic knowledge for a riskier immersion in the patient's unconscious. This process is analogous to Bachelard's idea of creatively reading a poem by entering so fully into its imagery that it is as if the reader himself were the author. And it contains, too, Winnicott's notion of transitional experience as the simultaneous appropriation and creation of some item of the world. The patient speaks the words the analyst was about to say.

The image of the "meditative spider" de Milosz's dreamer calls up from his hiding place concentrates this process. Once her web is spun, the spider's existence hovers, suspended, until the fly is caught. Then, at the very moment the fly enters her dreams, it appears also in her trap, and she revives. In the web of his room, the analyst dreams words that—given voice by his patient—recall him to life.

Such empathic, existential knowing raises deep epistemological questions. Who, in such cases, is the knower? And who is known? And what is the truth value of this knowledge? The person who comes to be known and to know himself through analysis is not the person "himself" but the patient-in-the-analytic-situation. In that situation, the couch "creates" the corner chair, and the chair, the couch. Or (perhaps more accurately) both the chair and the couch are dream contents of the consulting room.

Yet, while the couch and the chair are complementary elements of the same structure, there are two quite different transferences to the space itself. If analysts would more commonly tell their stories, we would see that their rooms are quite different from those of their patients.

A generous colleague revealed this image from his child-hood:

> When I was a little boy of seven or eight, my father bought
> a new easy chair and gave me his old one. But I had already
> made it mine. When I needed comfort, I would bury my
> face in its brown upholstery, burrowing into the corner
> made by the back cushion, the seat and the arm. The chair
> held me. My mother would have betrayed my secrets. This
> chair was my loyal confidante.

Here the chair is much more than a transitional object; it is a replacement. When he had approached his own mother with some childhood distress, she would become more anxious than he and would rush to alter the ostensive cause of his unhappiness (actually, her own), leaving him bewildered and alone. The chair simply listened, remaining perfectly calm and monumental. At once strong and yielding, it became his mother, so that each time he came to it for comfort, he took some of its warmth away with him. To a degree, he became his chair-mother. Nevertheless, the chair-mother was a mother *faute de mieux*—a compensatory object. Her softness and calm, however reliable, retained the quality of a *thing*. So, inevitably, to integrate these qualities entailed a certain deadness. Then, too, while the chair-mother gave him what she could, certain gifts were beyond her powers. Most importantly, she could not encircle him. All burrows—all places of safe retreat—must have an opening, and it is on this opening that the fears relating to external danger now became centered. For a while, he could maintain the illusion of safety offered by the chair. But then something would happen—a sudden noise, someone's entrance into the room—and his daydream of invulnerability would shatter.

As an analyst, his transference to the analytic situation retained these features. The consulting room as a whole, but especially his chair in the corner, recreated the chair-mother of his childhood. The rule-setting aspect of the role, which Serge Viderman (1979) illuminates, responded to a need for omnipotent control that his mother had failed to meet, and to which the chair responded only through the force of illusion. Because the patient-in-the-analytic-situation was controllable and predictable to a greater degree than any childhood situation, he found a great deal of satisfaction in his role. But the imperfection in its safety, the "opening," now turned on the patient's compliance with the rules. In the earliest phases of his career, any break in the frame would occasion the kind of anxiety he had felt in childhood when the illusion of the chair's protection had been spoiled. Time and sophistication had made it possible for him to maintain a sense of safety, even in the face of significant alterations. But its deepest *meaning* to him never changed.

Not everyone can manage such sophistication. For some, the illusion of safety, once ruptured, can never be repaired.

At the age of 86, a former analyst, who had practiced briefly in B_____ before the war, remembered her childhood. She came from an old family, and grew up on a country estate near_____. The main house, begun in the sixteenth century, had been classicized in the 1790s and remained full of anomalies: Palladian archways framed blank walls, winding corridors led to walled-up doorways. Her parents, though aristocrats, were intensely involved in revolutionary politics, leaving Ise's care largely to tutors and servants.

In that vast house, made vaster by her size and more alien by her loneliness, Ise came upon an abandoned apartment given over to storage. Its main room was so packed with furniture and trunks that only a child could have found its way to the corner where Ise made her nest. There, surrounded by the forgotten bibelots of three centuries, she dreamed herself into existence. As she put it, "I was like Descartes in his stove, except that it was not through reason but through imagination that I could finally say, 'I am.' " Lost in the tendrils of a rocaille girandole, Ise dreamed herself a Hapsburg duchess, eating ice cream at a *fête galante*. Alternatively, she became that infamous Bathory, allegedly her ancestress, who bathed herself in the blood of virgins to renew her youth. Far away, in B_____, her mother plotted a proletarian revolt. At home, Ise draped herself in a cape of silver-spangled *bleu du roi* and proclaimed herself "Queen of Heaven."

In her fantasy, Ise—herself a forgotten object—became something beyond price. As an analyst, this fantasy was realized. Enshrined in her corner, she shared her patients' dreams and received their adulation. In the environment of her office, and in her role, she had found the greatest satisfaction of her adult life. When the Germans were about to invade, she could not bring herself to leave. Then, one day, she returned from a visit to the country to find her office ransacked. Not only had all its paintings and objects been removed, but the very walls had been vandalized. Although she escaped B_____ and survived, she could not tolerate this violation; it was the end of her professional life.

THE FIT

One of the most provocative passages in Bléger's (1961) landmark article on the frame is the following: "The 'therapeutic alliance' is . . . an alliance with the healthiest part of the patient, and this is true of the process but not of the frame. In the latter, the alliance is established with the psychotic (or symbiotic) part of the patient's personality (*whether with the corresponding part of the psychoanalyst's personality I do not know yet*)" (p. 464; italics mine).

At least with respect to one aspect of the frame's spatial component, Bléger's parenthetical question can be answered. The analyst who has become the embracing corner, and the patient who comes for sanctuary there, find one another in the analytic space. This is not an alliance, which would indicate a fair degree of consciousness. It is more like a fortuitous inter-locking through which different needs are met simultaneously by the same gesture. For this reason, the analogy to mother-child symbiosis—or to one element in sexual relations—is apt. It is at this level that patients choose their analysts and analysts their patients. It is at this level, too, that the fit is found to be good or bad in a way that cannot be modified by analysis.

Patient and analyst may be said to be allied, in a loose sense, in their mutual creation of a *shared* space within the analytic situation—comparable to the shared space created by actors and audience in the theatre. But the primal spaces of the corner and the couch are not shared creations. They precede the analytic situation and meet there for the first time. The ideal analyst would be a corner capable of molding and remolding itself to fit the shape of each new patient. In actuality, his flexibility is limited, so that some fits are impossible, many are adequate, and a few are nearly perfect. Of these, the last are the most difficult to understand.

By means of their discrepancies, the shapes that enclose us—or that we enclose—inform us of our own shape. Floating blind and naked in a warm sea, we would lose our boundaries. When symbiosis works, we become equally lost. At such times, the process seems to take care of itself, and both patient and analyst experience a sense of well-being and growth that is almost effortless. Feelings of gratitude or mystery may come to us then, since we find ourselves in situations in which the will plays a negligible part, and yet by which we are benevolently sus-tained.

Analysis is possible and necessary in the large number of instances where the fit is good enough to support the relation-ship but impeded in discrete, manageable ways by discontinui-ties. The analysis of a good fit is no doubt possible, but we experience it as painful, even destructive. To question the good fit is not unlike questioning the child about the reality status of his transitional object. Implicitly we know this must not be done. Where there is a good fit—in contrast to an apparent one produced by compliance—the relationship itself is healing. The healing consists, in part, in the faith that we are understood— held fast by a love to which our own capacity for self-love will some day be anchored.

Is this experience regressive? I think that, for many, the experience of a good symbiosis in analysis is entirely new. The vulnerability that is its precondition may itself recapture the openness of infancy. But the experience that follows is not always a memory. In that new experience of mutual satisfaction, the analyst opens the corner-space he has become, and receives into it the child he once was.

3

The Patient's Space

Une maison dressée au coeur
Ma cathédrale de silence
Chaque matin reprise en rêve
Et chaque soir abandonée
Une maison couverte d'aube
Ouverte au vent de ma jeunesse

—Jean Laroche

Just as the transference exists in a potential way before the analysis begins, so the patient carries the consulting room within him until, after a long journey, he meets it finally in his analyst's office. Looking back, one can see his history as a labyrinth leading inexorably toward that room. Once there, however, it takes on new dimensions and becomes indeed the center of his life.

This is true whatever the frequency of visits. In fact, fewer, rather than more frequent ones may strengthen the room's position. Its place, after all, is established through a near-ritualistic repetition whose magic may decline with overfamiliarity. Every week at the same hours the patient returns to this unchanging space to sit in the same chair or recline on the same couch. Because of this sameness he can pick up the threads of the last session as if he had never left, and take them forward.

It is like returning to a summer house year after year—each time adding to its store of memories while, at the same time, bracketing the life led in between. A counterpoint of lives is thus set up in which the conscious ear can tune to each voice separately yet admit the other as it chooses, simultaneously or in alternation.

The space thus established is a poetic space—closer to dreams than to reality. In it the past can be evoked more palpably than in the spaces where its events actually took place. Here we visit the attics and cellars of childhood—as if in a vision. They are seen not as they were, nor as we should see them now if we could return to discover them miraculously unaltered. For we are no longer the same and would find the old lamps and strangely carved moldings disturbingly different. Instead, they are seen through a dim glass, as Miss Havisham saw her dining room on that eternal wedding day—veiled in its overgrowth of cobwebs and dust.

The room becomes associated with home. "Home" as in

children's play—the end or goal of the game, but also a sanctuary defined by rules whose feeling of safety somehow goes beyond rules. That sanctuary evokes the childhood home in faded, spliced, and fragmentary forms that can only be rebuilt in montage. Rilke (1910) speaks of the old house as "quite dissolved and distributed inside me: here one room, there another, and here a bit of corridor which, however, does not connect the two rooms, but is conserved in me in fragmentary form." Rilke's house kept its childhood feeling where motion and direction make qualitative differences. For this reason, some stairs "descended with ceremonious slowness while others were narrow cages that mounted in a spiral movement, in the darkness of which we advanced like the blood in our veins."

The home that is evoked in the consulting room is inseparable from the relationships that evolved within it. In fact, the specific qualities of those relationships may be forgotten but the memory of the spaces charts their contours. With this in mind, the subtlest and most pervasive childhood moods can be discerned through the present experience of space.

When analysis begins, the large-scale labyrinth that led to the office recreates itself in miniature. With what a mixture of yearning and terror its paths are traced! For there is indeed a monster at its heart, as well as a mother's arms. There must be both. Ultimately the idealized childhoods some people recall from which the minotaur has been expelled seem thin no matter how beautiful. Nabokov's (1966) memories are of this sort. For him, the end of childhood and exile from his childhood house occurred at the same moment, so that he came to attribute the inaccessibility of Vyra to the Bolsheviks. That exile, like the Expulsion, divided history into a glorious Before and an ordinary After. So, no matter how wonderfully detailed his recollection, Vyra never succeeds in becoming real; it remains forever under the spell of Nabokov's own enchantment.

It is not just simple repression that transforms childhood experience through the medium of space. Art is another and sexuality a third way. Both methods meet in pornographic literature, where the intense sufferings of childhood are screened through a latticework of passion.

There are profound affinities between the transformational efforts at work in art, perverse sexuality, and the analytic situation as they manifest themselves in the heightened perception of particular spaces saturated with feeling. The affinities are strong enough so that to explore them all in one context may be mutually illuminating.

* * * *

In the development of interior decoration, it took the emergence of an alienated historical consciousness—late in the nineteenth century—to create rooms that are the equivalent of Pound's *Cantos*. Such rooms are neither original creations (like the Art Nouveau) nor historical re-creations. Their designers scavenged through civilizations as if they were vast storehouses from which items could be abstracted entirely for their associative value—alone or in combination.

When space is treated in this way—as the occasion of a poetic assemblage for living—it reveals and expresses its maker's consciousness. One such consciousness that soared far above the demands of her trade and the sensibility of her peers was that of Rose Cumming. Until her death in 1968 this lady, eccentric and beautiful in old age, with odd clothes and a tangled mass of lavender hair, presided over a shop filled with objects as mysterious as they were valuable. Her work flourished most luxuriantly in the rooms she created for American millionaires of the 1920s. When she and her clients were well matched, and of course in the rooms of her own house, she was free to fabricate concrete dreams of extraordinary sophistication. Before discussing their relevance for psychoanalysis let me describe one of her spaces.

> On the walls of a stair landing, mirrored panels reflect three objects: an eighteenth-century chandelier in the form of a crystal galleon; an ancient, intricately tiered pagoda as tall as a man; and a sinuous Chinese goddess of white marble.

Through this vignette two essential features of her art are immediately visible in the poetic dislocation of space and time. The stair landing is a nonspace — a part of a house too small to permit perspective and thus allowing only fragmentary views. This basic half-reality is augmented by the mirrors, which reflect and rereflect a surreal collection of objects that can be seen assembled only in the glass. The boat and its reflections sail through the air above an oriental landscape that is monumental in relation to the ship but miniature in relation to real buildings. Yet, with respect to the people who find themselves in this space, the scale is neither miniature nor monumental: the pagoda, after all, is man-size. Time and space are collapsed by allusion as well. The joining of the Chinese sculpture and the galleon chandelier points to eighteenth-century orientalism — a fantasy Orient of proto-Romantic reveries based on objects the Orient never knew. In Miss Cumming's composition, all the objects are genuine enough — it is their conjunction that makes them dreamlike, the European eighteenth century no less than the erstwhile object of its fantasies.

Other, more useful, spaces she designed are equally mysterious — a mystery that can be analyzed without being quite dispelled. First, she made the walls evaporate by covering them with metallic or antique patterned papers in airy silver, blue, or mauve so that they disappeared as solid surfaces. She heightened this effect with old mirrors and fabrics that shimmered in the half-light of black candles set in rococo torchères. These ambiguous spaces were furnished with objects that suggested a past and were chosen for their evocative powers. Some had putative pedigrees ("said to have belonged to Catherine the Great"). Others simply recalled the times in which they were made. Even in photographs these rooms suggest the tents of Harun al-Rashid or St. Petersburg in the snow. But if we imagine their creator moving among them at dawn sixty years ago, naked under veils of chiffon after a winter's night of high wit and Veuve Clicquot, we have a silent film clip of the world into which this siren drew her sailors down.

The artist—a powerful dreamer—can take us up into his dreams. The patient is no less powerful as he invisibly transforms the room the analyst has prepared for him. The work of transformation is so swift and thorough that, simply by walking through the door, he can make comets whiz through the air and a forest grow up from the floor.

The art of assemblage, to which Rose Cumming's work belongs, makes use of items the world presents (*objets trouvés*). As such they are the least-altered descendants of the infant's creativity during the transitional phase. In the analytic situation, the furnishings of the analyst's office are the raw materials the patient is given to transform. If these are excessively neutral, this process is limited if not aborted. The patient can then suffer from a form of sensory deprivation that replicates a childhood in which stimulation was more inadequate than excessive (Kohut 1971).

The practice of furnishing the consulting room in a reticent way (Langs 1982) derives partly from the notion that objects with too much character will obscure the transference. If the development of the transference neurosis is seen as a creative process, the ideal material would approximate to a flawless piece of marble, which, because of its undifferentiated molecular structure, can be sculpted into virtually anything the patient can imagine. But the perfectly malleable substance exists only in theory. All media impose profound limitations on what can be expressed through them, so that in the end, conception and medium are inseparable. The transference, manifested in two different analytic relationships, is like a poem and its translation. Even should the structure and vocabulary of each language be perfectly homologous, the results of translation would nevertheless be two utterly different poems.

Creativity is not a monolith. The kind that prefers a tractable medium on which a preconceived form can be impressed is only one of several. Rose Cumming's creativity required the richest possible environment to manifest itself and a comparable sensibility to be perceived.

The purpose of a neutral environment is to allow the unconscious to gain its foothold with the least possible interference. As with so much of psychoanalytic thinking, what was a mere technical recommendation can later acquire canonical force so that the maintenance of neutrality becomes a goal in itself. But the consulting room is an enclosed garden in which the unconscious should flourish. "We admit [the repetition compulsion] into the transference," said Freud (1914), "as a playground in which it is allowed to expand in almost complete freedom." In this protected corner of his world, the patient can "admit the shaft of that third planet" (Stevens 1947) and experience his dreams awake. The manifest content of these waking dreams—including items from the consulting room—are charged from the very moment they are perceived. Indeed, they are likely to be perceived only because they already evoke something of significance.

The patient is present in the consulting room *as in a dream*. From the moment he enters there, the secondary process rules that govern his dealings with ordinary reality are suspended. However much he may seem to follow those rules—and although he may intermittently awake—<u>unconscious processes dominate the hour</u>. The transference, after all, is an acting out (*agieren*), an unconscious means of bringing the past into the present. And the transference constitutes the very *air* of the consulting room. Because it is dominated by the unconscious and by the *compulsion* to repeat, the consulting room has powerful affinities with the *mises en scènes* of perverse sexuality.

* * * *

Pornography, as the literature of perversity, captures a *state of mind* that centers on the sexualization of terror. The complaint that the characters of pornographic works lack dimension is a moralistic rather than an analytic one; if they were well developed and "realistic," the work would evoke a possible world rather than a state of mind. The novel is a social literature in which sex—an engagement of two individual people—has a social meaning. Pornography is a private literature in which sex is personal (masturbatory) and fantastic. The focus of the traditional novel is thus on the character; that of pornography is on a particular consciousness. "Perversity" here is defined not by an act's content but by the quality of that consciousness.

It is a consciousness that is particularly susceptible to spatial expression by means of sexualized objects and environments. The space itself becomes sexualized partly because perverse experience reworks a fragmented condition (originally experienced in terms of part objects) that was charged with high anxiety—now transformed into sexual frenzy. The household and later the world are taken for sexual objects. But also, the experience of perverse sexuality ionizes the atmosphere so that it shimmers like the air above a fire. This ionization—a compound of excitation and distress—is the chief characteristic of perverse pornographic space.

It is presented with great artistry in the works of Georges Bataille. His *Story of the Eye* (1928) is a surreal chronicle of sexual delirium by means of which the horrors of his childhood are redeemed. The chronicle moves from object to charged object, and from space to space, inexorably toward death. The depth of the original terror may be gauged precisely from the feverishness of the sexuality into which it has been turned, like the music of a wind instrument powered by hidden screams.

In the course of this dreamlike evocation, three principal characters—a girl, Simone, the unnamed boy narrator, and Marcelle (their mutual obsession)—pass through a series of sexualized situations and make use of objects (often innocent in themselves) that likewise become sexualized. Eggs are central—soon linked with eyes. The eggs/eyes are sexually enjoyed and abused—covered with urine or semen—both associated as well with tears. Sometimes the egg is an eyeball and its socket the vagina or anus. Eventually a third link is made between eggs, eyes, and testicles via those of a bull killed in the corrida whose horn has gouged out the matador's eye. The playful violence done to the eggs in earlier scenes becomes deadly in the end, when a priest is killed and his eyeball snipped out. This event provides the story's culminating, orgasmic image—an image the narrator has been expecting "in the same way that a guillotine waits for a neck to slice. I even felt as if my eyes were bulging from my head, erectile with horror . . ." This is what he saw: "In Simone's hairy vagina, I saw the wan blue eye of Marcelle, gazing at me through tears of urine." He describes this as a "dreary vision of disastrous sadness" (p. 103).

It is because Bataille, with rare generosity, correlates these images with some episodes in his childhood that we can make a certain sense of them. He tells us, for example, that he was conceived when his father was already blind and paralyzed with syphilis. Since the sick man was confined to a chair and could not use the bathroom, a container was kept by his side for urinating. He would use it in front of the boy, covered by a blanket that, however, was often askew. But what disturbed Bataille most at those moments was the look on his father's face. His huge, gaping eyes "went almost entirely blank . . . with a completely stupefying expression of abandon and aberration in a world that he alone could see and that aroused his vaguely sardonic and absent laughter . . ." (p. 112). Bataille concludes that his connection of eyes with eggs and their joint association with urine and tears had their origins here.

In 1915, Bataille and his mother had to abandon the sick man as the Germans advanced to occupy their town. He died before they could return home. Haunted by guilt and by the image of those vacant, terror-filled eyes, Bataille creates a pivotal episode in the book. Simone and the narrator are mutually obsessed with Marcelle, a girl trapped in a wardrobe during an orgy, driven mad, then imprisoned in an asylum. When they "rescue" her and bring her back, she recognizes them as her former tormentors and hangs herself. Marcelle's unbearable death immediately becomes a sexual occasion and their first consummation of intercourse. They experience this as a painful act whose value lies precisely in its pain. Simone, finding the corpse's open eyes supremely irritating, responds by urinating on its face. The lovers find themselves "blinded, as it were, very remote from anything we touched, in a world where gestures have no carrying power, like voices in a space that is absolutely soundless" (p. 68).

That space is precisely a perverse/pornographic space in which pain is transformed into sex without entirely losing contact with its source. The gesture has no "carrying power" because it has become a dream gesture—a purely poetic move-ment without face value. It exists only to stand for something else.

Bataille remembers loving his father in childhood as most other little boys love their mothers. "I was in love with my father," he says (p. 111). One may imagine the fate of this powerful idealizing love under the pressure of his father's sick-ness and insanity—and the intensification as well of the oedipal conflict. But Bataille's transformation of these primal experi-ences does more than instruct us about the origins of perverse experience. From his disillusionment, Bataille has made an art and a way of life. To stare open-eyed into the face of pain and terror becomes even a source of pride. "My father," he con-cludes, "having conceived me when blind (absolutely blind), I cannot tear out my eyes like Oedipus. Like Oedipus, I solved the riddle: no one divined it more deeply than I." "Today," he concludes, "I know I am 'blind,' immeasurable. I am man 'aban-doned' on the globe like my father at N" (p. 123).

By means of this obscene romance, Bataille restores to himself the repressed elements of the repeated (therefore ordi-nary) horrors of his childhood. As the repressed makes its return journey in the guise of sexualized objects, it charges the spaces through which it travels with the valence of the original scene. By itself, this would define the usual compulsive repetition of perverse sexuality. In Bataille's case, however, something unex-pected has happened. The startling appearance of the blue eye in Simone's vagina in that final scene represents, among other things, a restoration of sight to his father's—and his own—blind eyes and with it, through the stream of urine, a restoration of tears. These restorations, on the plane of the imagination, triggered actual memories of childhood. Thus memory and "insight" were also restored. Yet, these recovered memories have lost their poignancy: their emotional *valeur*[1] can be met with only in the tale.

For its author, the *Story of the Eye* has a twofold function. Most centrally it recreates through sexual fantasy the space of the little boy alone with his father—a space charged with "contradictory impulses" of such power that they cannot be tolerated. But it does not merely recreate that space in sexualized form—it transcends it by embracing the original horror and its associated guilt. Bataille refuses to sentimentalize. He cannot pluck out his eyes, through piety or any other means. Instead he takes the route of obscenity and betrayal. It is a dreadful route that accepts guilt without yielding to it; without living out the falsifying solutions guilt would dictate. It leads him ultimately to a space without coordinates—a space reduced to a single point of pain so total and so fully accepted that it constitutes a transfiguration.

Perversity defines an erotics of *situations*—situations that in their totality (i.e., seen from a larger perspective) recapture and rework the fragmented and dispersed elements of certain childhood relations. Masud Khan (1979), taking his cue from Winnicott (1952), considers these sexual events as dramatizing something that is before object relationships—that is, a sexual enactment where "the unit is not the individual, the unit is an environment-individual set-up" (p. 131). The function of such sexual events, therefore, is to "present the setting and the arena for [a particular] type of intrapsychic structure to be acted out, actualized, and known" (p. 133). Khan calls this structure the "collated internal object." To illustrate it, he presents a case history that has remarkable affinities with Bataille's novella and with that author's life. In the case of Khan's patient, her collated internal object consisted of "aspects of her father,

---

[1]"Value," as in English, but also "weight" and "meaning."

aspects of her mother . . . the mother's dissociated unconscious, and an amalgam of self-experiences from very early childhood, as well as what her mother fantasied her to be" (p. 133).

The father of Khan's patient, like Bataille's father, was paralyzed and confined to a chair—in his case through an automobile accident resulting ultimately from his alcoholism. He remained in this condition from shortly after her birth until his death when she was seven. The patient was her father's chief companion when her mother was at work, and she was instructed not to be "rowdy and restless" with him. Again, like Bataille's father, this man was forced to urinate at his chair and always smelled faintly of urine, and of alcohol as well since he drank more and more as the day wore on. This dismal picture was brightened somewhat by his fashioning for her, out of whatever scraps came to hand, ingenious little toys and models.

This scene—part of the daily life of her earliest childhood—remained buried and inaccessible until revived in sexual guise by means of an affair. When married and in her twenties she met a garage mechanic with whom she maintained a relationship—entirely confined to the enactment of a sexual fantasy—for a period of two years. First he would gag her, then, as she looked on in "terrorized fascination," he would tie her in different postures before the actual consummation. She described the mechanic as smelling of "cheap liquor, sweat and oil." Being gagged, of course, duplicated her own childhood condition, but the postures in which she was tied reproduced, often quite exactly, those of her father's partially paralyzed body. The man's dexterous working with the rope, meanwhile, was reminiscent of the gestures her father used when making her toys.

A later affair with a female French teacher revealed aspects of her relationship to her mother. The scenario developed as follows: the patient would work hard at her lesson until the teacher would notice some "naughtiness" (a minor error, an unfastened button) and she would be chastised. Afterward, the two would be reconciled with caresses, followed by intercourse with an artificial penis. This would start tenderly, but after a while she would see "a violent tension and dismay creep over the teacher's face, and it would fill [the patient] with helpless terror and acute concern. She would feel as if the teacher would either explode or exhaust herself to death" (p. 129).

Khan understood this fetishistic, artificial penis as the mother's dissociated unconscious, with which, without knowing it, the patient had had to cope throughout her childhood. This interpretation liberated a vivid recall of the mother as a woman who was never seen to be happy or relaxed, but cloaked her condition in unending and frenetic activity. Similarly, in both these affairs, the patient experienced frenzied passion and excitement, but never her real emotions.

"It's toward the gratifications of death," writes Susan Sontag (1967), "succeeding and surpassing those of eros, that every truly obscene quest ends." With a different inflection, Bataille (1928) posits a region of the mind "where certain images coincide . . . the *completely obscene ones* . . . those on which the conscious floats indefinitely, unable to endure them without an explosion or aberration" (p. 111). This consciousness linked with death pervades the spaces we have touched upon: Rose Cumming's surreal interiors as well as the loci of pornography and perversion. What are their coordinates? Rose Cumming defines them at their most abstract, where the space they shape merges with the unconscious itself. For there is a large shared territory between the imagery of dreams and death: the quality of time frozen, the simultaneous presence of disparate moments; objects and events joined by association in an indeterminately bounded space. The cultural netherworlds of heaven and hell after all are projections, more or less codified, of certain realms of the unconscious.

At what point, then, are we entitled to say that the imagery is not merely that of a dreamworld, but of a deathscape? Freud's (1924) description of the aims of the death instincts suggests a criterion. They strive for a state of eternal rest, therefore avoiding the new as they move backward toward a static, quiescent past. In their sublime way, Rose Cumming's rooms distill this striving. Even the power of eros, discernible in the beauty and unity of her spaces, cannot overshadow these trends. And yet, with the exception of one tour de force—a room filled with deadly objects that is more amusing than frightening—sadism per se is absent from her art. It is certainly not absent from the larger surrealist movement in which her work can be situated. Most obviously, writers like de Sade and Lautréamont were taken as mentors in an attempt to reintegrate the phenomena of cruelty, terror, and death, excluded by the *embourgeoisement* of art. The spaces of surrealist paintings—empty, razor-edged, and harshly lit—are often crueler than their contents. But their themes, too, are often perverse or else perversely handled. The motif of the Gradiva (which Freud gave to surrealism through his essay on Jensen's novel) becomes, in Masson's 1939 painting, butchered meat as it changes from stone to flesh. Delvaux's *Pygmalion* (1939) reverses that theme as well. In a stage-set world, a living Galatea worships the broken statue of her maker more, one feels, than she ever would after his metamorphosis into a banker with a bowler hat. If life is miraculous, on these views, it is a miracle of absurdity: the living themselves are halfway dead.

The spaces of surrealism are funereal and perverse not merely because of their *content*, but because they are an acting out. Their bizarre, gorgeous, erotic imagery, like perverse sex, combines surface sensuality with schizoid emptiness. Deep feeling is split off.

The associations with pornographic literature are pervasive. Max Ernst's "The Robing of the Bride" (1939) might have been an illustration for the *Story of O* (if written years earlier). The final palace scene in Buñuel's *L'âge d'or* refers directly to de Sade's *Cent Vingt Journées*. And the famous opening shots from his *Chien Andalou* (in which an eyeball is sliced with a razor) puts one in mind of Bataille's central theme. Yet, while Bataille supplies us with a key, these surrealist codes remain enigmatic. What they do is show us the world the analysand creates every time he enters the consulting room. For the analytic situation is equally a *mise en scène* for acting out the repressed and in that sense is a perverse environment pervaded by the death instincts.

These instincts, after all, are most obviously present in the repetition compulsion—the essence of the transference. Because the development of a transference neurosis is the *sine qua non* of cure, we can forget that it has no curative value per se. In itself, it is merely a resistance to remembering through acting out. But, of course, to assert that the repetition compulsion manifests the death instincts is to be doubly controversial. The concept of the death instincts is disputed, and the repetition compulsion can be seen as an independent phenomenon with integrative purposes.

To my mind, the compulsion to repeat represents a kind of programming. The configurations of childhood experience (relationships, for example) are laid down as paradigms to be followed again and again, at least in their broader outlines. What is striking is the *mindlessness* with which this is done. It is a mindlessness that cannot be understood simply as the workings of personal unconscious processes. One senses here the suprapersonal strivings of the species itself. In that sense it can be called instinctual and, because it is conservative, belongs to the death instincts by definition.

But it does not follow that the repetition compulsion is ultimately self-destructive. For if primary experience produced happier paradigms, the outcome of repeating them (with no less mindlessness) would be happier. The compulsion belongs to the

realm of the death instincts merely because it results in an
underlying sameness. Needless to say, it can, and often does,
work in tandem with masochism by satisfying guilt in repeated
situations of suffering.

The concept of the death instincts—viewed as a poetic
archetype rather than as a scientific hypothesis—crystallizes
certain human truths. However insupportable the idea of its
own extinction might be to a creature endowed with consciousness, the idea of immortality with its ontological status un-
changed is no less unthinkable. But whereas the former has the
weight of tragedy, the latter becomes bizarrely comic. The idea
of living unendingly a life designed for mortals is both ludicrous
and agonizing. The ordinary absurdity of a life measured out in
coffee spoons becomes an image of hell when taken to infinity.
Although consciousness carries our existence to another plane,
we remain members of a species like any other with a finite span
of life. The species demands of each individual that it live,
reproduce, and then die, since without ongoing deaths the
species could not survive. How can we imagine that such a basic
natural law can hold without resonating in the mind? Undoubtedly, most phenomena said to derive from the death instincts
could be understood without reference to them. And the concept is inherently so vague that its meaningfulness can well be
questioned. Yet, imprecision does not necessarily devalue a
concept. The tall, majestic figure of Death walks silently with us
throughout our lives—our enemy and our friend—just as He has
with all those who came before us. Freud simply gives new
expression to this ancient image—repeated over and over
throughout history and across so many cultures.

* * * *

This image haunted the life of a man whose history may
illuminate our inquiry. Since Khan does not report the ways in

which his patient brought her obsessions to the transference, her case sheds light (as it was meant to do) more on the framework of perversion than on that of analysis—except of course, by analogy. This was not the case with L., the patient of a South American colleague whose story I came to know through an extensive correspondence. By coincidence, I had acquired a small item (it was an ivory rosary bead in the form of a skull) from L.'s collection, which was sold at auction only a year or so before the analysis began. The bead formed part of a group of memento mori—the centerpiece of L.'s unusual holdings. The furnishings sold with it were individually unexceptional. But in the aggregate—upholstered in leather or rich Oriental fabrics and draped in zebra, leopard, and tiger hides—they created the dense Arabian atmosphere of Dulac's illustrations for *The Thousand and One Nights*.

Among the multitude of bibelots that filled the rooms of L.'s jewellike Venetian palazzetto, and apart from the memento mori, three groups of objects stand out: a collection of blackamoors, another of *ecorchés* (both animal and human), and a small but discerning group of arms and armor.

The perfection of his tastes and the strange subject matter of L.'s collections were striking in themselves. But when I read that he had sold the house and exchanged it for a white, bare-walled apartment stripped to the bone, I was all the more intrigued. Soon after, when my colleague began to write of his work with a new analysand, it was startling, but not very difficult, to guess his identity from a few unique details. I watched the unfolding of the case with great curiosity, and from it grew my interest in the spatial components of the analytic situation.

L. had resettled in B_____, a city without a past. In their grandiosity, the town planners had designed it in the shape of a jetliner, and, like all grandiose schemes, it never quite touched the ground. It was filled with people like L. himself who sought the illusion of starting anew.

In the weeks before beginning the analysis, L. reported, he mostly drove for miles and miles each day. The transport system around B_____ was extensive but still under construction, so that many roads ended abruptly in walls of jungle or trailed off into raw clearings where road gangs built their shanties. He felt nothing but an emptiness that could not even be called oppressive. To the first session he brought a fragment of a dream—the image of a man in a burnoose walking off with his head slightly turned. He associated it to a photograph album he'd seen as a boy in his grandmother's house—full of pictures of Egypt in the '90s taken on a grand tour. The rich umbers of the originals survived only at the edges, the rest having bleached to the palest yellow, where ghosts of pyramids and camels lay faded almost beyond recognition. "Wasn't Cleopatra called Egypt?" said L., who primarily saw himself in this image. But also, we should note, Dr. C. is a light-skinned Negro with a profound understanding of the psychological milieu of colonialism.

Whether in unconscious imitation of Freud or because of some common thread in their characters, Dr. C. had furnished his office with art objects that evoked the "archaic." Unlike Freud, however, he displayed only a few. On the wall perpendicular to that of the couch stood a monumental colonial vestment press whose luxuriant baroque carving evoked the jungle. It was surmounted by an emblem of the sixth seal. Dr. C.'s chair occupied the corner between this cabinet and the couch. Three African sculptures were arranged near the facing corner on pedestals of varying height: a Bakongo fetish studded with nails, an Ibibio mask of the Ekpo Njawhaw (society of ghosts and destroyers), and a stylized Poro mask from one of the Dan-Ngare peoples. On the wall parallel to that of the couch hung a large painting by a North American artist of a dog howling in a blue landscape.

In the first session, L. frequently closed his eyes. He had seen everything he needed to see but could not yet bear to take it in. In the second session he moved to the couch, where he again closed his eyes or else stared at the empty plane of the ceiling. In this way he maintained the blankness of the no man's land he had come to inhabit.

During the first few weeks L. revealed, in a desultory way, the events of the previous year: the decision to leave his business interests to a trusted assistant, to sell the house and its contents, and to move to B_____. At first he could not begin to say what had triggered this upheaval. All his life, it was true, he had oscillated between two ideals, which he called "the imperial and the coenobitic"—to live like a prince or like a hermit. Both, of course, represented strategies for power, either through mastery of the world or mastery of his own desires. But in reality, the imperial had prevailed, and with extraordinary visible success. Then at some point he had ceased to draw comfort from his power. It was, he said, as if all the objects in which so much had been invested were suddenly drained of color and flowed together into a kind of gray wash. At the same time his strivings in business began to seem pointless—a kind of drudgery not so different in the end from that of any laborer.

All at once, as he stared at the ceiling in the course of one session, it ceased to be a screen and became instead a *surface* , which described, through some irregularity of the plaster, a shape. It reminded him of "Lalage." Lalage was a porcelain figure he had loved very much and which had been accidentally broken by his housekeeper's little boy. L. had mourned its loss for weeks. To him it had somehow represented the essence of the eighteenth century: the century of Watteau, Constant, and of Rousseau's last "Promenades." Although, in fact, the restorers fixed it expertly, L. could not bring himself to return it to its shelf. Instead, it was *the space it had occupied* that increasingly commanded his attention. It became for him the equivalent of a "R" (ruh), that false door in Egyptian tombs through which the soul could come and go. In fact, the break had opened up a hole into another dimension.

Before long, everything he owned—indeed his entire way of life—got sucked out through it. L. began by pruning his rooms, creating clearings in the undergrowth. But the aesthetic of abundance that governed their design would not tolerate this treatment. Either the "foliage" had to grow again or the clearings had to expand. Bent unconsciously on a new course, L. packed more and more things away. At the same time, he was reducing his social and business activities, approaching in all spheres of his life an ultimate zero. It was at the borders of this zero that he now found himself.

Having said this, L. looked at Dr. C. for the first time in weeks. Without verbalizing an interpretation, C. felt that L. was assuring himself of his presence. In his aimless meanderings down the highways of B_____, C. had become the Ariadne whose thread drew him home.

In the eighth month of treatment, when C. missed two sessions to attend a conference, he returned to find L. disheveled and ominously silent. He had expected some reaction to the break, but the violence of L.'s rage (when, after several sessions, it at last came out) far exceeded his fantasy. With deadly insight, L. blasted him for his wish to be "the world's greatest black analyst," in pursuit of which he had left L. alone. "You use us," he said, "your *patients*, you further your own ends while you pretend to be the perfect fucking wet-nurse mammy, giving out tidy fifty-minute sucks. But I *see* you," he hissed, "looking so discreetly at your discreet, *masculine* Rolex—you Zulu mugger, you nigger whore!" When C. was able to regain an empathic stance, L. revealed what he'd been through. On the first day he'd simply driven around as he usually did, but came back somewhat earlier. On the second day he found himself immobilized. Unable to wash, dress, or eat, he sat in a chair the entire day like Beckett's Murphy, enveloped in oblivion.

In C.'s absence and before his rage emerged, L. reached the bottom of that zero in which his days were mostly spent. It was an emptiness beyond depression, dead at the core but surrounded by frenzy. He tried to masturbate but couldn't. From time to time he got up, walked around, sat down again. Whatever choices presented themselves (should he eat or dress? should he bathe?) could not begin to be made. Every possibility had equal weight or no weight at all. In the rooms themselves, background and foreground were lost. The space splintered into floating, undifferentiated shards, as if, in the aftermath of some Pompeiian disaster, meaning itself had been suspended.

To a degree, this fragmentation persisted in C.'s office, although L. had begun to coalesce even as he prepared for the visit. When the storm lifted at last, C. was able to draw the first links with the pervasive, nontraumatic features of L.'s childhood: the intensity of its loneliness, the barrenness of its landscape, and the rage with which these were associated. L. had a related "memory" that concerned the atmosphere of his childhood house on Saturdays, when the school and work week were over. He imagined himself lying on the floor of the living room, watching the motes in a sunbeam and daydreaming, as many children do, about the possibility of worlds within worlds. Might each mote be a planet like our own, and might ours be a mote in a still larger universe? Were we too observed by an eye so huge the sky itself was but a small section of its vast blue pupil? Mother, depleted of her usual frenzied energy, lay in a darkened room. Father was "away." L. wandered from place to place, unable to focus on anything. He must have been about seven.

The haze of those Saturday mornings enveloped his entire childhood. He remembered a great deal and, at least in the usual sense, had not dealt with the pain of it by repression. But the edges of these memories were soft. The sense of his child's body was likewise soft and permeable, having neither armature nor armor. Like the universe of Bishop Berkeley, his existence was ephemeral—to be wiped out by the blink of an eye. Berkeley, of course, believed that God would not blink. L. had no such faith.

Now, lying on the couch, L. wondered whether he were being held in C.'s gaze or whether C. were looking elsewhere, thinking of other things. Originally, he'd taken to the couch to blot out the room and maintain his isolation. Now he needed to see but, even more, to *be* seen. L. moved to the chair. There, in fact, he rarely met C.'s eye but began to notice more of the room itself. He did this casually and somewhat surreptitiously, concealing his interest with a vacant stare.

He began to talk of Anna. Anna was a black maid who'd worked for the family from the time he was three or four. L.'s mother had spoken of her as "infinitely patient," because, as she moved about on her hands and knees cleaning floors and table legs, she allowed L. to ride on her back. Now it seemed to L. that she was not so much "putting up" with him as enjoying giving him pleasure. His mother had never forgiven a friend for calling her a cow when her breasts had swelled during pregnancy. Anna, without losing any dignity, was quite content to be his horse.

From this and other clues, C. understood the role L. wanted him to play, and it is a tribute to his breadth that he understood the value of it. However, to the extent that Anna was L.'s paradigm for a supportive, comforting mother, the role was tinged with the contempt that adhered to her race and station. She became as well the target of split-off sadistic impulses deflected from his mother for her manifold failures to meet his unspoken demands.

This complex image became sexualized in adolescence, directly in erotic fantasies and also in the erotic *frisson* that attached to certain situations, objects, and spaces. L. described the central fantasy this way: "I am held by a huge Negro slave. He is so big that, though I myself am full grown, I am like a small boy in his arms. As I give myself up to him in the attitude of a *pietà*, he sucks my cock."

L. lived out this fantasy, and variations of it, with a succession of third-world male prostitutes. He brought some to the cheapest hotels, where the sheets were gray and often infested. Sex in these places was "dirty," more overtly sadoma-sochistic, and heightened by the smells of unwashed bodies, stale tobacco, and semen. There was no small degree of danger in such contacts; in fact, L. was robbed and beaten several times. But they preserved an erotic pull he could not resist.

Others he took home to a setting in which he was able to create the illusion of opulence even before he became rich. The effect he achieved (at first unconsciously but later with erudition) was of an oriental sensuality, closer to the innocence of Le Comte du Noüy's harem pictures (of which he came to own some splendid examples) than to the deliberate decadence of, say, Gustave Moreau. In contrast to the hotels, L. established himself within these rooms like a beetle among the overblown roses of a Dutch still life. At first, the working-class young men who came there felt flattered to be treated like tribal chiefs. Yet, however he ennobled them, for him they remained captives and savages.

Even before he began collecting memento mori, Death was a presence in these rooms. It was there in a preference for certain materials (leather, bone, rock crystal, and hides) and in a certain superabundance which, in nature, tends to precede extinction. Many of his sexual encounters courted death and he played with it—posing his Morani with spears and daggers, sometimes incorporating them in dangerous games. (He promised one boy a garnet pendant if he would wound himself from the sternum to the pubis so the stone should appear to bleed.) If the musculature is the organ system of the death instincts, L. was drawn to bodies modeled like Roman cuirasses. By handling them and controlling them, or being handled by them, his own molluscan body acquired—if only for moments—a degree of definition.

As one might expect, an alternation was present in the transference between a denigration of C. (seen as hired help; a whore) and an aggrandizement of him. But in the latter phase, there was always an edge of sarcasm in L.'s adulation. One important function of this complex maneuver was to resist a level of idealization that would have left him too vulnerable to disappointment. This profound resistance could never be entirely overcome.

As he oscillated in his feelings for C., the room took on different lights. It was largely through interpreting these shifts that C. built up a picture of L.'s childhood house and life. For example, L. was very drawn at one point to the African fetish and masks. He himself had not collected primitive art; he preferred European representations of "primitives," concentrating on blackamoors of the seventeenth and eighteenth centuries. Now, in looking at them, he felt chilled. He had the fantasy that C. would bind him to the couch, ritually slaughter and eat him. C. (who adhered to Kleinian concepts in a nonorthodox way) understood this as projective identification: it was L. who wished to kill and cannibalize him, incorporating his imagined powers or, perhaps, reincorporating his own, which had been projected into C. Fortunately, he kept this interpretation to himself, and L. went on to recollect a childhood terror that had persisted for many years. He had believed that a troll-like man lived under his bed who would grab him and eat him if even the smallest part (a finger or toe) hung over the edge. Because he was unable to leave the bed or even make the slightest sound, he was, in effect, imprisoned in his terror. Ultimately, C. interpreted this troll as an amalgam of L.'s own repressed sadistic impulses and his father's dissociated sadism. Elements of this distortion could be traced to each parent's childhood. L.'s father had been beaten viciously by his own father and therefore (as is so often the case with abused children) was impelled to do the same. However, he fought this (to him unacceptable) impulse massively and *never* hit his son. The effort flattened all his affective relations with L., who expressed his unconscious awareness of his father's dissociated cruelty in the bogeyman fantasy. Because his father never hit him, anger took on an apocalyptic dimension—the rage of the *Dies Irae*. For this same reason, L. could never integrate its power to make it his own in ordinary ways.

Another source of this distortion lay in his mother's idealization of her own father, by whom she was simultaneously awed and frightened. She married a man who inspired neither, reserving her idealizing impulses for L. with the proviso that he should never overwhelm her as her father had. The bogeyman can thus be seen as a dark ancestral spirit—the ghost of his grandfather's violent power. These African objects had related meanings for C., who, in contemplating them, attempted to recapture the lost values of his own ancestors. Although C., with a fine irony, was aware of the impossibility of this project as well as of its dense intimate and cultural meanings, it is nevertheless a tribute to the powers of the objects themselves (their "scriptability" in Barthes' sense) that each man could make of them a vehicle for so personal a search.

All his life L. had a compulsion to power that—no matter

how much he had got—remained elusive and external. Now, as he began actually to feel stronger in C.'s presence, he was also able to experience—for the first time—the paradoxical emptiness-in-fullness of his childhood. The emptiness had constituted a skeleton; the fullness the lamé of pettings and praise that draped it. In Venice he had replicated this set-up by deluging the vacancy with objects. In B_____ there was no conceal-ment, but equally no connection to the past. Now they came together, and L. suffered intensely for the first time since his boyhood.

The vacancy was filled with pain. L. awoke with it and went to bed with it and, when he came in, C. felt it pervade the room. He spoke of it as if it were a natural disaster—an earthquake.

When the planets finally moved, L. had been transformed. C. had first described him looking like a debauched baby. Now he seemed simply older. What C. had principally offered during this time was a holding environment. It was his talent to give this, and, for most of his patients, he believed, integrating this aspect of him during a period of breakdown deposited a foun-dation they had lacked. In his view, it was the basis for feelings of fullness and of a capacity for self-nourishment.

L. rejected this utterly. He discerned in the offer C.'s need to offer it and to have it accepted. He declined to see himself as a flayed, boneless thing, supported on C.'s armature and clothed in C.'s new skin. I tend to agree that internalizing the analyst as a strong, safe haven is a chief value of treatment—a value not necessarily weakened by the analyst's need to achieve it. Never-theless, I cannot but admire L.'s terrible rigor. For he now chose his homelessness, and with a full awareness. "Foxes have holes and birds of the air have nests, but the Son of Man," said Jesus, "hath not where to lay his head" (Luke 9:58).

L. terminated abruptly. Between the two alternatives of the

palace or the cell he had found a third, nomadic way, wandering almost haphazardly from one place to another and living in hotels that were nearly the same from New York to Istanbul. In society notices, when his name appeared at all, he was sometimes reported seen in different cities at the same time.

4

The Shared Space

PROLOGUE

The shared space of the consulting room can be defined only by complex multiple geometries. In one, analyst and patient are shaped by the room—warps in its topography. In another, having arrived there preformed, they systematically shape the room to their needs, establishing two spaces whose coexistence may barely be suspected. Finally, they jointly weave a space within the room of shared fantasies and countless minute negotiations.

The consulting room as a shared space, mutually created, is connected to the realms of play and theatre. We owe our thinking in these terms to Winnicott's (1968) work, which expands on the brilliant *aperçu* that "psychotherapy has to do with two people playing together" (p. 591). This concept of therapy as play is epitomized in his technique of the squiggle (1977)—a collaborative universe of shared discourse worked out on a playing field of paper.

But Winnicott's invention was itself preceded by the actuality of children's play. One small boy says to another: "Let's play 'Star Wars'," and as soon as his mate agrees, a new world comes into being. The words, "Let's play . . ." issue an invitation and, at the same time, mark the boundary between conventional reality and the world of "the play." This world is materially the same (to the eye of an onlooker) but transformed: the block of wood that was a portcullis now becomes a ray gun and the castle, demolished, a pile of Venusian debris. From behind the wardrobe's canyon wall an alien creature threatens. Inches from its jaws, the explorers clone a cell to power their weakened engines and the ship blasts off. The action is defined and props identified by a continuous dialogue with sound effects. There is no conscious scenario.[1]

Although such games are filled with clichés derived from TV and the films, the characters and situations remain archetypal. Within the framework of these archetypes—which are satisfying in themselves—feelings are expressed, adult roles rehearsed, and positions of power claimed and ceded between the players.

---

[1]Russell Hoban's *They Came from Aargh!* (New York: Philomel, 1980) captures this play world brilliantly.

At some age, fantasy play will yield to more formalized games in which fantasy itself becomes private and largely unconscious. Purposive adult activities are similarly informed by unconscious (repressed) fantasy. Only in sex, art, and religion is it permitted to resurface and sometimes to become central.

Some of this development has to do with the increasing rationalization of life and concomitantly, as Ariès (1960) has shown, with the increasingly sharp line drawn between adult and child since the Middle Ages.

A parallel development in the theatre is manifested in the fate of the commedia dell'arte. Like children's fantasy play, this improvisational theatre underwent a repression. Its origins are obscure, but the commedia flourished during the Renaissance in an already mature form. From its chief centers at Naples and Venice, it spread throughout Europe via traveling companies playing the fairs. Its end was signaled when Shakespeare and Molière took the commedia's stock plots and characters as inspiration. But Goldoni gave it the *coup de grâce*. What impelled this Venetian to kill off the great indigenous theatre of his homeland? It was done in two strokes, beginning with a play called *The Clever Woman*—the first to be written down in its entirety for a company of commedia players. Goldoni, who had retired to Pisa, knew nothing of its enormously successful performance and was surprised when the company's Pantaleone, Cesare d'Arbes, sought him out and begged him to come back as resident dramatist. Goldoni accepted, and its first production, *The Venetian Twins*, was performed in 1748. *It was played without masks!*

One cannot underestimate the profundity of this move. Borges (1952), seeking historical turning points that, like this one, passed unnoticed in their time, also gives an instance from the theatre: Aeschylus raised the number of actors from one to two. "With the second actor came the dialogue," Borges writes, "and the indefinite possibilities of the reaction of some characters on others" (p. 177). From this germ would flower *Hamlet*, *The Cherry Orchard*, and *Waiting for Godot*.

In 1748 a troupe of players dropped their masks. Within one hundred years, the commedia was already being studied as a historical phenomenon. In such studies (as in the contemporaneous studies of a moribund folklore) the repressed returns as an object of scrutiny. Three stages can thus be discerned: first, the unselfconscious production (the commedia; folk tales told by peasants); second, a transformation into "art" (Goldoni's comedies; La Fontaine's fables); finally, a scholarly treatment of the original material (Pierre Duchartre's *La Comédie Italienne*; Giuseppe Pitre's *Fiabe . . . siciliani*). Freud's investigations find their place in this progression.

In the psychoanalytic situation, the repressed is also allowed to return—as an object of study and as part of a therapy.

The same repressive process that found the old commedia too amoral and unformed (that is to say, a playground for the id) worked simultaneously in the family and in social interaction generally. Thus the sensibility that gave birth to Romanticism (an aesthetic of alienation that is the product of repression) gave birth to its twin: the symptom. Freud, divining the meaning of the symptom, created for the id a new playground in the safety of the consulting room.

But this playground is monitored by the analyst's observing ego. The observing ego functions, among other ways, as a form giver. Such processes are also at work in the improvisational theatre and in children's play. But here they function differently. Let us see how.

The observing ego, almost by definition, is an alienated part of the self that, partly because of its alienation, is accorded a special status whose capacity for "objectivity" is enjoyed by no other agency. It is held to have a privileged connection to reality and, from this point of view, comments upon the action, interpreting and shaping it. As it scans the mind's own productions, and those of its interlocutors, it judges what is and is not a therapeutic intervention, censoring and permitting accordingly.

But the analyst can also speak from a different part of his being and such ejaculations are, in some sense, beyond his control: they have the quality of oracular pronouncements. In making them, he is part of the action, although (since he tends to identify himself with his alienated observing ego) he may feel rather that the action has come to inhabit *him*.

The detached ego (like Redon's detached eye, prefiguring the TV camera) scans the patient's unconscious productions and the analyst's own. Patterns are discerned, and, by reference to a theoretical system, meanings are given to the action. The analyst here is not even in the position of an audience, which, having suspended disbelief, loses self-consciousness and gets caught up in the play. Rather he is in the position of a critic, whose task it is to retain self-consciousness and whose special status creates the illusion that he is in possession of a truer vision of reality.

Although they do not observe themselves as critics during the play, the actions of the commedia's characters and of children during fantasy play may yet be ways of working something out. That is to say, the players may move to a state of greater integration or to a higher level of mastery without the intervention of an interpretive consciousness. "[P]sychotherapy of a deep-going kind," Winnicott (1968) reminds us, "may be done without interpretive work." For "playing is itself a therapy" (p. 597). Not that a critical consciousness was lacking in the commedia's professional actors. Scenes would be critiqued by the troupes for structural defects and technical failures, and from this one may posit the presence of some sort of observing ego operating during the play itself. But this ego's intervention was aesthetic rather than interpretive and *it did not invade the action*. Moreover, this observing ego was the actor's own. By contrast, in the theatre of memorized lines and rehearsed scenes, the director functions as the actor's principal observing ego — now wholly other.

The intervention of an interpretive (i.e., meaning-giving) consciousness is not always necessary to development. If the scenario and the roles are chosen well, an internal logic will bring the characters through.

It is no accident that comedies dominated the repertories of commedia troupes. This type of theatre moves, according to the classic formula, from a state of relative disintegration (confusions of identity, estrangements through misunderstanding) to one of happy resolution (true identities revealed, lovers united again). This formula is no less archetypal than the characters who play it out. Which is to say that anyone caught up in it must unconsciously follow the scheme to its conclusion. In fact, comedy (and tragedy, its counterpart) is the only form of theatre that develops under laws of internal necessity. Goldoni's comedies — as with all the theatrical forms that replaced the commedia — are controlled externally by the individual playwright's personality and ideology — including that of "realism."

The psychoanalytic situation is likewise a theatre whose "play" can develop according to internal or external necessity. Allowing it to evolve by it own rules, however, requires the highest level of expertise.

One reason that the classical improvisational comedy is so hard to reestablish is that its performance required not only unique talents but a unique training (the French word *formation* captures this better). Commedia actors were able to switch roles as necessity required, but to do so was the exception. Usually, in a company of a dozen players, Harlequin would be Harlequin for life. Often his father had been Harlequin before him and his wife – like her mother – played opposite him as Columbine.

The experience of playing an impromptu role for life must be very different from the conventional actor's experience of playing a lifetime of unrelated parts, each overseen by a director and written by a playwright. Not only would the improvisational actor become intensely identified with his role – his own character would evolve within it. Here the affinities with the psychoanalyst's experience are very close.

The analyst, too, for the life of his career, plays an impromptu part with which he becomes identified and which becomes a central vehicle for the evolution of his character. For the duration of the treatment the patient likewise plays his part, developing it as he goes. Together they create a theatre *à deux*.

There are other affinities as well: in both actors and analysts, narcissistic character traits predominate. And the effectiveness of both – since they bring their very beings to their roles – depends upon their personal depth and flexibility. From the sixteenth century to the eighteenth, people of great cultivation were drawn to the commedia. To offer one example, Francesco Andreini (fl. 1558), manager of the Gelosi, could play every kind of musical instrument, spoke Italian, French, Greek, Turkish, and Slavic, served with acclaim as a soldier, and was a poet and a member of the Spensierati – an important Florentine literary academy. His brilliant and beautiful wife, Isabella, herself elected to the Padovan Accademia degli Intenti, was no less accomplished in the classics, theology, and poetry. Tasso, in a Platonizing mode, spoke of nature forming her body as an exquisite framework for her features, as the sky is a setting for the stars. Then to guard her from envy she is identified with her name itself, a word written by Love which expresses only beauty (*sol bellezza esprima*). Throughout their careers, Isabella was the company's prima donna and Francesco either the Captain or the

Sicilian Doctor, a character of his own invention. Beyond all
this, the ordinary requirements of the roles demanded great skill
in singing, dancing, and acrobatics.

Such actors embodied civilization itself in a highly refined
yet robust form. Rather than dampening their work, civilization
gave depth to their roles, otherwise powered by the energies of
great unconscious forces.

In the less spirited style of his time, Freud expressed the
same combination in the analytic milieu. Consider the qualities,
interests, and aptitudes he combined: an aesthetic and anthro-
pological knowledge of biblical and classical antiquity; an accomplished literary style; a profound immersion in postclassical
European literature, philosophy, and scientific thought; access
to his own unconscious and its expression in dreams, humor,
and everyday life; ambition, charisma, and a compelling personal presence. At its best, the analytic tradition continues this
marriage of high civilization animated by primitive drives on a
model of the process as theatre or play. I contrast this with the
technicist's ideal, where analysis becomes the curative treatment
of an emotional disease.

THE PLAY BEGINS

Who begins the game? This question has no single answer,
because analyst/analysand is one of those pairs, each member of
which is unthinkable without the other. In some sense, therefore, it is the game that begins the players. Nevertheless, each
has his part in the beginning. The analyst sets the stage,
proposes the rules, and issues an invitation by advertising his
availability. He must do this, because without a patient he
cannot be an analyst. And he needs to be an analyst. The game

is structured as if the patient's need to be analyzed were its sole *raison d'être*, and this too is part of the game. The patient plays his part by presenting himself for analysis *as an analytic patient*. That is to say, his presentation is already modified by the existence in the culture of the analytic situation, with its theoretical structure and conventions. Thus the actors never appear before one another outside their roles.

The patient's anxiety in coming for the first interview must be understood, therefore, not only as a sign (or manifestation) of a threat to his defenses, as well as of an awakening of desire, but as *part of his role*. For his part, the analyst receives the patient with a calm and welcoming demeanor. His ease and control are thus the counterparts of the patient's excitation and fear. There is a certain sexuality inherent in this set-up, which has many features of a classical seduction scene. According to that scene's archetypal rules, the analyst, as analyst, is always male, sadistic, and parental while the patient, as patient, is always female, masochistic, and childlike. Much of the first phase of treatment, whatever its duration, is taken up with the patient's conflictual struggle with this primal arrangement. Nevertheless the game proceeds, because the players tacitly agree to support one another in their roles.

One might say that all beginnings in psychoanalysis are seduction scenes. The patient—vulnerable merely in presenting himself for analysis—must be courted and wooed until at last he yields.

Of the extant commedia scenarios, most are comedies, and all of these are based on love intrigues. Seductions, of course, are central features of such intrigues. In essence they show the seducer—without the use of force—gaining his ends by overcoming a series of obstacles, both circumstantial (such as husbands or fathers) and moral. The great seducers use rhetorical means almost exclusively. They work from the knowledge that the "victim" wants to be seduced and is prevented only by moral conflict, fear of betrayal, or fear of reprisals. The "victim" too plays her part—fluttering, attempting to escape, seeming to yield, then changing her mind, allowing herself to be caught only when the seducer seems to have proven himself.

In this light, Freud can be seen as a very great seducer—in the high tradition of Casanova and of Ninon de Lenclos. Not that the object of analytic seduction is ever direct sexual pleasure. On the contrary. But the horror we feel at the scandal of an analyst sexually seducing his patient may be less related to the psychic pain the act might cause or to its affinities with breaking the incest taboo than to its rupture of the space of the play. When the gun, loaded with blanks, goes off in the theatre, the hearts of the spectators beat wildly—but also pleasurably. Yet if real bullets should be substituted and the actor, not the character, be killed—we would find ourselves merely sickened. At the moment reality obtrudes, the game is over.

In the game of seduction, all is fair provided the boundaries of the game are not lost. The lover's weapons, as we have said, are chiefly rhetorical—the skillful use of spoken and sometimes of written words. His aim is not merely to convince his beloved—but to win her heart. We must not forget that these words are spoken not merely in fulfillment of a role. The roles go to the very core of the actors' characters.

The rhetoric of seduction can be understood as promoting what Kohut designates self-object transferences. It does this in either of two ways—and often in both. First, as a precondition, the seducer holds the object in his gaze, communicating rapt attention. Then he mirrors her grandiose-exhibitionistic self, which his attentive, admiring presence calls forth. Finally, he projects an image of strength and reliability that can be readily idealized.

As in all seductions, the lovers cannot be truly spontaneous until the relationship is well established.

THE SECOND ACT

When the analysand is committed to the treatment, the analyst can at last afford to be at odds with him. Now, if he is able, he can speak from the tripod—which is to say from an unconscious but not overtly empathic connection. True, he must then respond to the disequilibrium such interventions (or, more properly, outbursts) can produce, but I would distinguish between a disruptive utterance that jumps out of a connected unconscious, and an empathic failure per se.

In a sense, the first phase *establishes* a mutual space. Together, analyst and patient weave a nest of symbiotic illusions in which they take up residence. Frequently the analysand plays with the rules, and the analyst indulges him. Similarly, resistances are often not analyzed or—if the patient himself should note them—the analyst accepts them and even interprets them as necessary and valuable. With each such reassurance, the analyst plucks a bit of down from his breast to line the nest for its occupants' comfort. Bachelard (1969), cataloguing the imagery of primal spaces, makes a prominent heading of nests. Under it he quotes Jules Michelet: "In reality a bird's tool is its own body, that is, its breast, with which it presses and tightens its materials until they have become absolutely pliant, well blended and adapted to the general plan." He adds that "the nest is [the bird's] form and its most immediate effort, I shall even say, its suffering" (*L'Oiseau*, 4th ed., 1858, p. 208).

The analyst's effort to make a nest *for the other* as well as for himself contains an element of sacrifice—a sacrifice of his spontaneity. Its result is the illusion of a good symbiotic container.

Held in that container, the patient can take up a journey abandoned of necessity long ago. Far from being inert, however, the container has energy—which derives in part from the analyst's effort to sustain the symbiosis through countless minute adjustments to the patient's moment-to-moment needs. Another part of its energy derives from the mobilization of the patient's own developmental strivings. Like an infant, the patient flourishes in an environment carefully attuned to his cries and smiles—in the ubiquitous ether of his analyst's love. Even the unavoidable failures of empathic connection promote development as long as the nest remains fundamentally intact.

But at some point, in order for the play to advance, the analyst must introduce what Freud and Antonin Artaud, each in different contexts, have called "the plague." In fact the nest, the symbiotic container, is an illusion. The analyst has allowed himself (partly in fulfillment of his own needs, partly in sacrifice of them) to be used as a self-object for the patient. But he is, in fact, wholly other. To introduce himself as other is to introduce death and chaos.

There are those (e.g., Stolorow et al. 1983) who suggest that in the context of an adequately empathic relationship offered in analysis, the patient will ultimately grow to confront the most archaic critical situations, which were originally insupportable. This is true of most crises, but not of confronting the ultimate arbitrariness of human experience symbolized by death. This confrontation puts the person on a fundamentally different footing with life. To be sure, a solid foundation is required to do this. But the analyst who, having provided this foundation, deprives his patient of the opportunity to go beyond it promotes an illusory, infantilizing vision.

The denial of death is so universal in western culture that

it should not surprise us if analysts succumb to it. Particularly in
the United States (but by no means there exclusively), the part
of Freud's theory that did not deny it—that sought to confront
it and to develop its ramifications—was soon excised. The fact
that this excision was performed by analysts who otherwise
considered themselves entirely orthodox suggests the level of
normal resistance to the meeting with death. For this same
reason, it would not usually be considered an analytic failure for
a patient to terminate without having made that confrontation.
One result has been to trivialize the analytic project as a
branch—a particularly long-drawn and expensive branch—of
the self-improvement industry.

High comedy (one thinks, for example, of *The Tempest*)
does not avoid death; chaos and death are included within it.

Chaos—"the void of primordial matter"—is a concept that
points to an experience of primal reality, unstructured by symbolic forms (culture). Chaos is thus the condition of the perceived world before its elements are named. Since we wear the
spectacles of culture unremittingly, we do not guess at the fictive
nature of the reality they show us. And any hint that this *might*
be the case—that the reality we experience daily might be a
tissue of illusion—is occasion for the greatest anxiety. From the
social side, such an opening up is a taboo.

Breaks in the fabric are introduced by the analyst's empathic failures, by fee raises, vacations, and the like. Breaks of
this sort are not introduced with the express intent of dislocating
the patient's sense of reality, nor are his reactions to them
exploited for this purpose. But when the analyst does do this
intentionally, he moves the play in an entirely different direction.

The value of such a move is to produce a heightened sense
of the conventionality of the ordinary world—an awareness that
the modes of perception and action we take for reality derive

from a ubiquitous cultural screen (with highly individualized warps) interposed between ourselves and the uncategorized world. To know this experientially is to be freer to perceive and to act in unprogrammed ways.

When an analysis enters this phase, the scene of the play shifts radically, and we enter the theatre Artaud (1938) envisioned in *Le Théatre et son Double*.[2]

The Artaudian theatre is not one of naturalistic character development through dialogue. It is a theatre of *gesture*, where words become sounds whose meaning has been lost—intensifying the power of the noise itself. Like a syllable in a mantra, the vibration of these primal vowels can produce a state of mind. The purpose of speech here is not to enlighten through interpretation. It is to *reveal*. "To make metaphysics out of a spoken language," Artaud (1939) wrote, "is to make the language express what it does not ordinarily express; to make use of it in a new, exceptional and unaccustomed fashion; to reveal its possibilities for producing physical shock; to divide and distribute it actively in space; to deal with intonations in an absolutely concrete manner, restoring their power to shatter as well as really to manifest something; to turn against language and its basically utilitarian, one could say alimentary source, against its trapped-beast origins; and finally, to consider language as the form of Incantation."

Artaud proposed to turn language toward madness by intentionally using for moral/aesthetic ends the entire arsenal of

---

[2]There are more than conceptual links between Artaud's visionary theatre and that of psychoanalysis. Through his friends, the Thévenins, Artaud was linked to Marie Bonaparte, but an even stronger link to the analytic movement came through his friendship with Dr. and Mme. Allendy, who contributed generously to his experimental theatre projects. Allendy, one of the founders of psychoanalysis in France, thought of Artaud as a son. He was also part of the circle of *Nouvelle Revue Française* contributors through which psychoanalysis made its entry into France and to which Lacan—the most Artaudian of analysts—belonged.

schizophrenic speech disorders. His purpose was to deeply dis-orient the audience—to drive them mad.

To be driven mad is a deep yearning of all people—a yearning countered by an equally profound terror. Historically, the deconstruction of conventional reality has been understood as a spiritual project. In the last two centuries it came to be seen as an aesthetic and also as a therapeutic project. It is a leitmotif of the Romantic movement's interest in the Other, variously conceived as the exotic, the eastern, the primitive, and the historically remote. It is, of course, a prime force in Dada and Surrealism. And it was central to the initial phases of the psychoanalytic movement before its shift in focus to the ego.

The capacity of the ego to coopt these efforts at its decon-struction is astounding. Therefore the analyst who pits himself against the ego in an analytic theatre of cruelty finds himself facing a formidable opponent.

If we accept Lacan's formulation (1949), then the ego is a precipitate of identifications linked by an illusion of fortresslike solidity that belies its ontological flimsiness. To attack it is to attack any one of its major components (identifications) or its sense of cohesion generally. This is precisely what God did when he decimated Job's "substance": first his sons, daughters, camels, and sheep, then his body. Into Job's comfortable existence, He introduced chaos (which is to say, life) through the agency of Satan—God's destructive (vital) aspect.

God functions here as Job's pestilent analyst, attacking his ego to put his life on a more secure foundation—which is no foundation at all. He does this, however, not as a technique but out of His own nature, that is, out of His desire to be loved exclusively and to dominate (to be lord)—out of His Being.

If God functions as Job's analyst, then the analyst, in the present context, functions as God, who, on Nicholas of Cusa's

formulation, is wholly Other—unapproachable and inconceivable. He can only be desired and longed for, as we desire that
which is in its essence out of reach. The same is true of our inner
selves—that part of ourselves which is experienced as Other. If
God (in Nicholas' brilliant formula) is "He whose center is
everywhere and whose circumference is nowhere," then it is only
possible to contact God by contacting our own centers—a place
beyond the citadel of the ego.

Because it is not a technique but comes solely from his
desire, the gesture that will penetrate (shatter) the patient's ego is
unpremeditated and cannot be discussed prescriptively. Nor, for
that matter, can we warn against it.

The stage of the analysis that corresponds to a theatre of
cruelty begins with the analyst's willingness to accept the role of
God in his patient's life; to be the agent of the ego's collapse and
the only perfect object of his patient's love.

To be God—to take God as model for one's role as a
therapist—is to act in a completely unitary way, undivided and
unselfconscious. From this position, an action—a God's action
or a godlike action—is a manifestation of Being. As such it can
never be a mistake.

The purest statement of this truth is found, not in any
psychoanalytic text, but in Heinrich von Kleist's (1810) "On the
Marionette Theatre." The marionette, Kleist argues, is much
superior to the human dancer, because when operated by a
puppeteer who places himself at the marionette's own center of
gravity, it acts quite without affectation. "For affectation sets in
. . . when the soul, the *vis motrix*, is elsewhere than at the center
of gravity during its movement" (p. 44).

Affectation is a form of self-consciousness—that is, of the
human condition; its entails the awkward gesture. "Such mis-
takes are unavoidable," says Kleist, "since we have eaten of the
tree of knowledge. The gates of Eden are barred against us and

the angel drives us on. We must make a journey round the world and see whether we can perhaps find another place to creep in at" (p. 46). Such a place is suggested by the fact that while a god can perhaps rival a puppet in purity of gesture, a man cannot. The place to creep in, then, "is where god and marionette intersect, . . . where both ends of the world's circle fit into each other" (p. 46).

As an example of the loss of grace through self-consciousness (an example that uncannily prefigures Lacan's mirror-stage essay) Kleist gives the case of a young man who notices, quite innocently, the resemblance between a chance posture of his own and that of the Spinero, a well-known classical sculpture. The resemblance is indeed exact, but the observer, to whom the young man points it out, perversely denies it. The youth repeats the gesture over and over, attempting to prove the resemblance—and of course fails. This attempt signals the end of innocence. From then on "he would spend the whole day in front of the mirror, and one by one his charms began to fade. An invisible, intangible force seemed to spread itself like an iron net over his free, unselfconscious gestures, and within a year he had completely lost the extraordinary charm which had delighted everyone who saw him" (p. 48).

How shall we recover that lost innocence? Kleist, without being too precise, suggests an answer: ". . . as one line, when it crosses another, suddenly appears on the other side of the intersecting point after its passage through infinity . . . so too, when knowledge has likewise passed through infinity, grace will reappear." He asks whether "we must eat again of the tree of knowledge in order to relapse into a state of Innocence?" and replies, "Certainly . . . that is the last chapter of the history of the world" (p. 49).

The medium of the ego is symbolic form (culture), so that

the disruption of the ego's false sense of reality is accomplished through the disruption of its acculturated expectations—especially, but not exclusively, in the realm of language. Language must be made "to reveal its possibilities for producing physical shock," to produce a shattering visceral experience.

The recovery of innocence is possible when the links of the ego's iron net are broken. Since the person identifies himself with his ego, this can only be experienced as a breakdown—a passage through infinity.

A CASE HISTORY

When J. entered the room I had the sensation of being swept by pulsing lights like green Loie Fuller veils, edged with orange and melting into gold. The audience screamed with excitement! One decibel higher, I thought, and we'll all be inundated.

But the lights stopped and dimmed, the crowd grew silent, and J. began her song. It was an old-fashioned song about a woman who gives everything to a man and gives more the more he takes and the less he cares. In singing it her voice had the raw, street-whore rasp of Joplin and the openness of the young Yvette Guilbert melting hearts at the Divan Japonais. Yet, she was nothing less than herself, and that was sensational. Imagine a tall, Burne-Jones redhead (her hair was that rich) with an elegant body sheathed in black sequins whose beauty keeps flickering like a strobe light between cold passion (impossible to touch) and the utmost accessibility. . . .

This vignette extracted from my journals was an attempt to epitomize the effect J. produced in the first interview. It also evokes the shape the relationship assumed from the start: J. was to be the star and I her enraptured audience. The value of this set-up—a narrow mirror transference in Kohut's (1971) taxonomy—would be in part to move her from a masochistic, persecuted position to a sadistic one.

J. had always been involved with bikers and ex-marines in relationships that more or less victimized her. R., her present lover, had left a military career to be an artist. He devoted himself mainly to sculpture as a performance art, to body-building, and to women. According to J., he made love like a satyr and smelled like a goat.

The image J. herself projected was gentle and sweet na-tured. She had had a few parts in showcase productions, but otherwise earned her living by waitressing and modeling; money worries were constant. Until fairly recently, she had been active in a religion that stressed universal love and a rather strict morality.

Within the first year of treatment, J. withdrew from acting and worked minimally. She spent her days at home. Her guitar—an old love—was taken up again and she began com-posing songs. Within the loft space she shared with R., J. built herself a little room.

The room she built at home was the double of the one we built together—twig by twig. And there is a sense in which both rooms were the counterparts of an interior room in which she had taken up residence—for in those days she lived more fully in her unconscious than she did in everyday reality. The dreams she brought me from it were luxurious, baroque canvases— panoramic descents into a netherworld both dangerous and magnificent. They contrasted markedly with the cloistered sim-plicity of her waking life.

My eyes registered every shadow that passed across her face. Although a kind of symbiotic attunement, like an aeolian harp, may be part of the therapist's condition, with J. this sensitivity was unusually heightened. J. banqueted on my atten-tion and grew voluptuous. Eventually this *volupté* spilled over into an affair with N. that translated the therapeutic relation-

ship to a physical plane. It was a mostly sexual relationship in
which an exquisitely refined tactile language took the place of
words. Eventually, as that affair ended, J. developed this relationship with herself as a kind of instrument. She took delight in
the broadening of its range, the adding of registers and timbres,
the mixtures of sound it could produce—and ultimately in her
own capacity to play it with increasing control and refinement.
Simultaneously, the range of her compositions broadened and
had to be scored for synthetic as well as for conventional sounds.

The sessions of this first period—which lasted over two
years—were a kind of sustained *Magnificat*. My adoration magnified her as her performance magnified me. When the great
ballerina Maria Taglioni gave a command performance for
Nicholas I, who, after all, commanded whom? The aggrandizement was mutual. Likewise, in the theatre of the family, the
child's grandiose–exhibitionistic display puts the parent in the
royal box.

In my own hall of mirrors, J.'s sense of her own value
doubled and redoubled while, at the same time, her creative
drives expanded. Eventually she needed to move beyond the
walls of our miniature theatre and of her own cozy room. Of the
many things that made this possible, three stand out in particular. The first was a dream in which she is pursued through a
Piranesian cellar by a rat. Just as it gains on her at the top of a
stair she finds a knife in her hands, turns, and kills it.

In another dream fragment, she is a child playing board
games with another little girl in a gingerbread gazebo. Suddenly
they are menaced by a madwoman who shatters their absorption, and J. awakens terrified.

The dream of the rat in the cellar was the last in a long
series of dreams of being threatened by some terrifying thing,
but the first in which she returned the attack. Beyond noting
this, I said nothing.

The second fragment had one obvious interpretation and another less obvious and more powerful one. J.'s mother had been subject to psychotic episodes (she may have been manic-depressive) and would, at such times, burst in on J. in the room she shared with her sister with the same terrifying effects as the madwoman in the dream. Since these episodes were not part of the everyday fabric of J.'s childhood, they constituted true *traumata*, easily subject to isolation and difficult to integrate. But, as Kohut (1971) has observed, traumatic events "must be understood in the context of the parents' personality and of the history of the parents' whole relationship with the child prior to the external event ... around which the child's psychopathology crystalized" (p. 80). In this light, the madwoman was an aspect of J.'s character—disallowed and split off.

Simply to be told in an admiring way that she was powerful and crazy had an electrifying effect. Her body and face seemed suffused with a new energy. In time, it spilled over into her work, which became more sinister, anodized, and bloodthirsty; she became a vampire.

As a vampire, J. turned on R., whose goatishness was no match for her now. She kicked him out and felt no remorse. When she'd removed every vestige of his presence (she would like to have fumigated the place), J. assembled a band of adoring boys. She lined them up behind her like Busby Berkeley galley slaves and planted herself in their midst—a combination of Venus in Furs and playful High Chicaboom.

At this point I raised her fee.

Because of the current state of the transference, she accepted the raise as a recognition of her new status. It spurred her on and, for the first time in her life, she became serious about money. First she invested in real estate and made money. Then she opened a restaurant (called J.'s) and made even more money. The more she made from these sources, the more aggressively she pursued her stage career. When a major label turned her down, J. formed her own recording company and promoted herself furiously. At first she achieved an underground *succès d'estime*. Then, with "Love Me," she hit the charts. For nearly two years her popularity climbed like a rocket. And then, without any warning, it fell.

Until then my role had been well defined. I was J.'s adoring audience, a mirror reflecting and rereflecting not only what she saw of herself and its idealization, but also what she did not see, so that her dimensions grew in number as well as in size. Beyond these, I was the thread that held this collaged self in place while the new tissue put down roots and grew cohesive. But something different was demanded of me now.

J. was not a manic-depressive, but she had a manic-depressive's world view. Despite the reintegration of alienated fragments and the subsequent release of creative energies, her sense of life remained fundamentally either/or. Either angelic or demonic, famous or obscure, beautiful or ugly, cruel or victimized. With the collapse of her career a switch was thrown: the room trembled, the walls swiveled on hidden pins, and this shimmering rococo space with its apotheosis and its glass became a Bedlam.

Midway in the transformation I said (without knowing why, and with the feeling that I was doing "something wrong"): "There is no success like failure and failure's no success at all" (from Bob Dylan's song "Love Minus Zero"). In retrospect, I had grasped the impossibility of her Manichean split and reformulated it as a paradox. But I did not do this consciously, and that, no doubt, was the source of its accuracy and its power.

The immediate effect was unremarkable. At first she looked somewhat irritated, then smiled in a puzzled way and lapsed into silence. In a few minutes the session ended; J. slipped on her rhinestone stilettos and left. When she came back two days later, she looked like a ship battered on the rocks.

She hadn't washed or changed her clothes; her hair was tangled and her skin so pale I could see the outlines of her skull. She walked jerkily across the floor and sank down like a puppet in a chair. After our last session she'd gone home and fallen into a troubled, dream-filled sleep. In it, she'd found herself transported to a new-wave lamasery nightclub called (in icy neon letters) False Dawn. The high mountain air was thin and the aurora borealis played like a light show. The great revolving sky seemed like a crystal dome on which the stars were etched, ringing as it turned with an indescribable sound. When her eyes had adjusted to the light, she realized that the landscape mirrored the sky—a great *tapis vert* stretched for miles ahead of her, gray-green in the half-light and dotted with white flowers. On her left stood a monumental gray boulder carved like a skull whose mouth she guessed would lead to Hell. On her right, as high as the skull, stood a truncated marble pyramid surmounted by a throne. On it sat a luminous and beautiful Presence—the very center of the Universe. J., standing at the apex of this celestial stage set, gazed up at the throne in adoration and felt herself adored in return. After a long while, when she felt full and had turned to walk away, she heard the warning: "Do not look back!" But she could not help herself. What she then saw horrified her: the face whose beauty was beyond description had been transformed, merging the death's head and the god's into one.

At this point in her narration, J. cried—doubled up and holding herself as if physically tormented. For my part, I felt neither moved by what I saw nor impelled to comfort her. Not that my feelings were alienated. But I had somehow grasped the necessity of this condition and understood its larger value.

This distance from her suffering—in marked contrast to my former high sensitivity—pervaded the sessions of the ensuing months. One might say that in making that paradoxical statement I had taken up a position outside the symbiosis and declared my separateness. This betrayal—like sexual infidelities in other contexts—broke the illusion of two-in-one. In becoming a person apart, I also became good-and-bad. The loss of the sense of unity, therefore, entails a loss of the ideal.

J.'s mood changes during this period were rapid and violent. Some days she was so depressed she could not get out of bed. She would miss a number of sessions and then appear, wraithlike, moving like a sleepwalker across the room. In this state, whole sessions might be passed in silence. Then something would ignite her and she would vilify me, hissing from the edge of the couch like a gargoyle Medusa. The songs she wrote during this period were equally extreme: some were love songs (among them the haunting "Double Suicide" which begins, "We should melt in air, our bones, our hair"). Others were songs of social protest—an alien genre for her and among the worst she ever produced.

That year I took my vacation in July. Despite the violence of her moods, I was not afraid to leave her. Nor did she seem to care. I took our mutual indifference as a sign that the process she was in had become entirely her own.

I put her out of my mind (or thought I had) until, at a Gesualdo concert at Maser, I suddenly saw her sitting opposite me across the round Palladian chapel. The shock precipitated a severe tachycardia episode. Perhaps my anxiety was heightened by the bizarre harmonics of *Moro lasso* in which the words *chi dar vita mia può,/ ahi, mi dà morte* are repeated endlessly in vertiginous and clashing chromatic cascades. J. did not seem to see me, even though my eyes compulsively sought hers. As I hurried toward the exit, I saw her red hair a few yards ahead of me. Outside, she stood on the porch, lighting a cigarette. I rushed past her, hoping to cross the piazza and get to my car without our meeting, but, somehow, I could not restrain myself from checking. I turned around. *It was not J.!*

When I came back in mid-August, J. was visibly transformed. In April she had been commissioned by the American Evangelical Union to write a rock opera. Although she was free to choose her own subject and was assured of doctrinal and aesthetic freedom, she was asked to address specifically the theme of challenges to faith. Throughout that spring she spent her days at the Krikorian Institute, reviewing genocide documents and taped interviews. At first she was listening for the attitudes of survivors—Gypsies, Jews, Armenians—to these unfathomable, cataclysmic events. J. thought it miraculous that any of them should have felt redeemed by their experiences. What made this possible?

Then, inevitably, her attention turned toward the persecutors. Victim and persecutor are, after all, mutually entailed, each unthinkable without the other. This meant that if any survivor should have felt redeemed, his persecutors were necessary to his redemption. Others have noted this paradox and its theological implications, but for J. the awareness was fresh and awesome. This is as far as she'd come when I'd left.

When I returned six weeks later, the piece was nearly finished. In a fever of inspiration that had its defensive aspects (keeping the self-object present through constant work) she had found her theme, sketched the plot, and composed nearly all the music. Later she would call it *The Redeemer*, but its working title was *Judas*.

Her audacious thesis, simply put, was that Judas had chosen the role of traitor, and the infinite suffering it entailed, as an act of sacrifice to make the Resurrection possible.[3] As Jesus ascended into heaven to sit at God's right hand, Judas by a parallel route descended into Hell to be unceasingly tormented. Which sacrifice, she asked, was the greater—those few hours on the cross or that eternity of pain? Finally, since it is inconceivable that the divine sacrifice should be inferior to any other, in whom was the word truly made flesh—in the body of the Nazarene or of the Sicarian?

Working largely with a synthesizer and the great organ at St. John's, J. had produced sounds that combined the complex harmonic dissonances of the *Art of the Fugue* (the last, unfinished segments) with the transparent veils of sound one associates with Messiaen. The effect produced a musical experience different in kind from either of its elements: a kind of unearthly peace in which the sense of a terrible reality is not lost.

Of the many wonderful passages in the opera, a few stand out in my memory. The first is Judas's acceptance of the thirty pieces of silver. In the more usual passion play, our sadness at this betrayal is mitigated: if the Crucifixion is now in sight, the Resurrection at least has been advanced; we have little but contempt for the traitor. But in J.'s work, Judas's acceptance of his role had already been established, so that the kiss and the money seal his fate no less than they do his victim's. They become poignant acts of an incomprehensible heroism.

In the finale, J. capitalizes on the contrasts offered in the gospels between the *lignum crucis* on which Jesus hung—a dead wood that, in the remarkable symbolism of the Easter liturgy, bursts into bloom at the moment of the Resurrection—and the blasted tree in Aceldama whose fruit is a hanged man and whose field becomes a graveyard. Because she makes us feel the love in

---

[3]Some readers may have noticed that J-L. Borges treats this theme in his "Three Versions of Judas" (1964) in exactly the same way, but J., always original, discovered it independently.

that betrayal and the acceptance of damnation in that suicide, we are turned inside out by Judas's death—an offering to Jesus and to the world.

This is not the place to detail how the A.E.U. reneged on its promise, the specious arguments its spokesmen offered, the court battle that followed, and the (on the whole) beneficial effects all this had on J.'s career. What I do want to outline here is the place of this creation in J.'s analysis and development. She had followed the paradox I'd given her beyond its Aristotelian borders to a place where the principle of contradiction does not apply. There, in a state of great upheaval, the secret of Judas was revealed to her—which is to say, that good and evil are inextricable concomitants of one another—the same insight that Freud grasped in postulating the joint operation of eros and the death instincts. Because this awareness entails the loss of the purity of the good object, it also entails unparalleled grief. But this is mitigated in the end by the redemption of the bad object. The energy bound up in maintaining the split is now available—as it was for J.—to fuel a steady creativity, while the work itself is informed by a new complexity of vision.

The character reorganization that was accomplished in writing *The Redeemer* was paralleled by a reworking of the transference. *I* had betrayed J. (and gotten paid for it as well) by failing to respond empathically when her popularity had waned. Until then, I had functioned, in part, as an idealized self-object anchoring her in the world. My paradoxical exclamation cut her loose—without compass, without sails. Sometimes the sea itself boiled with her rage and sometimes, filled with self-contempt, she nearly sank beneath the waves. With my support and admiration to hold her she could have tolerated the world's rejection. Their loss was shattering. It evoked, I think, the shattering effects of her mother's psychotic episodes, made doubly unbearable by her father's simultaneous withdrawal. On a still more primitive level, she entered and navigated a developmental passage she had never properly passed through—the integration of the split good and bad object that characterizes the depressive position. This was done in an ingenious way that revealed, however, a certain incompleteness. I, as Judas the traitor, am idealized, indeed glorified, yet simultaneously killed and tormented. She recognizes the redemption entailed by the betrayal and feels grateful for it. Yet she cannot help but hate me for disillusioning her.

To take the process further would mean to leave the split behind, since the integration of the good and bad object goes beyond a mixture of traits to produce a new condition, one quite unlike its predecessor. J. herself was aware of a desire to move in this direction. "Do you remember that dream," she asked, "the one with the nightclub called False Dawn? On the one side was the skull and on the other the throne. But between them was a field of flowers. They weren't unusual flowers or remarkable in any way. But they were the most beautiful I've ever seen. When I think of that field I want to be there and be there and never have to leave."

Analysis may be like theatre, but it is not, in the end, governed by the same aesthetic rules. If it were, J. would have terminated then. Instead, she lingered on for nearly a year, cutting down to one session a week and often missing that until, at last, she was able to acknowledge that the end had already taken place.

Time

5

The Psychoanalysis
of Time

INTRODUCTION

Time frames the analytic hour. If we take the metaphor
seriously, this frame gets linked with other frames, but
especially with those of pictures. The framing of pictures
is very ancient, for even frescoes were contained in
plaster moldings or else in trompe l'oeil, painted ones.
We have to go back to the caves of Lascaux to discover

pictures that are truly uncontained. The difference is profound.

The frame, translated into words, declares that "this is Other." The portrait peers out from its frame; the viewer gazes into the landscape. Whatever the genre, a boundary exists that is part of the concept of the painting. Not at Lascaux. That is how we know that the minds of its artists—perhaps too of its culture—were utterly different from our own. An art with no boundaries. An art that is not Other.

The analytic hour has a frame that declares and guards its otherness. And, unique among frames, it has no style. The Dutch still life has a carved ebony frame like a solid piece of furniture. It *is* a piece of furniture. The Boucher has a gilded, leafy frame. It melts at its edges into the room. The analytic frame, by contrast, is simply "Beginning" and "End." In its ideal, at least, it is neutral.

If this frame is offered as a neutral field, patients will treat its boundaries in different and revealing ways. To be overly punctual or to be consistently early or late, to calculate the end or be surprised by it are each quite different behaviors. Yet all are more alike than simply to take the boundaries into account. Within this dimension, the uses of the time frame in diagnosing the ego's condition and building its strengths have been relatively well studied. Peter Hartocollis (1983), for example, has explored time-sense disturbances in various diagnostic categories. He concludes that the felt sense of past–present–future is determined by the ego's sense of adequacy in the face of some difficult reality. No matter when the traumatic event actually took place, the painful experience of inadequacy is perceived as present.

Less well studied are the implications of self psychology for understanding experienced time. From that more recent perspective, a marked concern with time in a patient whose narcissistic development has been impaired functions primarily to produce cohesion in a self threatened with fragmentation. For such a person, the watched clock helps string together bits of time that would otherwise drift apart. By contrast, a more cohesive self can permit the time to move along organically, without relying on a mechanical structuring of the day. Technically, this understanding suggests that time-related obsessive behaviors, when the result of narcissistic damage, are best treated by promoting greater cohesion—a broad effort in which the analysis of time experience may itself play only a small part.

In what follows, I hope to draw out some of the implications of self psychology for understanding time experience. I also want to examine certain questions raised by different psychoanalytic systems—those of ego psychology, self psychology, and Lacanian theory—with regard to the place of fixed-time sessions in the analytic process.

Before beginning, we must be careful not to reduce time experiences entirely to the vicissitudes of individual histories. Time itself has a history—a particular, documentable history in the development of human communities. Beyond that, the origins of time can be traced to the general tendency toward structuring—a tendency that alternates in tension with a tendency toward freedom from structure. We shall examine the one through David Landes's (1983) authoritative book on the history of time and the other through Michel Tournier's novel, *Friday* (1969).

THE ORIGINS OF TIME

We live in a culture that worships the clock—emblem of the god of time. As we shall see, however, it was an already fragmented experience of life that led to the invention of the clock—thus creating a loop that furthered the impossibility of an organic unfolding of the day. According to Landes, mechanical clocks did not appear until the thirteenth century. They were made in response to the monasteries' need for accurately kept services ("hours") demanded by their rules—and especially for the observance of the nocturnal office called matins. The first use of clocks was thus to function as alarms. Since collective prayer was the focal value of monastic life, to have been forced to shorten an office through lateness would have constituted a core offense.

The Cistercian reforms of the early twelfth century had paved the way for the invention of the clock through their emphasis on uniformity and punctuality. But St. Benedict's *Regula*, the foundation of Western monasticism, themselves rested on the innovations of Pachomius—an Egyptian monk of the early fourth century. Those who had preceded him in the desert had lived as hermits or in loose collectives without formal structure. Pachomius virtually created the monasticism we know by proposing an order that prescribed every detail of the day.

Here we may speculate on the psychological roots of Pachomius's institution—and its enormous success—in order to illuminate the experience of time in the analytic situation.

The early desert fathers, inspired by Jesus's example, went alone into the marginal regions of the Middle East to spend their days at prayer and labor. Although the physical rigors of such a life are great, the mental ones are even greater. After all, the line between mystical vision and transient psychosis is a fine one; the hallucinations these men suffered, understood by them as the Devil's temptations, attest to the extraordinary stresses of an eremitical life. Those who emerged from years of isolation with their minds intact must surely have had strong characters. With this kind of strength and the spiritual knowledge their devotion won them, they tended to attract disciples.

Now the character of a disciple is not that of a master (otherwise, he would not remain a disciple for long). The disciple tends to lack the strength to discover his own way unguided. Left alone he is, like a child, threatened with a degree of confusion and fragmentation his character cannot withstand. The disciple requires a discipline. This is precisely what Pachomius offered. The discipline he devised parallels the orthodox structuring of the early Church (exemplified by the efforts of Irenaeus), directed against the individualistic and antihierarchical (hence uncodifiable) doctrines of the Gnostics. Without the orthodoxy of Irenaeus and the rule of Pachomius, Christianity could not have persisted. Social existence inheres in rules.

To be cast out of society is to be cast out of time—and vice versa. Because society, embodied in its rules, is a character-sustaining framework, to be threatened with exile is to face decompensation. Michel Tournier's novel *Friday* (1969), based on Defoe's *Robinson Crusoe*, is a kind of thought experiment to understand the state of mind produced by exile. Cast up on the island of Esperanza, Robinson's first, desperate response is to attempt escape. When the boat he builds cannot be launched, he falls into a state of despair and regression in which even the most basic rules, such as toilet training, are suspended. Then, moved by a residual shame, he begins to order his life by rigorous statutes.

Among his first efforts at recivilization are to begin a calendar and to fabricate a clepsydra (water clock) to regulate his days. "What suddenly dawned upon me with overwhelming certainty," writes Robinson in his journal, "is my need to fight against time, that is to say, to imprison time. Insofar as I live from day to day, I let myself drift; time slips through my fingers, and in losing time I lose myself. When I began a calendar I regained possession of myself" (p. 60).

At first the dripping of the water clock assures him that

time has been tamed. But eventually its consoling plop becomes ominous: "the inexorable dripping of water that can wear away a stone" (p. 66). It is a terrifying image of disintegration, tiny fragments of the self being lost, bit by bit. Then, one night, Robinson forgets to fill the clock and sleeps late. When he realizes that time has stopped, he declares himself a holiday and sets out on a years-long exploration that culminates in a transformed sense of time and being. Here is how he describes that new sense:

> What has changed most in my life is the passing of time, its speed and even its duration. Formerly every day, hour and minute leaned in a sense toward the day, hour and minute that was to follow . . . so time passed rapidly and usefully . . . leaving behind it an accumulation of achievement and wastage which was my history. [p. 203]

But now, the cycle of hours and seasons has merged in the moment, making each instant separate and fresh. Robinson wonders, "Are we not now living in eternity, Friday and I?" (p. 204).

The capacity for self-regulation in sensitive attunement with necessity and desire results from a parenting relationship of similar sensitivity (Kohut 1977). Like Robinson, the patient often enters the analytic situation with poor self-regulating capacities, compensated and revealed by his relationship to the clock. The hour then becomes his Esperanza—his island-mother and his hope.

TIME-SENSE TRANSFORMATIONS

The process that takes Robinson from one sense of time to another is experienced as a rebirth and is analogous to the

transformation that occurs in the successful analysis of a narcissistically damaged patient. We begin with an adult who has
developed a pathological relationship to time in reaction to a
fragmented self-experience. I shall take an obsession with time as
paradigmatic, although it is one of many possible strategies to
counter the anxiety of fragmentation. That anxiety itself derives
from inadequate holding—the lack of a sustaining relationship
sufficiently attuned to changing developmental needs.

Integumented by a fragile net, rather than by strong internal bonds, the patient enters the analytic hour—itself a time
out of time. On the stage created by the time frame, everything
that happens is charged with significance. Consequently the
patient's usual sense of time will be revealed within the hour in
a heightened way.

In the first year of treatment, Evelyn was always punctual, coming to
sessions with a list of topics kept in mind or written out. She proceeded
through the list, speaking in interminable paragraphs linked by the
copulative "and." If I managed to interject some comment, her thread
would be taken up again immediately after I had spoken, acknowl-
edging my words but interweaving them according to the design of her
predetermined discourse. At home she would work at recalling sessions in detail. Likewise, after conversations with certain other people
she would take the equivalent of process notes, sometimes following
up with letters that addressed subtle mood changes or unexplained
lacunae in the interaction. Finally, although she came three times a
week, she called quite regularly between sessions.

All these behaviors can be understood as strategies to make
of time a seamless web—avoiding tears or, if unavoidable, sewing
them up again as fast as possible. This structuring of time had
several, mutually reinforcing origins. Most importantly, Evelyn
had suffered the central trauma of her childhood at the age of six

when Frank, her father, abruptly left home. She was present at the blow-up when he packed his bags and she herself had begged him unsuccessfully to stay. The divorce was violent and ugly. Afterward, her mother coerced her to break off seeing Frank, and when she remarried two years later, Evelyn was made to call the new spouse "Dad." Frank's face was snipped out of all her childhood photos so that where her father had been was, quite literally, a hole. We may say, therefore, that one meaning of her relationship to time was founded on the denial of this primary rupture.

The departure of her father left Evelyn in the care of her mother, who was too narcissistically damaged to respond to Evelyn as an individuated person. Since the mother so often failed to confirm Evelyn's sense of reality, insisting on her own, Evelyn came to lack confidence in the reliability of her feelings. From an early age she would scrupulously examine her interactions, compensating through intellectual discernment for the intuition she could not trust. Her structuring of the hour through lists was an aspect of her distrust of letting the interaction flow along unanalyzed affective channels. At the same time, it was a way of keeping herself intact in the absence of a sustaining milieu.

In this matrix of narcissistic failure, instinctual conflicts, as Kohut (1977) suggests, are inevitably traumatic. The narcissistically damaged parent always discourages libidinal expression (understood as an avenue of individuating, autonomous expression) in favor of a false self that is rule-abiding and compliant. Evelyn could not abandon herself to passion—an experience beyond the clock—any more than she could to the unstructured flow of her own associations. In the act of love she was always aware of an observer whose presence made the situation an *event*—an objective happening rather than a subjective experience. In the jungle of overdetermination that bears upon this inhibition, we must not lose sight of the underlying terrain. In Evelyn's case, this was formed by her mother's inability to attune herself to the flow of her child's changing needs and desires, interposing her own instead.

A turning point in Evelyn's treatment was heralded when she announced, "I don't know what to say today." It was the moment when an arbitrary and defensive structure could be tentatively abandoned in favor of a more natural one. Now the unmeasured segments of the hour could lengthen or contract in sync with the content, and especially with the affective tone of what was being said. This kind of development is precluded by a structured, goal-oriented psychotherapy. It is also precluded by a psychoanalysis structured through formulaic responses. How, after all, can the patient develop an authentic flow of associations if they are met with predetermined interpretations? No less than the patient, the analyst must "not know what to say today." The analyst's highly sensitive and receptive ignorance ("evenly hovering attention") establishes a timeless matrix in which the relationship unfolds. It is this matrix that the patient needs to internalize, no less than the object himself.

Like his silence (see Chapter 8), the analyst's timelessness replicates the mother-as-environment—an environment that, at its best, forms and reforms itself in accord with the infant's fluctuating demands. Writing of an allied concept of space, E. James Anthony (1975) suggests that if the therapist can divest himself of the idea that "nothing will happen unless he makes it happen or helps it to happen" (p. 330), this space will become a fertile transitional zone for quiet development. But the analyst may see this role of environment-mother as degrading. It requires him, after all, not only to subordinate his personal demands in the usual way but continually to become what his patient needs him to be so that even the sanctioned gratifications of a professional persona (the pleasure of offering interpretations, for example) may be lost. Without this sacrifice his function as environment will crumble. But if he is able to maintain it reasonably well, the patient will ultimately find his own rhythm of expression—and then grow to accommodate the demands of conventional reality.

Richard usually began sessions cut off from emotion, filling the hour with chatty news of the intervening days, recounted by a charming yet superficial self. He was protected by wit and urbanity from the devastating feelings his words should often have entailed. Yet these feelings would sometimes start to surface toward the end of a session. For a long time I ended punctually, understanding and interpreting to him the resistive function of his timing. Yet nothing changed until one day when the appointment following his had been canceled and we ran over into the vacant hour. I had "lost track" of the time—a slip I came to understand as a wish to respond to his own timing. Through my correctly punctual endings and my interpretations I had been denying my own empathic messages, informing me of Richard's need for a self-object attuned to his affective states—a developmental requirement Richard's alcoholic mother had never adequately met.

Now, with this extra time, the feelings that would have been choked off by my obedience to the clock flowed on. The sense of emptiness he'd had at a recent party evoked a childhood scene: he was a little boy in a bar with his parents on a Saturday afternoon. As the hours dragged on, Richard—terribly bored and lonely—watched the two adults get increasingly drunk. He felt not only lost and forgotten, but also terrified because he knew the drive home could literally kill them. As he relived this scene and others like it, Richard's pity and love for the child he'd been grew until at last he could cry for him. Throughout this development, we were connected by a bond that transcended the ending, when it did come, leaving us both deeply satisfied.

In this instance, if the therapist's role is understood as largely concerned with the analysis of resistance, then the expression of feeling and the satisfying bond that resulted from this expanded session may be seen as gratuitous outcomes, rather than as legitimate analytic goals. We have then two profoundly different views of the purpose of analytic practice—the difference between a classical/ego psychology understanding and that of self psychology. If Richard's timing is understood as resistance, then that resistance must be analyzed. Assuming the analysis is correct and well timed, a continuing series of associations will be opened up. If, on the other hand, it is seen as analogous to a baby's hunger cycles—in which time is measured by digestive processes rather than by the clock—then the analyst must respond by attuning himself to it. The first approach follows from the idea that the behavior is the outcome of unconscious conflict—a conflict revealed in the transference itself as a manifestation of the repetition compulsion and thus an acting out rather than a remembering. The second (self psychology) approach follows from the idea that the behavior is out of sync with the time frame not as resistance but because a legitimate developmental need—in this case to be responded to on the baby's time, not on the mother's—has never been properly met, causing a part of the self to split off and weakening the capacity to function "realistically." This split-off, infantile self and its needs are revived in the transference—a self-object rather than a neurotic transference. In the context of a self-object transference, the expression of feeling and a satisfying bond are treatment goals, because, according to D. Socarides and R. Stolorow (1984), it is in the context of this bond, achieved through affective expression, that the analyst's parenting functions are internalized.

In the next session I proposed we move his hour to the end of the day to keep this flexibility possible. Whether this change constitutes a parameter depends on whether the fixed-time session is taken as a rule. If it is, the outcome is the only test for the validity of altering it.

Sometimes it would be clear that, despite an open end, no emotional bedrock could be reached. But even then there was value in the obviousness of this to both of us, and its independence of the time frame. On the other hand, when Richard did connect to feelings, these could be experienced fully. As we worked on, this tended to happen not only more often but within shorter spans of time.

Parallel to this development was a change in my (our) handling of the end. At first, even though we ran over, I would signal the end by saying, for example, "Let's stop now." I allowed myself to be guided by my feeling either that the natural end had come or that it would not be reached in the amount of time I was willing to continue. ("Natural," here, indicates the achievement of a state of mutual satisfaction such as that of a symbiotically attuned mother and infant. The end is signaled by feelings of fullness and completion rather than by an external agent.) Nevertheless, he experienced all endings as abrupt and painful and asked me to prepare him for them shortly beforehand. After a while, he began to do this himself, and increasingly, sessions ended within the standard hour. Eventually, the lateness of the session outweighed for him the value of its flexible length and he asked for an earlier time.

Because it involved the introduction of what would usually be called a parameter, this example might be viewed as a special case. Nevertheless, I believe it embodies a principle that can be universalized. No one comes to treatment with an undistorted sense of time. After all, the same forces that work to make the transference possible (resulting in a distorted perception of the analyst) function equally to distort the experience of the analytic situation in the dimensions of time and space. If the analyst and the situation provide an open framework with no more than a beginning and end, the patient will begin by structuring the span in characteristic and revealing ways. But eventually he will respond by exchanging a false and defensive time structure for one that flows with his feelings. To accomplish this change may or may not require the use of a flexible hour—but, *provided the analyst's own time sense is open*, the patient will eventually be able to take clock time into account without losing its affective measure.

THE AXIOM OF TIME

The introduction of a parameter does not alter the fundamental axioms of the system—it merely suspends one for a specific reason with the expectation that it will ultimately be reaffirmed. To deny an axiom, on the other hand, is to introduce a fundamental change. A psychoanalysis without fixed-time sessions is like Euclid's geometry without the fifth postulate: it defines a different universe.[1] Here I will describe three psychoanalytic universes deriving from different axioms of the time frame.

• An ego-psychology analysis values the fixed-time session as itself a curative framework. At the most general level (and at the risk of oversimplification), the goal of treatment is to strengthen the ego's capacity to recognize and negotiate reality while mediating among the other agencies, so that needs and desires can be satisfied. Reality here is not a remote construct but rather the totality of social conventions and practical arrangements that sustain daily life in the world. From this point of view, the fixed-time session is instituted to make a professional life possible for the analyst and to allow patients to slot sessions into their own scheduled existences. Since the fixed-time session

---

[1]The postulate that one and only one line parallel to a given line can be drawn through a point external to the line. Substitution for this postulate in the nineteenth century produced the non-euclidean geometries of Lobatchevsky/Bolyai and of Riemann—the latter providing Einstein with the mathematical basis for the general theory of relativity.

is reality, the analyst supports the regulating functions of the ego by maintaining it. The time frame functions more axiomatically on this system than on any other.

The weakness here turns on the limitations of a common-sense view of the real. According to that view, it is possible to speak of an objective reality that exists externally—a reality that groups of individuals can perceive, free from the distortions of personal history or culture, thereby permitting true descriptions of it to be readily produced and shared. This confidence in the possibility of objective perception requires a perspective that ignores history and anthropology—treating the contemporary culture of the perceiver as absolute. Undoubtedly this is a serviceable attitude in facilitating communication and maintaining social cohesion. But we are concerned here with the truth value of this position and its clinical consequences. Analysts are trained to winnow the distortions arising out of personal history from their perceptions of the patient. They are not similarly trained to filter out distortions in perception arising from culture. When a common-sense view of the real is enshrined in psychoanalytic theory, the possibility of arriving at a skeptical perspective toward received views of reality is further compromised.

Beyond this, there are two particular cases in which doubt is least likely to arise: first, when patient and analyst are in agreement on reality and, second, when a view of reality is embedded in the frame, which, by virtue of its background status, is less visible than content. With respect to time, the behavior of consistently early, late, or punctual patients will be available for interpretation in terms, say, of unconscious conflict. But the behavior of the reasonably on-time patient (one who tends to arrive perhaps five minutes before his hour) can easily escape notice. Similarly, the analyst's own transference to the time dimension of the frame will tend to escape interpretation. *We are blind to behavior that conforms to the frame, taken as reality* (Bléger 1967).

Jacob Arlow's (1984) article on "Disturbances of the Sense of Time" is a case in point. It reveals that Arlow appreciates the concept of objective time as intrinsic to the highly valued project of a scientific inquiry. Yet the values of science are not themselves held "scientifically." The failure to make this distinction leads to an objectification of scientific concepts, so that clock time becomes real time (or "time" t.c.). This in turn leads to errors in cultural/historical interpretation, as if technologically sophisticated societies were the only ones oriented in reality.

More seriously, it leads to clinical misinterpretations. Arlow understands an ecstatic "timeless" experience, for example, as a disturbance of the sense of time in a performer he treated. But such experiences are "disturbances" only if clock time—an ego-centered notion—is identified with real time. Much of artistic experience is outside the ego's domain and thus must seem aberrant to a therapist (or patient) who takes the ego's constructs for reality itself.

• Neither Kohut nor others who might identify themselves as self psychologists have defined a clear position with respect to time as an element of the frame. To the extent that the fixed-time session is an unexamined inheritance from a classical, and especially an ego psychology, model, the failure to define its place can lead to contradictory efforts within the treatment. To remedy this deficit in a preliminary sketch, I shall take it that a self psychology-oriented analysis would be more likely to give weight to the holding value of predictable and repeated elements of the frame as ways of providing a secure, confidence-inspiring setting. I say this because such a setting functions to enable the establishment of some form of narcissistic transference (mir-

roring or idealizing). A transference of this sort is understood as
the reestablishment of a developmental trend that was truncated in childhood (Kohut 1971). The overriding value of reestablishing it is less to make repressed childhood experience
accessible to consciousness via interpretation than to complete
the truncated process through the analytic relationship. Self
psychology therefore requires the analyst to be active in the
fulfillment of this effort, since he is offering himself not in a
neutral way but rather as an attuned self-object. Similarly, if the
analytic frame is seen in this light as a situational self-object, its
elements can be altered to maintain the empathic attunement
on which development depends.

The practical requirements that establish the fixed-time
session in an ego psychology psychoanalysis would apply here as
well, but with this difference: they would not be taken as Reality
t.c. If it can be shown, therefore, that the fixed-time session does
not respond to the patient's developmental needs and a practical
alternative can be found, the self-psychologist will be prepared
to give it up. Consequently, since fixed-time sessions are not
axiomatic, the decision to provide a flexible hour would not
constitute the introduction of a parameter.

However different, this system has problems of its own. If a
rule no longer determines the length of the hour (for at least part
of the treatment of some patients), the decision to end becomes
more obviously the analyst's choice. It is no less his choice on the
system outlined first, but there that fact is camouflaged by the
analyst's subscription to a rule and by the patient's implicit
agreement. In the present case, the analyst proposes an ending
based on an equation that includes both the patient's and his
own present status. The countertransference dangers are perhaps no greater than on another, more axiomatic system (ad-
herence to rules can as well mask as inhibit countertransference
behavior), but here the analyst must be prepared to handle the

patient's reaction to his self-interested assertions and to the foreground position they give him.

But there are more serious problems. Unlike a classically based or ego psychology analysis, a self psychology analysis entails gratification (White and Weiner 1986). For an arrested developmental trend to begin again and find completion, it is not enough to recover the past. Nor can the patient be expected to find such reactivated primitive needs met outside the analytic setting. The analyst himself and the situation as self-objects are the only agencies through which this process can be accomplished. With this in mind, the flexible hour offers a nuanced way for the situation to remain attuned to the patient's changing needs. What happens, however, when the needs mobilized by this effort seem bottomless? After all, the addictive personality is a principal category to which self psychology is addressed (Kohut 1971)—a very large category with protean manifestations. If the addict's fathomless hunger shifts from its usual object (alcohol, sex, work, etc.) to the analytic situation, and gets manifested as a demand for more and more time, will not treatment become impossible?

Despite this extremely difficult development, we ought not to conclude that the approach itself is wrong. After all, the shift from a behavior that is both destructive and unsatisfying to an attempt at satisfaction through relationship must be seen as positive. The problem is only that the analyst cannot be on twenty-four-hour call to meet the needs of a ravenous baby. It is at this junction that one of the self-help organizations—such as Alcoholics Anonymous or one of the groups modeled on it— may become a valuable adjunct. Because members do make themselves available to one another without time restrictions, they function effectively as holding environments. With the patient established in such a group, the need for the analyst can be scaled down to a manageable level, and more conventional boundaries can be reestablished. But if we take the boundaries of the session for Reality and assert them prematurely, the patient cannot help but experience this as a rejection and devaluation of his needs—and thus a repetition in the analysis of the primal trauma of his childhood.

• In the final system I shall consider, the duration of the hour is equally unfixed. The session does not end in accord with a rule, nor is it determined by an equation of current needs. The session ends to dislocate the ego. Jacques Lacan's (1953) short sessions function like a Zen master's rap on the head as assaults on the attempt to grasp reality—and to reduce reality to what can be grasped. The hour's length here is not an axiom of the system—a part of the frame—but a manipulable weapon in dueling with the fiction-making ego. The analyst wields it to stop the establishment of patterns and the predictability they yield, so that a different and destructured reality can unfold.

The risk here—as in all psychoanalytic systems—lies in the potential for misuse of a powerful technique. It can be handled capriciously, exploitatively, or sadistically. More simply, it can be mistimed. But no system can be absolutely safeguarded from the possibilities of error and perverse intent. A more serious problem concerns whether this "cure" of the ego, through treating what might be called its structural *méconnaissances*, works at the same time to undo those distortions that result from a particular developmental history. If that were the case, its superiority would be apparent. But it may be that only an ego well grounded in conventional reality can afford to experience this ground as illusory. The consideration of this question—so central to the advance of psychoanalysis—has been fraught with political partisanship. It is not possible to eliminate questions of power from these deliberations. At the same time, something no less weighty than power is at stake here, namely, each partisan's sense of the real.

TIME AND REALITY

Each analytic theory, then, is embedded in a metaphysic that profoundly affects the direction of treatment. Because of this, time and all the other elements of the frame should be understood less as axioms of a geometry-like system than as themselves deriving from different assumptions about the nature of reality, knowledge, and experience.

On an ego psychology model, for example, there is a direct attempt to strengthen the capacity to distinguish and negotiate a common-sense reality. The framework of treatment is thought of as real, so that the patient's distorting attitudes toward the frame and his attempts to alter its conditions are necessarily "unrealistic" and therefore constitute evidence of ego failures. Every effort would be made to keep the frame intact, since to alter it would advance the weakness.

A self psychology analysis would hold that the capacity to recognize and negotiate a common-sense reality are by-products of the parent's (and the analyst's) attunement to developmental needs. To meet those needs, however, may require a departure from common-sense reality behavior. In this way the analyst may allow himself and the situation to be experienced and manipulated in accord with the patient's needs, expecting that a combination of manageable failures and a predominant sensitivity will allow the patient eventually to recognize what is actually, in common-sense terms, the case. Although self psychology leaves the question of the nature of reality open, its sense of the real is not obviously different from that of ego psychology. Both systems have as a goal the capacity to satisfy needs in the world defined by common sense. It is on the question of what blocks—and unblocks—the achievement of that goal that they differ.

The Lacanian system is radically different from the others

in its very concept of reality. The analyst is not present as emblem and guardian of a common-sense reality, nor does he offer himself as self-object—an illusion deemed necessary for development. He remains the unpossessable, incomprehensible, Other—the unknowable x beyond the ego's illusory construct. The "cure" here is not just a reorganization of the personality that makes satisfaction obtainable in everyday reality. The ego is indeed cured, but of its very function. One result is to transform the experience of time.

Let us reexamine Tournier's Robinson from this perspective. When Robinson's escape plans fail, he regresses to a primitive condition in which internalized social rules are suspended. It is an experience of decompensation that threatens both his self-esteem and his sense of identity. From the Lacanian (1949) point of view, it is a regression to the mirror stage, and Robinson responds, as does the child of six to eighteen months by imposing a fictive order on this humiliating and fragmented experience. The creation and maintenance of this order is the labor of the ego. It works ceaselessly at making and fortifying its boundaries as well as increasing its domains of control, always deferring pleasure to the future, taking satisfaction only in its efforts (often pointless in themselves) at transforming the primeval land into a rationalized landscape.

Here Friday enters the scene as Robinson's Lacanian analyst. His impact is, quite literally, explosive. Although he goes along at first with the order Robinson imposes, it clearly has no meaning for him, so that even his conformity takes on a subversive, undermining meaning. But he also literally transgresses the rules. One day, in the course of smoking a forbidden pipe of tobacco, Friday accidentally detonates a powder keg. The explosion destroys Robinson's calendar and clepsydra, together with many other whatnots of civilization and stores hoarded for the future. The destruction of time effected by the blow-up has been partially anticipated by Robinson's stopping the clepsydra occasionally and withdrawing to a dark rock-womb deep inside a cave. Consequently, he is prepared to begin learning from Friday a new order—to experience the natural condition of the island, and his own impulses as something other than chaotic—as possessing indeed a logic of their own that makes survival possible without sacrificing the life of the moment. The structure of time is lost; Robinson learns to live in an endless present.

If the gestalt made by the mirror-stage ego is punctured, the fictive nature of conventional reality (which Friday understands intuitively) becomes apparent. It remains a recognizable and negotiable system, but it is not taken for reality itself. As a result, it can be even more easily manipulated than by one who believes it to be hard-core. But the vulnerability of this condition can be equally great, particularly for those visionaries who arrive at it independently and who find themselves without the holding value of a conventional sense of the real. The analyst who can sustain this vision offers a uniquely flexible and empathic self to his patients—a capacity for responsiveness that does not stop short of his personal sense of the real.

WHAT IS TIME?

If clock time is an aspect of the fictive reality created by the mirror-stage ego, what then is time? Beyond the ordering, gestalt-making function of that ego, there can be no time. Since the rational use of language belongs to that same realm, all discussions of time necessarily belong to it as well. Only in poetic language do we get a different sense—and then it is not time at all that gets evoked. That is because time is not so much an actuality of experience as a dimension of the ordering of experience. Without the effort of ordering, therefore, there is no time.

To put it another way, time is an artifact of the ordering function of the acculturated mirror-stage ego—a function embodied in language. At this nexus Wittgenstein's (1960) thought intersects Lacan's to illuminate difficulties in the concept. " It is helpful here to remember," Wittgenstein reminds us, "that it is sometimes almost impossible for a child to believe that one word can have two meanings" (p. 26). "Philosophy," seen in this light, "is a fight against the fascination which forms of language exert upon us" (p. 27). The fact that we can *ask* the question, as St. Augustine (c. 400) did, "What is it I measure . . . when I say . . . 'This time is longer than that'?" seduces us into thinking that "measure" has a consistent usage. In fact, Wittgenstein demonstrates, it is used quite differently with respect to length and time.

Wittgenstein's linguistic philosophy and Lacan's linguistic psychoanalysis have the effect of peeling language from the surface of Reality. In the process, language as exemplar of the symbolic (which includes all of culture) is shown to create a reality so seductively that we take it for Reality itself. The value of traditional psychoanalyses is to cure the patient of the *méconnaissances* deriving from the repetition compulsion, from neurotic compromise, or from developmental arrests. The value of a Lacanian analysis is to cure the patient of a primal *méconnaissance* that is central to the ego's way of knowing. Reality is not revealed in this way: it remains the irreducible *x* of presymbolic experience. Consequently we know no more about time as an aspect of that reality than we did before. We learn only that the time of ordinary discourse is part of a cultural/linguistic game whose elements and rules (some well, some vaguely defined) constitute reality with a small r. This revelation frees us not only from the past but from the present and the future as well.

6

Time and Death

"[T]he idea of death," said Ernest Becker (1973), ". . . is a mainspring of human activity—activity designed largely to avoid the fatality of death . . . by denying in some way that it is the final destiny of man" (p. ix). There is no doubt that Becker's thought captures a human truth. But for death to be denied, it must also be acknowledgeable. The notion of denial suggests a trick of mind—an act of pretending if not of outright lying—that what is known to be the case somehow is not. As used in psychoanalytic discourse, denial is an unconscious process that protects against perception when awareness itself is felt to be a danger. The concept would not be meaningful unless perception were possible, and unless the process could be reversed, bringing into awareness what was formerly held outside. But if awareness hinges on maturation, for some period preceding it neither acknowledgment nor denial can be predicated. That is how it is with death.

Why this should be the case we cannot say. But whatever the reason, no one can imagine his own end in a way that makes a difference until a certain time.

That moment of ripeness arrives in middle age—roughly the fifth and sixth decades of life. The impact of death in these years is a counterpart to the explosion of desire in adolescence. In traditional symbolism, the figure of Amor stands over one's youth, loosing his arrows into unprepared hearts. His pendant in middle life is Death, the skeleton of the *danse macabre* who appears at the height of their powers to men and women of every station. It is in symbolic form that Death makes himself felt—in images and words irradiated with feeling.

Death's first unambiguous visit has all the shock of an icy hand on warm skin. This imagery is clichéd because—in reverse form—it is well grounded in experience. Who can forget, touching the corpse of someone they've loved, the horror of that cold, stonelike surface? It is a true trauma for which no one is prepared. Consequently the experience has no "place" and requires, if integration is to happen at all, ample time and the matrix of a rich symbolic system. In our impoverished culture, such a matrix is weak or absent. For that reason, the experience gets submerged and brought, along with everything else, to the psychoanalytic situation.

Unfortunately, because analysts are members of that same culture, patients often find no help in their need to confront death. Instead, they meet with a more sophisticated but still impenetrable wall of denial. The analyst interprets the patient's death imagery as "something else."

Anything, of course, that can be interpreted can be variously interpreted. And yet, in analytic practice, there is a tendency to take some images (sexual ones especially) at face value while treating others (death images especially) as metaphorical. We shall not fall into the trap of positing what Wallace Stevens called the "irreducible x at the bottom of imagined artifice." For we are all, in the same poet's vision, "men made out of words." Therefore, we must cast the problem, as best we can, largely in the modes of symbolized experience and discourse.

Let us return with this in mind to the case of L., introduced in Chapter 3. If we now reframe the loss of Lalage as an encounter with death, L.'s disengagement from his analyst can illuminate a central passage in facing one's mortality, namely, its neutralization through faith.

Briefly, to recapitulate, the breaking of the porcelain figure opened up a hole in the fabric of L.'s life that could not be closed. In the context of his analysis, the opening led to a recovery of the void his childhood had been when a frenetic mother and an abstracted father left him prone to states of agitated vacancy. But we may note also that the break took place in L.'s middle life, when the defenses that had staved off a lifetime's emptiness had grown weaker. Because of this, the demise of Lalage may also be seen as a death signifier: the irreparable awareness of his own irreparability.

Coming to terms with this may be seen as a developmental task. The solution—when there is one—consists in rebuilding one's life by refounding it; an act of faith. There is a counterpart to this process in analysis, centering on a suspension of disbelief—a faith that the analytic theatre is not "merely" a game. In analysis, as in life, L. would not or could not believe.

Faith, after all, is a mode of experience—antecedent to it and transcendent of it. Tertullian's aphorism, *Credo quia absurdum*, puts a fine point on this thought: faith is not acquired through experience. With it, whenever possible, experience is taken as confirming of what faith already holds. Religious belief is merely a specific instance of faith in a basic fit between ourselves and the world—the faith that our bodies can use its contents as our minds can comprehend its structure. We take ourselves and the world to be interpenetrating realms—ultimately compatible. Complete faithlessness, if it were possible, would mean experiencing the world as deeply arbitrary and inhospitable. It would mean experiencing the network of its apparent laws as a tissue of fictions capable of unraveling at any moment and reconstituting themselves in new and unpredictable ways. Indeed, what are called crises of faith usually take this form—a form of which Job's trials are the paradigm. The fabric of a life is rent through the unimagined loss of some primary good—the death of a mate or child, a substantial loss of property or income, and so forth. Especially if multiple losses of this kind occur in a brief span of time, the world can seem a chaos. To negotiate such trials successfully is to ground one's faith at a relatively unshakable new level where it becomes more independent of the accidents of life.

Arriving at faith in this or that credo, and at whatever level, entails decision. It is the nature of faith in *x* that the believer moves from what is known to a high-level interpretive position through which further experience is screened. That move is never "justified"—but, having made it, we open up one line of development and foreclose others. The path we open may itself be a very difficult one that requires considerable courage to pursue. But to have no faith whatever is a different order of experience. "To live without a goal," said E. M. Cioran (1970), "is more difficult than to live for a bad cause."

How, then, are we to understand L.'s faithlessness? If we look at his life deterministically (an expression of our own faith), we may conclude that childhood experience undermined his capacity to believe in the analytic situation. Alternatively, but from this same perspective, we can examine the analytic relationship to see if the analyst himself unwittingly spoiled L.'s capacity to believe in him. Both lines of inquiry view L.'s ultimate faithlessness as a failure produced by different causal chains. Knowing L.'s case, it would certainly be possible in some nonrigorous but convincing way to establish one or another of these premises. But there is a different way of looking at the outcome that, because it challenges our deepest presuppositions, is more difficult to pursue.

"Psychotherapy," said Winnicott (1968), "has to do with two people playing together" (p. 591). For the play to happen, both players must suspend disbelief. Often that suspension is an achievement that requires, especially for the patient, the laying aside of a profound distrust. Afterward, in order for the play to advance and "succeed," it is imperative that neither participant awake from the "dream" of the action and question its status in reality. For the proscription against questioning the status of a child's transitional objects applies with equal strength to the analytic play. A patient is most likely to question that reality following an empathic failure or a disruption of the frame. But if the analyst recognizes the patient's deep desire to return to the play, it is not difficult to work toward reestablishing a bond and the security of the setting. For in the end it is desire that keeps the play going; desire is the fuel and motor of the patient's faith.

L. felt that desire as keenly as the rest of us, but at the same time he could not deny the truth.

We must not romanticize the truth. However much we may suffer for our beliefs and values, they give structure and meaning to our lives. Yet, as they are neither empirically nor logically grounded, there is never a finally compelling reason for their acceptance. Because of this, the decision to take one up and to base one's life on it means putting a stop to questions at some ultimately arbitrary point: a leap of faith.

The place that religious belief takes in one life is held by revolutionary politics in another, or by feeding the hungry, exterminating the Jews, the psychoanalytic movement, or the Jacobite restoration. Glorious, odd, or evil, these credos focus us. Without cynicism L. saw them all as equally impossible. The hole opened up by the breaking of Lalage remained unfilled—by his analyst or by any other object of belief. Whether or not this faithless life revealed epiphanies of its own I cannot say. When his analyst lost sight of L., he seemed to be wandering like a planet without a sun along paths that looked varied but were always the same.

If we understand that initial break as a glimpse of death, its effect upon L. was to make all of life seem an illusion—a complex of patterns woven in the air. It may be that the awareness of mortality has this disorienting effect upon everyone, but there are different responses to it. Perhaps the most common is amnesia and the resumption of one's former life. Or else there is the return to an old faith or the acquisition of a new one that renders the believer more impervious to dread. Other reactions that keep the initial vision open are rarer, and even among these L.'s was unusual for its purity. It was a dreadful response, but we may also wonder, from a psychoanalytic point of view, about its clinical significance. Before turning to this question, let us look into the case of another man whose testimony to the confrontation with death in midlife is among the most poignant our civilization has produced.

* * * *

T. S. Eliot's *Four Quartets* (1935–1942) record the struggle of a middle-aged man of faith with the problem of death. His faith, however, came first. Christianity, from the time at which Eliot found it, answered demands of his character that were ongoing and independent of crises. Eliot's cultural traditionalism can equally be understood in this way, along with his austere habits, precise manners, and intellectuality. All are the qualities of a single man. As such they must cohere amongst themselves and with other traits as well. They must be related, for example, to what we know of his marriage and private sufferings, to his work as a banker, publisher, and committee member. Most of all, they must fit with his collagist methods of composition and with such lines as these, alternately gorgeous and full of terror ("East Coker," 1940):

> Whisper of running streams, and winter lightning,
> The wild thyme unseen and the wild strawberry,
> The laughter in the garden, echoed ecstasy. [p. 187]

and:

> Oh dark dark dark. They all go into the dark. [p. 185]

A generic death does not confront a generic man. It was with a particular character that Eliot met his particular "death" at the age of forty-six amidst the shambles of his private life and a hideous European war. What was this character? Not enough is known of Eliot's intimate childhood to produce a definitive psychobiography. But, given this limitation, Leon Edel's (1982) work offers the most consistent and insightful portrait anyone has yet made. What I propose here is to summarize Edel's findings and to supplement them from several sources. First, I shall make use of some of Leonard Unger's (1966) critical essays. Since Unger's work was not psychoanalytically informed, it has the advantage of being free of the limitations of psychoanalytic theory as it then stood. His understanding of fragmentation in Eliot's work, for example, was achieved independently of Kohut's use of this concept in tracing narcissistic development. And it is to Kohut's work especially that I shall turn to reinterpret Edel's findings. Lacking that theory, Edel — who is otherwise marvelously perceptive — could not give adequate expression to what he saw. By passing Edel's thought through the lens of Kohut's theory, what we attain is not so much a new image as a sharper, more coherent focus.

* * * *

Edel begins by inquiring into the source of Eliot's depression, "out of which [his] poetry came into being" (p. 164). Eliot himself referred to his condition as *aboulia* — "loss of will, despair, and apathy." Because he uses one classical notion of depression as symptomatic (a consequence) of loss, Edel is obliged to discover such a loss of object or condition in Eliot's past. But there was none. Eliot's *aboulia* was not depression in any classical sense; it was, as I hope to show, a narcissistic condition of fragmentation and depletion. Lacking this latter concept, Edel draws instead on the work of Ernest Schachtel (*Metamorphosis*, 1959), who posits an intrauterine paradise that persists in attenuated ways through childhood. For some, he claims, the loss of that primal paradise cannot be transcended. They long for its restoration or else dream of reconstructing it in a utopian future. As Edel puts it, ". . . they deprive themselves of time present by looking always for time past or for a problematical future . . ." (p. 167). *Aboulia* defines this limbo as a chronic and pathological condition.

Unwittingly, Schachtel's theory itself repeats the human tendency to create paradises and to protect their status by locating them in times and places experience cannot test. But no human condition is truly Edenic. We achieve and maintain such "memories" only by splitting off the painful features of actual experience. This is so certain that we can make a diagnostic rule of it: the more perfect the childhood someone presents, the more terrible it is likely to have been. If Eliot indeed longed for a paradisiacal past, it was for a past he'd never lived. But Edel cannot demonstrate that Eliot had such a notion of a childhood paradise whose loss dominated his life. Not only the theory but also its application are weak. Nevertheless, his *aboulia* can be accounted for through what we know of his early years. Because of the scarcity of facts, however, this account cannot be certain; it can only be more or less convincing.

Eliot was the unexpected last child of middle-aged parents. His closest sibling was already eight when he was born, and an older sister was away at college. His situation in the family thus approximated that of an only child. According to Edel, Eliot's father "was already deaf and so seemed remote and distant to his youngest child" (p. 168). His mother, Charlotte, is described as "an exaltée and religious poet . . ." (p. 168). Edel takes these lines from *"The Family Reunion"* (1939) to be more or less autobiographical:

> The rule of conduct was simply pleasing mother;
> Misconduct was simply being unkind to mother;
> What was wrong was whatever made her suffer,
> And whatever made her happy was what was virtuous—
>   [pp. 89–90]

"On her youngest son," Edel goes on to say, "Charlotte Eliot placed the mantle of her own poetic strivings. He was to perform the work she longed to perform, and he had to win the world's praise and acknowledgement she most desired" (p. 170). At times, Eliot was treated as a wunderkind and as a "special late gift of God." This preciousness was "reinforced by certain phys-ical ailments, in particular a hernia which kept him from sports" (p. 170). His mother did not raise him herself, however, but entrusted his care to an Irish nurse.

This is a familiar picture. It is the picture Alice Miller (1981) sketches, for example, of the sensitive only child who becomes the object of his mother's narcissistic attachment. As such, he may be lavished with affection and treated as a little god. But it is the idealized projection of her self the mother loves—the real little boy behind the projection is unknown, neglected, and painfully alone. No surrogate mother, however good, can ade-quately compensate for such a set-up.

Of the many possible consequences of this kind of mother-ing, three are immediately evident in Eliot's work: profound isolation, difficulties in communicating (attaining satisfaction both in expressing himself and in feeling understood), and experiences of fragmentation.

Unger goes so far as to say that all of Eliot's works are "variations on the theme of isolation" (p. 114). In "The Waste Land" (1922), for example, are the lines:

> We think of the key, each in his prison
> Thinking of the key, each confirms a prison. [p. 69]

and, more explicitly, we find in *The Cocktail Party* (1950):

> No . . . it isn't that I *want* to be alone.
> But that everyone's alone—or so it seems to me.
> They make noises, and think that they are talking to each
>   other:

They make faces and think they understand each other.
And I'm sure that they don't. [p. 134]

The <u>sense of isolation</u> is linked to the failure of communication: <u>the inability to *say*; the impossibility of being *heard*</u>. Take
these famous lines from "Prufrock" (1917):

To have squeezed the universe into a ball
To roll it toward some overwhelming question,
To say: 'I am Lazarus, come from the dead,
Come back to tell you all, I shall tell you all'—
If one, settling a pillow by her head,
  Should say: 'That is not what I meant at all.
  That is not it, at all.' [p. 6]

and later in the same poem: "It is impossible to say just what I
mean!" (p. 6).

The primary results of the foregoing are feelings of discontinuity, emptiness, paralysis, and dispersion. In "Gerontion"
(1920) Eliot writes:

I have lost my sight, smell, hearing, taste, and touch:
How should I use them for your closer contact? [p. 31]

and in "Burnt Norton" (1935):

Internal darkness, deprivation
And destitution of all property,
Dessication of the world of sense,
Evacuation of the world of fancy,
Inoperancy of the world of spirit [p. 179]

Many of Eliot's poems, "The Waste Land" most notably, are
collages of fragments—fragments of poetry sewn together and
themselves stuck with fragments from other, past poets. "Burnt

Norton" opens the *Four Quartets* with a fragment from Hera-
clitus (who is known to us only through fragments). And "The
Waste Land" contains the well-known lines: "These fragments
have I shored against my ruins" (p. 69).

Isolation in childhood produces fragmentation. The development of a cohesive self depends upon being "held" in a
reasonably consistent way by a mother attuned to her child's
affective states and developmental needs—a mother who loves
the whole child. Idealization rules out a sensitive attunement.
The child of vomit, shit, fear and rage, embarrassing outbursts
and insistent demands is exiled by the idealizing mother, who
attends and rewards only those bits that sustain her idealization.
In addition to experiencing fragmentation, the idealized child
also comes to loathe his dirty self—which is also his true self—
filled with energy and a palpable reality. It was thus a broken,
weak, and self-hating child that Mrs. Eliot sent out into the
world to be her champion.

This child nevertheless retained his creativity—not, I think,
because of his suffering (as Edel suggests), but despite it. Yet, to
be open to the unconscious, as the poet must, is dangerous to a
character prone to disintegration. Eliot's youthful intellectuality
was a first line of defense against this threat. He himself, years
later, could barely understand the doctoral thesis he'd written
on the philosophy of F. H. Bradley. That Eliot should have
chosen to explicate Bradley's work on appearance and reality is
itself telling, but I am concerned here less with the content of his
thinking (which always reveals aspects of character) than with
its defensive function. At this early stage, thinking was at odds
with creating and seems an attempt to dominate it. When he
declined an academic career, Eliot ceased to use his intellect as a
bulwark against the imaginative life and began instead to use it
as a support.

This early decision was made in the context of settling in

England and marrying Vivienne Haigh-Wood at the age of
twenty-six. The marriage, the move, and the rejection of an
academic life were all deep acts of rebellion. And it was precisely
in this way that Eliot's family understood them. When he
returned briefly in 1915 to present his decisions after the fact, his
father cut him off without a cent.

Such a rebellion must be seen as an attempt to differentiate
himself from an engulfing family that tended to assimilate its
members' talents to their own ends. In 1915 the authority of the
family, and especially of a patrician family such as Eliot's, was
still very great. Its implicit rules would have required that he
marry an American girl of his own class—known to the family
and on good terms with them. The rules would also have
required that he pursue the academic career to which his talents
disposed him. (He was virtually assured a Harvard professorship,
had he completed his doctorate.) If Eliot had met these conditions, the family would happily have continued to supplement
his income. And his talents as a poet would have been no less
appreciated.

With these three gestures, then, Eliot cut himself off from
his family and so preserved his identity intact. But he paid
heavily in guilt. Beyond that, no comparable gesture could wipe
out the character weaknesses that were the legacy of his childhood.

The refusal of a professorship and the loss of an allowance
forced Eliot to work very hard—briefly as a teacher, then for
eight years in a department of Lloyd's bank, and finally as an
editor and director of Faber & Faber. While he was at the bank,
Ezra Pound tried to get up a subscription for him, but Eliot
refused. He refused, I think, not only out of pride, but also
because the tedium and the obligations of the job helped structure his life. Given the tendency to fragment, after all, Eliot
could not have sustained long stretches of unstructured time

devoted to creative work; the grind helped hold him together. In addition, the split in his daily life mirrored that of his character. It was the same Walter Mitty split Kohut (1971) picked out as defining the narcissistically damaged personality: a grandiose–exhibitionistic self that knows only a secret or circumscribed life and a more visible, clerkish self—dry, colorless, and depleted.

Rather naively, many of Eliot's friends and biographers have blamed Vivienne for the unhappiness of his years with her. But all marriages are *folies à deux*. The madness is always apparent; only the jointness of the enterprise gets obscured. When they met, Eliot's genius was beginning to be recognized but he was personally off-putting—punctilious, reserved, sexually timid. In Virginia Woolf's (1919) words: "how sharp, narrow, & much of a stick Eliot has come to be . . ." (p. 262). Eliot hungered for affection yet, in his extreme inhibition, could not begin to secure it for himself. He *had* to be seduced—and, by all accounts, Vivienne was exceedingly seductive.

No seducer is without self-interest. Vivienne's demands upon her husband—demands not unlike the mother's in *The Family Reunion*—were soon revealed as the haze of early love began to lift. How else, after all, but on the unconscious paradigm of his mother could Eliot have chosen a wife? His "devotion" to Vivienne for all those years derives from the same primal source. It is sheer partiality to read that devotion as love, or to think that he was any more capable of loving her than she him. By all accounts, Vivienne displayed a seductive charm that overlay a character no less narcissistically damaged than his own. The web she cast over him was meant, in the end, to secure his support for her own weakened self.

When Eliot broke with her, he did it with shocking abruptness and finality, never contacting her again before her death. A pattern can be established between this break, the earlier one

with his family, and the later, equally abrupt one with his friend
John Heyward at the time of his remarriage. (The two men had
shared a household for many years, and Eliot feared Heyward's
jealous disapproval.) These ruptures reveal Eliot's sense of relationships as stifling, enmeshing ties. He had to slash them like
Gordian knots in order to get on with his life.

His friendship with Pound, however, was formed on a
different model. In Pound he secured the powerful support of a
powerful man—an armature and container for his fragmented
self and a veritable Niagara of energy. It was an idealizing
transference that Eliot established, not unlike Freud's to Fliess,
except that, in this case, the friends were truly equals. Pound
filled the function of a primal father—supporting Eliot's creative
self like Hermes the infant Dionysus. He introduced Eliot to the
English literary world, got him published in the most influential
journals, and, of course, edited his work. The structuring function that Pound assumed in Eliot's life is most obvious in his
editing of "The Waste Land." Unaided, Eliot simply could not
hold a poem of this length together. All his longer works are
cut-and-paste jobs that depend for their aesthetic wholeness on
skillful editing, subtle linkages of voice, theme, and imagery, and
the reader's own cooperative ear. To read one of Eliot's longer
works is to create a gestalt out of fragments.

But this partnership could not be reparative. Pound's functions were Pound's and Eliot, however grateful, could not make
them his own. Pound stayed, in this sense at least, *il miglior
fabbro*. Although he would never establish a comparable relationship with another *person*, Eliot came to rely upon institu-
tions, belief systems, and work in much the same way. In this,
his development also parallels Freud's after the attenuation of
his friendship with Fliess. There is a sense in which he institutionalized himself, for example, in his editorship of *The Criterion*,
as well as in his lectures and essays on literature and culture. But

it was religion that offered him the richest, most complex and enduring resource for his idealizing needs.

Eliot had been raised a Unitarian—essentially an eighteenth-century deistic and rationalized religion. It did not answer to his sense of the immanence of mystery nor to his need for continuity with the past. In becoming an Anglican, Eliot could experience himself reunited with an ancient tradition containing the fullness of mystery in its liturgy and sacraments.

Eliot valued impersonality—freedom from the trivia of particular lives. But reason is impersonal in a nonhuman way. Aristotle's rules of logic or Russell's *Principia* do not speak to us in a particular voice. The rational functions of mind, therefore, are the easiest to reproduce electronically. The affective, spiritual, ecstatic senses are, on the other hand, deeply personal. In the anthems of Orlando Gibbons or the sermons of Lancelot Andrewes, in the Book of Common Prayer and the King James Bible, Eliot could hear particular voices that answered to his own. The timelessness of sublime experience, unlike that of reason, is touching because it is evoked by human voices. Communicating in a sublime mode, those voices seem to transcend time. They manage to be at once universal and particular, seventeenth and twentieth century, the listener's and the speaker's. In this realm, Eliot could hear and be heard; he was not alone.

As I see it, Eliot was permitted these comforts through the survival of his capacity for transitional experience. The moments in the rose garden—pools of light in those dark and broken years of childhood—could at least sometimes be recaptured with new meaning. When he did find them again, he found them especially in religious experience and in the making of poetry.

Needless to say, the greater part of Eliot's experience of art and religion was conscious and effortful. In writing poetry, the intervals of self-criticism far outnumbered the flashes of inspiration. In his religious life, too, he was a daily communicant. He served for years as an officer of his parish church and on national committees as well. Moments of "echoed ecstasy" cannot have been frequent. What mattered is that Eliot believed in them; *he did not doubt their status in reality* (Winnicott 1953).[1]

When, in about 1934, he came to confront his own mortality, those experiences were part of the repertoire with which he did it. The *Four Quartets* can be seen as an arena—and a trophy—of that confrontation.

* * * *

Because of their richness, these poems can be discussed in many ways—none of which will "translate" them, because, like a dream, a poem belongs to a different realm of mind. For that same reason Eliot thought—and I agree—that one can "get" the meaning of a poem and be deeply moved by it without being able to articulate its meaning in expository language. I want to examine the poems as a middle-aged man's attempt to reconcile himself with a new, concrete, and terrible awareness of his mortality—an awareness that has all the force and immediacy of sexual desire in adolescence. I should say that I am myself deeply moved by these poems. I feel in discussing them the same discomfort I sometimes feel in analyzing a patient's creative work. Analysts and Western thinkers generally tend to give primacy to expository thought—to the work of consciousness and the language of the ego. But art belongs especially to the

---

[1]Winnicott (1953, *op. cit.*) makes the central point about the transitional object that "it is a matter of agreement between us and the baby that we will never ask the question, 'Did you conceive of this or was it presented to you from without?' The important point is that no decision on this point is expected. The question is not to be formulated" (pp. 239–240). This is precisely the attitude taken by Eliot toward the moments of ecstasy and toward the ground of his faith.

realm of transitional experience. The conscious voice can talk *about* that experience, but the two languages are not equivalent. The insistence on translation—which is what interpretation amounts to—can work to devalue and derealize all forms of transitional experience. It is the equivalent of questioning the reality status of a child's transitional objects. Transitional experience has its own integrative movement and must not be probed unnecessarily with the scalpel of interpretation. If I feel justified in examining the *Four Quartets* in this way, it is in the hope that it will advance the psychoanalytic project in a neglected yet critical area.

Writing of Shakespeare, Eliot (1927) remarked that he was "occupied with the struggle—which alone constitutes life for a poet—to transmute his personal and private agonies into something rich and strange, something universal and impersonal" (p. 49). For this reason we shall find few direct references to Eliot's own struggle in the *Quartets*. "Burnt Norton" (1935), written somewhat before the rest, contains no references at all to middle age or death. Seeing it as the work of one who finds himself "at the still point of the turning world," midway between past and future and forced to conjure with the reality of these dual perspectives, may be valuable to our understanding. But no personal and private agonies are present in the poem. They enter only with "East Coker" and its Solomonic first words, "In my beginning is my end."

For a Christian, there is a unity of beginning and end— Jesus the alpha and omega of an existence founded on His incarnation and resurrection—present, historical, and eternal.

But these words are also an elegant expression of mortality. Because all men are mortal, death is implicit in birth. Death lies curled up in the baby like the new flower at the heart of the bulb. These two themes, interlaced throughout the poems, are uttered here in a single breath. In unfolding the mystery of time we are offered a certain "solution," but in the fixity of an end we have the primary, inexorable problem. These words were first said, after all, by Mary Queen of Scots when she found herself living under her cousin's sentence of death.

Once we have heard that sentence, all of time is transformed. The past—and not only one's personal past but the history of the race and of the universe—becomes a densely patterned whole. We are here, first, because of the long enchainment of couplings of male and female—a chain that stretches back before humanity itself to the chemical couplings of the stars. At the same time that the past assumes the solidity and grandeur of a monument—a Hadrian's column in which to take one's place—the patterns are revealed as false and the monuments crumble. For "the pattern is new in every moment." That moment is the present, which is apprehended now with a new and shocking intensity from the standpoint of "the middle of the way"—that is, within sight of the end.

The future presents no comparable problem. For youth the future is full of terrors and excitements. The question in middle age is no longer *how* to live, but how to *live* when we can see, gaping ahead of us, a black vacancy. "O dark dark dark," Eliot wrote. "They all go into the dark." In these words he voices a terror of vacancy that is everyone's but that is first of all his own. Then he moves—somewhat too quickly—to a response: "I said to my soul, be still, and let the dark come upon you/which shall be the darkness of God" (p. 196). *If it is the darkness of God, then it is not darkness.* God must be absent as well to record and evoke an absolute blackness. Nevertheless, good counsel remains possible. Some part of the self can stay intact to say, "Let the dark come upon you, wait without hope, without love, without thought" (p. 186). The capacities to wait, to be passive, to relinquish the urge to control what cannot be controlled, are acquired capacities. Because they embody a knowledge that cannot be had without time, they deserve to be called wisdom. "The only wisdom we can hope to acquire is the wisdom of humility: humility is endless" (p. 185).

Because they contain the core of his initial feeling, I shall quote in full from "East Coker" those first ten lines of Part III:

> O dark dark dark. They all go into the dark,
> The vacant interstellar spaces, the vacant into the vacant,
> The captains, merchant bankers, eminent men of letters,
> The generous patrons of art, the statesmen and the rulers,
> Distinguished civil servants, chairmen of many
>   committees,
> Industrial lords and petty contractors, all go into the dark,
> And dark the Sun and Moon, and the Almanach de Gotha
> And the Stock Exchange Gazette, the Directory of
>   Directors,
> And cold the sense and lost the motive of action.
> And we all go with them, into the silent funeral . . .
>   [pp. 185–186]

These lines, and especially the first, are Eliot's cry from the cross. This is the black hole at the core of the four poems. Constellated around it are other reactions, thoughts, epiphanies, and, above all, a redemptive meditation on the mystery of time. Without these lines, however, we would have what amounts to a hollow philosophical discourse, laced with passages of great beauty, but built on avoidance.

The felt prospect of death is a blow to everyone. But what in particular may this experience have meant to someone with Eliot's character?

To the extent that our actions, as Becker suggests, are assays at immortality, their failure becomes terribly evident at that stage of life when the Dark becomes real. It swallows everything and everyone, from the descendants of Charlemagne's knights to builders of suburban subdivisions, from petty bureaucrats to the Sun itself. In the process it makes us all equal—equally nothing. "As it was in the beginning," goes the Anglican doxology, "is now and ever shall be, world without end." To this, Eliot's "O dark dark dark" poses a direct contradiction. These words represent, experientially, the sense of the finality of death and the futility of all effort. Everything we do is empty and stupid: nothing can redeem the pointlessness of our lives.

The central point of Eliot's life was his writing. It was through the act of writing that he tried most to feel alive, whole, full, and valuable. Like all compulsive efforts that would compensate for narcissistic failure, it could not work once for all, but had to be repeated over and over. It, too, went into the dark. Part V of "East Coker" is a meditation of his life as a writer, from the standpoint of "the middle." There is no satisfaction in past accomplishment, for "every attempt is a wholly new start, and a different kind of failure . . ." (p. 188). "Because one has only learnt to get the better of words for the things one no longer has to say, or the way in which one is no longer disposed to say it" (pp. 188–189). Moreover, the writer is only discovering and conquering territory that has already been found and conquered by greater masters. Here Eliot pulls back—much as in Part III—from the anguished dead end to which this line of thinking leads. He says, in midsentence, "but there is no competition." And adds soon after, "But perhaps neither gain nor loss. For us there is only the trying. The rest is not our business" (p. 189). By refounding his sense of value from achievement to the effort itself—an exploration, not necessarily successful, "for a further union and deeper communion"—Eliot pulls himself from an empty dark to one that contains at least a possibility of fullness. Now he can conclude with the words, "In my end is my beginning" (p. 190).

This is the movement of the poem. We are creatures in and of time, which leads inexorably into the dark. Time itself is not redemptive—yet, if redemption is possible at all, it is possible only in time.

After the dark has come upon us, what can lead us out?

To my mind, the *Quartets* contain an abortive response to this question. Eliot's character did not permit him to pursue his despair to an authentic conclusion. If it had, two possibilities would have opened up: either he would have become lost in it—a wanderer without hope like L.—or he would have emerged from it with a sense of illumination. That he did neither was not a failure of will. Indeed, he lived fully and courageously, stretching the boundaries of his character to their limits of tension. But no one can go very much beyond his or her boundaries.

What was it about him that brought his movement along this path to a halt? These lines from "The Dry Salvages" (1941) offer a clue:

> . . . to apprehend
> The point of intersection of the timeless
> With time is an occupation for the saint—
> No occupation either but something given
> And taken, in a lifetime's death in love,
> Ardour and selflessness and self-surrender
> For most of us, there is only the unattended Moment, the
>   moment in and out of time,
> The distraction fit, lost in a shaft of sunlight,
> The wild thyme unseen, or the winter lightning
> Or the waterfall, or music heard so deeply
> That it is not music at all, but you are the music
> while the music lasts. These are only hints and guesses.
> Hints followed by guesses: and the rest
> Is prayer, observance, discipline, thought and action.
>   [pp. 198–199]

". . .[H]umankind," he had said in "Burnt Norton" (1935), "cannot bear very much reality" (p. 176). If reality is, precisely, the Incarnation, the intersection of the timeless with time, why is it so hard to bear and what makes it possible for some people to sustain it better than others?

The psychic "organ" of apprehension is the ego, which following Lacan (1949), structures experience (at least from the mirror stage) in ways that offer an illusion of order and comprehensibility. This structuring function, increasingly socialized, yields a sense of reality seamless enough to be taken for reality itself. Included in this sense are various identities: an entity-like personality or character with its attitudes, its tastes and distastes, mannerisms and credos; social roles (Nobel laureate, son, chairman of many committees); and body. The "saint" is someone who can withstand—indeed works toward—the demolition of this false structure to live increasingly in an aleatoric reality, accepted, not made. The capacity to go this route depends in part on adequate narcissistic development. That, at least, is how I would translate the notions of grace and its sustained reception into the conceptual system of developmental self psychology. Because narcissistic damage is so universal—virtually a given of the human condition—there are few saints among us. (I tend to think of grace as ubiquitous; it's the capacity to receive it that's lacking.) It takes, after all, considerable success in development to assume an adequate set of false identities in the first place. It is an extraordinary being, then, who can give them up.

The felt prospect of death is a missile aimed at the conventional sense of reality. Since the ego's various identities are used as bulwarks against chaos, to experience the meaninglessness of them has all the impact of madness, fragmentation, disintegration. The weaker the character (again, from the standpoint of narcissistic development) the more it relies on these identities for

cohesion, wholeness, and value. At the same time these identities are edifices requiring constant maintenance, making life a
hell of tedium and labor. Into that hell breaks the shaft of
sunlight, the wild thyme unseen, the music, the hidden laughter
of children—brief glimpses of another reality.

Eliot's narcissistic weaknesses obliged him to devote considerable energy to the cultivation of his personae. His traditionalism in religion and government can partly be understood in
this context. Traditional social structures are rich and relatively
solid sources of narcissistic support: they are the very matrix of
unquestioned social roles and practices. Not that Eliot held to a
simpleminded conservatism. After all, the Almanach de Gotha
too went into the dark. (We might wonder, however, who but a
snob would have included it in the list?) But he had a deep and
sound distrust of avant-gardism. There is, after all, a secret
affinity between the conservative and the avant-gardist: the one
establishes his being by finding place and value in ancient social
structures, the other establishes his through an unending push
beyond the present limits of the acceptable. There is romanticism and desperation in both. Eliot's position was more modest.
He felt the need for an elision between the present and the past—
neither the dead end of historicism (cultivating the illusion of
living in the past) nor that of living in the ever-moving edge of
the future.

But, despite the modesty of this position, it too had a
narcissistic function not unlike that of Proust's *Remembrance*
(Kohut 1977)—an effort to hold together a self prone to disintegration in the dimension of time.

To openly explore "a further union and deeper communion" requires a sturdy character structure that can withstand the
threat (indeed the actuality) of disintegration. Among psychoanalysts Bion (1965) has given profound thought to this movement, which he expressed symbolically as the transformation of

K (the realm of knowledge) into O. "O" stands for the thing-in-itself, which is "been" (requiring a transitive form of the verb "to be") rather than apprehended. Approaches to O, even those that stay within the realm of K, can create great psychological turbulence. Bion adduces in this context Newton's breakdown in connection with formulating the differential calculus.

To elucidate the meaning of "psychological turbulence" Bion quotes St. John of the Cross—the very passage to which Eliot alludes in "East Coker." That passage concludes: "The third [night of the soul] has to do with the point to which [the soul] travels—namely, God, who, equally, is dark night to the soul in this life" (p. 159). Bion associates this night with the transformation in O, that is, from K → O. "The transformation that involves 'becoming' is felt as inseparable from becoming God, ultimate reality, the First Cause. The 'dark night' pain is fear of megalomania" (p. 159). Certainly this goes a way toward explaining Eliot's resistance to sainthood. Eliot would have been particularly vulnerable in the domain of "megalomania," that is, of the grandiose–exhibitionistic self.

Freud (1914) rightly understood megalomania as a narcissistic phenomenon, although the terms in which he couched its dynamics ("The libido that has been withdrawn from the external world has been directed to the ego . . ." p. 74) are mystifying. Kohut's account, as I would extrapolate it, makes more sense. An adequate response to the child's spontaneous grandiose–exhibitionistic displays fosters their transformation into socialized forms of ambition and achievement pursued with energy. An inadequate response fosters splitting and repression. The consequences of such a reaction vary in severity and range. In the case of megalomania, the split is radical, indicating a gross and sadistic rejection of this aspect of the child—an origin revealed in the persecutory or dictatorial character of the grandiose delusions. More commonly we see attenuated and/or disguised remnants of the original "drive" in a depleted character that has learned to fear its own (largely unconscious) grandiosity. The daily life of such people is gray, slogging, joyless, routinized, dutiful. Or, as Eliot put it, full of "prayer, observance, discipline, thought and action."

What may have happened when Eliot, as a small boy, showed off and boasted to his mother? I suspect that as he played the Superman of 1892 she would not have admired his biceps and his x-ray vision. Rather she would have fixed him with a withering kryptonite gaze and warned him about the delicacy of his health. Her admiration would have been selective—directed especially toward precocious intellectual, academic, and artistic achievement—not the body but the mind. Even then, I imagine, her approval would have been selective, since she would have been too invested in his excellence to be uncritically loving and thus to mirror *his* sense of achievement. Such interactions underlie the splitting and partial repression of the grandiose-exhibitionistic self as well as the proneness to fragmentation; the child is loved only in bits.

The emergence of primitive grandiosity is necessarily disintegrating, since to be everything is also to be nothing. Therefore, be content with moments in the sunlight and with the hidden laughter in the garden.

* * * *

Despite the pain that flowed like a ground bass through his life, which of us would not choose Eliot's occasional moments and creative achievements over L.'s wanderings in the void? After all, didn't he produce a large *oeuvre* of undeniable quality and enjoy great power in shaping the taste of his time? He never lacked for recognition, was ultimately accorded the highest honors, and even made a happy marriage late in life. By contrast, what could L.'s existence offer? He had no country, no occupation, no friends, no home, no possessions. He created nothing and loved no one. In Cioran's (1964/1970) words, he had fallen out of time into the "wrong" eternity—the one that "lies beneath" (p. 174).

We would tend to choose Eliot's way because we value love, honor, achievement, and creativity. We see them as redemptive—as making life worthwhile. Freud shared this notion, summed up in the adage ascribed to him about love and work (Erikson 1950). If not both love *and* work, then at least one or the other can make life seem good enough. But neither?

The belief in the *value* of love and work can indeed sustain us. But no belief system can stand up to analysis. However convincingly we offer rationales, these credos are founded only on conviction. We sustain them because at some point the line of questioning has ceased. Pick it up again and the subject of the analysis disintegrates. To be freed through analysis from neurotic patterns or the unconscious imprint of the past is a liberation; to be freed from faith is a curse. This was L.'s position, for, unlike Eliot, he could not brake his plunge into the Dark.

For someone like this, there is no going back. The darkness has indeed covered him, and it is blacker than anything Eliot knew, because it is unlit by the conviction that it is God's or that it leads to anything at all.

Does it lead to anything? Does it lead, in particular, to "O"? We cannot answer this question. In Bion's terms, O cannot be spoken of, nor can it be pursued. The obstacles to it can be removed in some sense, and, if you like, we can call this the pursuit of O. But it may be that, in the end, O must come to us . . . or not. We can think of L. as caught in the time warp between K and O. In this position there is nothing anyone can "do."

Bion interprets reports of mystical experience as indicative of becoming O—an experience of ultimate reality unstructured by K. This is, of course, an interpretation. It might be that such experiences are protective states induced by the unbearable condition of "→" (the warp or passage "between" K and O). On this interpretation, "→" would itself be the ultimate reality, preceded, and sometimes followed, by the illusions of K and O. *But we have no criteria for choosing between these interpretations.* Nor have we answers to the many questions to which they give rise. For example, is becoming O good? Is it better than the normal state represented by the relationship to K? Finally, is becoming O worth risking entrapment in the limbo of "→"?

Neither the conflict between civilization and instinct nor the destructive potential of aggression is the worst disease of the human condition, but consciousness itself. Because we have the capacity to analyze—a capacity so full of power and exhilaration—a wedge is inserted between ourselves and the world, and the space grows ever wider. In the end, the universe is atomized and man himself falls into bits.

If this is true, how modest the analyst's role must be! How can he know where to lead his patient? To what end? Is there a single value we cannot question? We think it good, for example, to help mitigate a harsh and primitive superego. Yet how can we be sure that the suffering, however great, isn't preventing a still greater suffering? Alternatively, how can we be sure that this suffering, left alone, will not lead to an unspeakable joy?

* * * *

Between Eliot's aborted venture and L.'s circular one we cannot ultimately choose. Even Pascal's wager becomes impossible, since it may turn out, after all, that the way to O leads through the dark night of unbelief and that faith itself is an obstacle to it. The experience of anticipating one's death that L. faced in the breaking of Lalage can rend the dimension of time in which life is ordinarily lived and throw us into deepest psychological turmoil. Cioran called this the "fall out of time" and saw it as the inevitable consequence of consciousness. To the extent that denial remains possible, this consequence is not inevitable. It is ironic, therefore, that a stronger character who can sustain this experience without denying it becomes subject to a devastating ennui, "incapable of manifesting himself or even wanting to leave some trace of his existence" (Cioran 1964, p. 181). And that may be all he will ever know.

7

Lost in Time

INTRODUCTION

In the winter of 1981 I received a strange yet captivating letter. It was my introduction to the patient who is my subject in this chapter and makes perhaps the best introduction to a discussion of her case. Except for altering or omitting certain identifying information, I give it here in full:

Dear Mr. Kurtz,

I have just come from Weimar, where I spent many hours with your former patient, M_____. The gardens there were laid out in Goethe's time, you know, with his theories in mind. They manage to be both beautiful and unobtrusively instructive, like an English border: seemingly natural but full of hidden intelligence. M_____ spoke of the *Metamorphose der Pflanzen*. He is such a plant, he says, and you have been his master gardener. We played that silly parlor game—which plant would you be if you were a plant? A broken pitcher plant, I said, or a cabbage rose with the blight. When I told him I would be in New York later this month, he suggested I see you and so, if you have the time, I shall. I cannot stay long enough for a proper analysis but perhaps that will not matter. I had a great friend whose life was quite changed by a single afternoon with Freud (or was it Ferenczi?). I can't imagine what they could have accomplished in those brief hours. Even so, I am encouraged. Already I am half in love with you. This is what is meant by "transference," is it not? I was in love with my father, but this was too terrible to know so I repressed it and became hysterical. Now I shall fall in love with you and shall know again the wish (with all its primal innocence and terror), "I want to **** my father!" Tears! Shame! Uncontrollable sobbing on your couch! (You will not say "Our time is up" then, will you?) Finally, relief. So, I was in love with my father. *Tant pis!* Like every other little girl. I am like every other little girl! But now I'm all grown up; I shall meet a man and have babies and repossess the penis I thought I'd lost. I can hardly wait. Like Mme de Gaulle. Do you know the famous interview when an Englishman asked her what she wanted most when she retired? "A penis, of course, a penis." Embarrassed silence. Then a Frenchman came to the rescue. "Just so, Madame, 'appiness, and we all wish it to you for years to come." Except, you know, that will not work for me; I've been spayed. This hysteric has no 'υστέρα.

But at the same time that I write tongue in cheek, I do expect this letter will be opened and then cleverly resealed. Intrigue in the palace, intrigue and poison. Not to mention wars of faith or in the name of faith over sins and heresies no one even remembers now. Monophysitism, incest: who still cares about these things? Oh, we sometimes punish the fathers for doing it. But the daughters? For dreaming of it?

I was taught never to tell my dreams, but I'm supposed to tell you mine, am I not? Let me tell you the dream which decided me to write to you. It is set in Venice. I am entering a small theatre with my old friend Y——————— who, however, looks not like herself but rather like Julie de Krüdener (an evil sort of parlor mystic of Chateaubriand's time). Another lady is with us but I cannot recall her face; perhaps she has none. We are about to hear a lecture on time. The lecturer stands before an oval clock whose hands are hinged (no doubt so they can fold in passing through the narrow parts). When the lecture is over, I ask a question. I ask it innocently, yet I soon sense it is taboo, something that breaks an unspoken code and must never be said. I ask, "But what sort of time do you mean?" Immediately, the lecturer, in a dramatic deus-ex-machina gesture, mounts his pointer and shoots like a missile toward the clock face. There is a gap — not readily visible to the audience — between the face and the frame. If the trick goes well the man will seem to disappear into the clock by entering this gap and descending on hidden chains below the stage. But something does go wrong. Instead of disappearing, he bongs up again and smashes his head on one of the hands (pointing to three?). The mechanism goes crazy; he is jerked up and down on the chain, up and down again and again, crushing his head . . . Obviously he is being killed. It takes me a while to realize this. When I do, I scream and scream until I wake myself up.

Are you a Blue or a Green? By birth I'm a Blue, but in spirit . . . And now we have the Greens again. But I'm always on the other side of the side I'm on. Blues and Greens — one thinks of a Mediterranean peace: sun, beaches. Not a battlefield. A Homeric one at that, with journalistic descriptions of the arrow entering the body of the hero. ἀκρότατον δ' ἄρ' ὀϊστὸς ἐπέγραψε χρόα φωτός αὐτίκα δ' ἔρρεεν αἷμα κελαινεφὲς ἐξ ὠτειλῆς. Blue, green, and the red-brown of dried blood. Not that I'm nostalgic for blood except, perhaps, for a few drops of it.

I shall call you on the twentieth.

(signed)
Lydia Paleologus

And she did call me on the twentieth. Whether she had grown less cohesive in the interval or whether the act of writing enabled more coherence than she could normally manage, I can't say. But by the time I saw her, she was rambling very loosely. In this kind of discourse with the usual rules of communication suspended, it's impossible to know whether the patterns one hears are imposed or discerned. For this reason, and for others that shall be made evident later, my introductory comments will be brief. Instead I shall proceed with an attempt—in some ways more difficult than interpretation—to simply reproduce the quality of her speech.

To guide the reader through this labyrinth it may help to say that Lydia believed herself to be a sort of female Ahasuerus. Not a Wandering *Jew*, however (she was, in fact, somewhat anti-Semitic), but a Wandering Byzantine. The Paleologi were the last dynasty before the Turkish conquest. (Their name, incidentally, means "ancient word," where "word" keeps its old connotation of "spirit.") They were scholarly people, instrumental in preserving a thread of Greek culture under Turkish rule and in spreading it through Europe, where several branches of the family continued. Whether in fact Lydia was entitled to the name I have never been certain; the delusion, however (if that is what to call it), centered mainly on the belief that she had herself persisted through not less than 500 years. She meandered freely through this enormous timespan, although certain times and places were frequently connected (Rome, for example, in the sixteenth century, where she claimed to have sat for Michelangelo, or New York in the early 1960s), together with the languages of those places. For this reason, I could not even begin to make sense of much of what she said. The basic language she used was English, and I could also understand some of her French and German. But when she used Greek or a Slavic language, of which I have none, I could not even be sure which one it was. There were also times when it seemed to me she spoke a purely personal language—a speech that Lydia herself may not have understood. What immediately follows, therefore—full of ellipses of her silences and coughing fits—is not a reproduction but rather an *impression* of what it was like to be with her. I have not translated the foreign-language bits, since that would create the impression of more understanding than in fact was available to me.

LYDIA

I'm supposed to begin at the beginning, I know. But I don't know what the beginning is and . . . interrupted all the . . . all the . . . Doesn't seem any likelihood of an end . . . In my end is my beginning. Who was it said that? Mary Queen of Scots, I think . . . and Eliot too, much later. The words keep going round and round—the same words. Perhaps it's the Word that writes them all. " Ἐν 'αρ χῆν 'ο λόγος." The Word created us . . . in the Word's image. So we are words. I am a word. No body. *** Can the Word, shall we say, "make love"?

Well, the Word impregnated a virgin. "Do it unto me" etc. A penis-word. The Word erects itself, plunges itself into that virgin womb and pumps away . . . "Oh Baby!" An explosion of seed-words. *Ein echt Göttlich Wörterbuch.*

The *jouissance* of the Word creates, among other things, the Savior of the world. The Savior, needless to say, is male. The Word is male. The father is male. How can there be females if we're all made in the image of males? There can't. The female is a dream of the male. I am somebody's dream. Trying to become flesh, you say? Who writes your lines?

Not that I'm a feminist. Lesbian bitches! How can licking another woman's tits or becoming prime minister make me any less of a dream? A dream lesbian; a dream prime minister. Wake up!

> Jak mówić? Jak rozedrzeć skórę słow?
> Co napisałem, wydaje się teraz nie to.
> I co przeyłem, wydaje się teraz nie to.[1]

---

[1] From Czeslaw Milosz, *The Separate Notebooks.* New York: Ecco Press, 1984, p. 70.

Torn up. Torn up by Turks, factions, fans of the Ramones. By
devotees of Miss Piggy or Yosemite Sam. Torn up by fears, Mouse-
keteers, ideas of reason and disorder. By Montefiore and Estense. By
Nationalist Socialist Post-Modernist Marxist Lacanian Monophysit-
ists. Sons of fucking bitches!

Do you mind if I smoke?

In the Topkapi Museum I saw my dress. Even in tatters it's . . .
I'm an interesting garbage heap, don't you think? An attic. [She
winks.] Let's try on Auntie Lydia's flapper dress. Oooo! Doo waka doo
waka doo. Let's do it. Let's go to Istanbul. Let's go to Rome. Let's do
the Via Crucis. No need to conquer the world. It's an Adventure Park.
*** Le Roy . . . Le Roy est environé de gens qui ne pensent qu'à divertir le
Roy, et l'empêcher de penser à lui. Like me. I think of nothing but myself.
I watch over my existence . . . like Berkeley's insomniac God. It's
exhausting.

So, if women are God's dream and dreams are wish fulfillments,
does God want to be a woman? You like that, yes? But, if the dream
shifts—to war, or hunting, or boys—or if He wakes up. What then? Is
that why I can't think sometimes? Or is it my brain? Should I get a
CAT scan? Would you recommend I get a CAT scan?

I used to be able to think before I stopped masturbating. (How I
hate that word.) That was in the convent. Didn't I tell you I'd been in
a convent? Our Lady of Perpetual Orgasm, we called it. You smile.
Yes, God smiles too, sometimes. But I did not smile! I prayed ceaselessly for the end of desire:

> Galamatho, Jesu
> Brach, rabama me
> Me de galama.

The winds blew over the desert—cold winds in the daytime, hot
winds in the night. My camel was my only shield. Then, a voice came!

> Hora, Lydia,
> Rado me gala,
> Signo do . . .

It was a commandment. Of course I knew what it was; I understood. So I readied myself, bathed, dressed in white. And then . . . nothing. I had no will. No will. I took off my white robes and lay down.

Do you know what God does to those who fail Him this way? Who hear His Word and do nothing? He gives them *eternal life*.

My dear, if you live long enough, time begins to flatten out. Perhaps you've begun to notice this already. You were born in, say . . . 1940? Your father in . . . 1910? When you were young, 1910 could just as well have been 1810 or 1710—a different era. Then, at some moment, you saw that it was only thirty years. Thirty years! *Nur ein Augenblick.* Well, I had much the same realization, but with centuries. And, of course, I forget. We all forget. When did I buy that brownish dress (the color they used to call "kaka dauphin"), twenty years ago, two hundred years—for a ball at the Breakers or at Marly? Perfectly logical, or would be if I could think. But I can't *think.* Maybe if I could fall in love . . . if I could make love . . . if the two halves of my brain could . . . *Shit!*

* * * *

I call it "The Fortress" but really it's just a piece of eternity—a wall surrounding eternity, keeping out time; you know, you've read Frazer: a sacred grove. (We *are* being bugged . . . and I don't want you to . . .) *** We were all wolves, I suppose. You know how wolves urinate to claim their territories? My mother couldn't stand the stench, poor thing. Tripping through the forest with her jellies and cigarettes. Timeless days of blue flickering light, long corridors and those salmon-pink chairs, you know, with the little boomerang flecks. I've counted those flecks; I've *memorized* those chairs! Unintelligible voices on the loudspeaker. Metallic fish. Someone would give me a shot and the days would lose vertical hold: upper and lower body split, Lucy and Ethel and Ricky and Fred, scrambled and quartered like a coat of arms. Betty Furness says, "Will you take the Amana freezer or the complete set of American Tourister luggage?" Take the luggage, I want to say, and the trip. But *she* wants the freezer so I just scream it in my head.

* * * *

You and I, we're like two asteroids, each with a slightly different, although thin atmosphere; not really able to support life and yet life happens: pigeons, woodlice, even tiny mammals. You look up at the sun and see a certain light—pale green, perhaps, watery and sti . . . shimmering (I was going to say "stammering"). But would *you* identify it that way? You won't answer, so I won't pursue it. But you can see that these reticences are atmospheres that do sustain a kind of life, however secret. And at the edges, where they almost meet, there's an aurora effect . . . dawns that, in any other world, would be called sunsets. So time gets wrapped around itself. What we see is an endless, or seemingly endless series of diminishing circles with the illusion— because of the refractive index—that they're connected. Anna Comnenus wrote a treatise on that illusion. She called it "History." All we've got is an Arabic translation which, needless to say, attributes it to a *man*. And also distorts her ideas so much we'll never know what she really meant. But, of course, Anna may not have known what she meant either. We think clearly—or think we do—and then, looking back, we see that that was not what we meant at all. And so it goes— within the same person (if a meaning can be given to "same") and even more so between two people. I say "even more so," but perhaps there's no discernible difference. You're thinking I'm solipsistic, aren't you? Or does your heart go out to me? You send it at the end of an arrow— flying from your little planet to mine. You imagine I'm lonely. But it could just be the index so that what you think is my loneliness is actually your . . . Or perhaps it's neither yours nor mine—just a property of the two atmospheres at their barely touching edges.

Suppose we could *be* the edge. That's your dream, isn't it, to be an angel moving along the edge, conscious and yet not conscious? You move and the lights of the aurora play through you. In this way you hope to give up knowledge and yet still know. But when you come to inhabit the globular interior of a flower—a rose, for example, a big Bourbon rose—the scent is so dense it knocks you out. So, don't send your heart to me. After all, it may just be some ionization of the air that produces these lights and sounds of the sort they arrange for tourists at the big old châteaux.

You look perplexed. You must stop listening with the third ear. Listen with the *fourth* ear. What's the fourth ear? The fourth ear has a long canal like an underwater tunnel. The wind rushes through it producing little eddies when it meets an obstacle, or little storms when the pressure changes . . . that's all.

When you live in the rose you don't know that you live in it, except at those moments when a space opens up between the petals or in a place where an insect has bored a small hole and an alien light shines through. But some of those moments—and you can't tell which—are dreams or hallucinations. The light suddenly is not rose-colored and the scent gets thinner—but not for long. *You are not to solve this problem because it is not a problem.* Anyhow, a problem that can be solved is not worth solving; don't you know that? Leave those things to the engineers.

I don't want to hurt your feelings, but when you make sense you make no sense. I can see you trying and then out comes this extraordinarily intelligent gobbledygook. I must give you credit—not only for trying, but for the rectangular purity of your nonsense. Like Christmas presents carefully (even obsessively) piled under the tree, or like the crystalline structure of certain substances. Molybdenum comes to mind. If I remember correctly, molybdenum is one of those elements that's never found in nature and only passes fleetingly through the retort on its way to becoming something else.

And yet sometimes—even though what you've said has no meaning to me—the sound becomes a presence, like a great tree a farmer leaves in the field. Then the field begins to revolve around it, this axle, this last representative of an old forest. The memory of the forest is gone but the tree remains. Later, people will think it's been planted there. But a shadow of "no intention" clings to it. Linnaeus can give it a name, but it won't stick.

That's what I mean by "nobility." The tree is noble because of "no intention." You don't understand, do you? Never mind. And "divine" too. *** Didn't Swedenborg say that trees were our ancestors? So God made them first—great forests and jungles reflecting His face. After all, God does want company. But the company of Newton? Of someone who sees Him as a sort of Louis XVI? Yet even Louis, on the scaffold at least, poor man, came out from behind his automata and showed himself . . . I want to say "glorious" but only the French can say that with a straight face.

In my case, the whole tree's been chopped down . . . boutiques and tract housing over and around me . . . but the old root won't die. I'm the shadow of a shadow of that tree, which, after all, was itself only a representative.

And even if I were restored, which is impossible, who would recognize this *revenant*? They'd think it was just a trick of the light or a promotional scheme for something. You don't see either, but at least you . . .

But that's not enough! What *is* enough is following that shadow there around the ear of the cup, over the lip and *in*—a new element, Chinese. In this smoked light the cup disappears, *and* the company— calling taxis and going their separate ways, leaving their host with fragments of old music. I remember the Dutch queen, waltzing alone in a ballroom after her daughter had married. Spinning in the green-gold chinoiserie of pagodas and palm trees. It was simple happiness. Not that *Wienerblut* and champagne didn't play their parts, but the whole was more than the sum. The whole had no name, although it had color and sound. The color of the sun on the goldfish pond— flickers of orange in the algae, pinpoints of white and washes of pale yellow. Down among the lily roots the fish swam. They were the gift of an emperor and had outlived a . . .

ANALYSIS

I must interrupt Lydia here, much as I have grown to take great pleasure in her voice. But other voices call us—most forcefully the one that feels itself to be drowning and cries out for an explanation. What does all this mean? In responding to this question—which is a quite different project from answering it— I want to start with Kohut's (1979) landmark paper, "The Two Analyses of Mr. Z." Beyond advancing self psychology theory, this paper had another, no doubt unintended, result: it demonstrated the absolute relativity of a psychoanalysis. Whether successful or not (judged by whatever standards), the analysis of a patient by one analyst is wholly different from the analysis of that patient by another or, for that matter, by the same one at different times in their lives. I say "wholly different" because, unlike mechanical processes where many things can be held constant for purposes of comparison, nothing can be held this way between two analyses. The subjects—the people involved—are fluid, changing constantly. Since it is an *interaction* between fluid subjects that describes the ephemeral vector we call an analysis, each one is a unique and irreducibly two-person complex. This is all the more true when we realize that the theory by which the analysis proceeds unfolds as well over time. Psychoanalysis began with a more naive notion of its subject matter as a process taking place between more-or-less constant entities according to more-or-less fixed rules. Case histories were, and continue to be, written as if they were describing solitary journeys guided by an omniscient, invisible hand along routes as inevitable as railroad tracks. As we have grown more sophisticated, we have come to see that this model does not fit at all. Robert Stolorow's (1987) reconceptualization, focusing on the intersubjective field as the actual subject matter of an analysis, constitutes an important theoretical advance because it takes the fluid mutuality of relationship into account.

But there are certain radical consequences of this rethinking that have yet to be followed out. And, as so often happens in a fractured field, the consequences have actually preceded the reformulation. I think especially of Searles's (1975) "The Patient as Therapist to His Analyst," which implies the following question: If the subject matter of an analysis is the intersubjective field, how can we distinguish and hierarchize within it the two roles of patient and analyst?

In the orthodox framework, this question does not arise.

Since the analyst is held to have been adequately trained and analyzed, countertransference phenomena (in the stricter sense) are aberrative and manageable. Therefore, the analyst can be counted on to perform in a good-enough way his blank-screen function and to give correct interpretations.

When we distance ourselves from orthodoxy, its myths become more visible. The analyst is, in reality and of necessity, very partially analyzed and imperfectly trained. If nothing else, he has not analyzed his addiction to the analytic role. I think especially of its cohesion-producing functions enabled by the rapt attention he gives his patients (see Chapter 2, "The Analyst's Space"). But I think also of the sense-making functions of offering interpretations and weaving narratives that make a mess of data into a comprehensible portrait. One might say that the analyst is addicted to understanding. Understanding here is a route to power—over the other person, to be sure, but more importantly over his own discomfort with unstructured experience. And bound up with this is an aesthetic function—the artistic satisfaction of making a life into a biography.

Proceeding in the orthodox way, there is always the danger of reproducing in the analytic situation the deadness of its mechanical model. (I'm using "mechanical" loosely here to mean "rationalizing" or "systematizing.") The well-oiled analyst/computer follows his program (however subtle the program may be), and out comes the cure.

We know, of course, that there is no final "cure"—if, indeed, a meaning can be given to that term in this nonmedical context. More importantly, we know how far from mechanical the process really is. Nothing of consequence happens unless both parties are deeply engaged. The analyst's countertransference, far from being circumscribed and aberrative, must be integral and profound (Roustang 1980). All this becomes most explosive when the analyst is called upon to face reactions that are integral to his role and therefore held invisibly within it. I am speaking of those situations—often involving patients called psychotic or hysterical—where it is the analyst's need to understand that is being challenged. Can he allow the patient to cure him of this need and to open up a world that does not make sense?

This was the challenge Lydia presented to me as, week after week, she spoke in the manner I have tried to recreate. It wasn't that I couldn't make *any* sense of it. To listen to a series of words and *not* make a kind of sense of them may not even be possible. Rather, I lost confidence that the sense *I* happened to make had any particular authority. The central meaning of "meaning," after all, is in relation to ordinary language—a shared communication system—a system of elements, structures, and rules of usage held in common. There are, of course, continua of meaningfulness in ordinary discourse and strategies for the resolution of ambiguity. But at some (perhaps unspecifiable) point we fall into meaninglessness. It is then that systems of interpretation can come into play—psychoanalysis being one of them. But, without denying its therapeutic value, psychoanalysis is epistemologically very weak. We say, for example, that an interpretation is "correct" when, in apparent consequence of it, a memory is recovered (or seems to be, since we can rarely check its accuracy), a fruitful line of associations is opened up, or an emotional release is obtained. Yet, there is no way of demonstrating that these *post hoc* events happened because of the interpretation or of its correctness, thereby affirming its correctness and its efficacy.

When a system of interpretation, empirically unverifiable, is held dogmatically, doubt is warded off. Kohut's "Two Analyses," by moving us from one to two, opened up infinity. Because of the anxiety evoked by infinity, our tendency is to dogmaticize each new interpretive system. For a student there may be value in acquiring some unquestioned system so that development can proceed. That, at least, has been a principal received idea in psychoanalytic education. But for a seasoned practitioner to develop, he must face the challenge of "no system."

Analysis is not alone in presenting this challenge. Most fundamentally, it is a challenge of living, but one that art can offer us in a particularly concentrated form. Among the arts, poetry especially may use language in eccentric and disorienting ways. Psychoanalysis has always opened itself to the influences of science and more recently to those of linguistics and conceptual analysis. But its relationship to art has been more ambivalent. There is a kind of condescending admiration of poets and novelists whose insights can be said to prefigure those of analysis. It is that same sentiment to which Jews object when Christians read the Old Testament as a preparation for the New. But to actually submit to the influence of poets—to take Antonin Artaud, for example, or John Ashbery as seriously as we take Saussure or John Austen, simply doesn't happen. We hold tenaciously not only to the distinction between primary and secondary process, but to an implicit ranking of them.

Lydia's discourse—like Artaud's and Ashbery's—questions that distinction. In a long speech of which we can make no sense we happen upon a perfectly intelligible passage. Because of its setting, however, we have no way of deciding whether that passage is a bit of sense stuck in the nonsense like a raisin in a fruitcake or whether its sense-making appearance is just that—appearance—and it is actually as nutty as the rest. The same problem arises at a larger scale. How can we know whether the seemingly rational discourse of ordinary and professional life—indeed the very chapter you are reading now—is not actually embedded in a lifelong but covert word salad of which it is part and parcel?

The language of so-called secondary process is the language of practical and intellectual achievement: the co-op on Central

Park West; the membership in The Club; the paper presented, the theory constructed, the book published, the kids in Harvard. And, at the end of it all, a well-attended memorial service and an obit in the *Times*.

The scheming and the intelligent figuring that go into these achievements are called secondary process. Persons capable of sustaining it are held to be successfully functioning members of society: definitely not crazy. This judgment is made possible, however, only by selectively ignoring—or concealing—the crazy epic poem in which these reasonable paragraphs are set.

* * * *

Lydia required that I give up the labor of selective ignorance that makes sense possible. She did not want to be understood—to have a meaning given to her words. In this she echoed Artaud (1946), who said, "I have never been able to stand someone meddling with the lines of a great poet from a semantical, historical, archeological or mythological point of view—lines of poetry are not explained."

Lydia herself put it in theological terms: "God does not want to be understood," she said. "God wants to be loved."

We must distinguish between the wish not to be understood and the wish to conceal. A murder mystery—which is a sort of puzzle—can be solved. But a true mystery cannot. When we treat mysteries as if they were puzzles we trivialize them.

Why do we do this?

Partly we are just expressing the view of a post-Enlightenment world—a view so pervasive it has become like the air. From that perspective, there are no mysteries that are not puzzles. And if something cannot be formulated as a puzzle—solved or to be solved—then it is not real.

More personally, I had had, in adolescence, a taste of

unstructured experience that I could not sustain. Paralleling a psychotic withdrawal, I flew up into the rafters of rationality as high as I could go. I have been trying to get down ever since. Psychoanalysis has not been of much help. It, too, is a child of the Enlightenment, trying to make sense of everything, treating the mysterious as a puzzle. Good, therefore, for providing structure; useless for enabling unstructure. Looking back at the various inter-subjective fields in which I have played, the one I shared with Lydia was the only one to make a difference of this sort. As long as I tried to understand her, the analysis went nowhere.

One might say that Lydia presented me with the equivalent of Zen kōans: paradoxical statements one is required to puzzle out, but which resist comprehension. Yet, in struggling with them, the mind, if all goes well, will make a sort of quantum jump into another mode. And, in a modest way, that was what mine did.

One central strategy of analysis, after all, is to make sense of a life through the making of constructions. If the construction is accurate, Freud (1895) found, it will unlock a repressed memory. But even if this doesn't happen it has value because, if well timed and well put, "we produce in [the patient] an assured conviction of the truth of the construction which achieves the same therapeutic result as a recaptured memory" (p. 291). More profoundly, the process of construction follows, or claims to follow, the secret lines of unconscious structure and is itself structuring. In the patient's discourse, Freud says, "the whole spatially extended mass of psychogenic material is . . . drawn through a narrow cleft and thus arrives in consciousness cut up, as it were, into pieces or strips. It is the psychotherapist's business to put these together once more into the organization which he presumes to have existed. Anyone who has a craving for further similes," Freud continues, "may think at this point of a Chinese puzzle."

My craving for similes notwithstanding, I can't help but find off-putting Freud's primary image—of a mass squeezed through a narrow orifice and extruded in lumps and strips. Yet, if I drop this first picture and follow the second, I think only of an interminable weekend in the country: rain, dull guests, nothing decent to read. To relieve its *longueur* I'm reduced to doing an immensely complicated Chinese puzzle—an Alice-in-Wonderland puzzle, moreover—whose pieces keep changing as I use them and whose ultimate plan is unknowable. If not for the intervention of a consciousness that sometimes appreciates absurdity, I'd pack my bags and leave.

Even if such trivial pursuits were what psychoanalysis turned out to be, the "psychogenic mass" Lydia presented me defied this kind of organization. For biography to be possible, time's arrow must fly in one direction. In Lydia's case, the arrow split into multiple parts, any one of which might fly sideways, backward, circularly, randomly, and sometimes even forward.

Without distinguishing between them, Lydia's offerings combined memories (with every degree of accuracy and distortion), false memories, clairvoyant experiences (both pre- and retrodictive), hallucinations, and inventions. In the case of the predictive ones, Lydia believed she'd sometimes lived to actually see the events she had clairvoyantly foreseen. Yet the image had become a memory (with all the force and weight of a memory) long before the event took place. The flattening effect on time that comes from simply living long enough then wiped out whatever residual distinctions remained between these categories. Thus Lydia could honestly say that witnessing the king's death on the scaffold in 1793 (it took two whacks of the blade to do it) had given her the courage to face her own death when the Turks stormed her father's palace 300 years before.

* * * *

Smashing my head repeatedly against the wall of Lydia's wishes and her incomprehensible past eventually provoked a crisis. It was one of those moments when the analyst, circling round and round the patient like an electron around a nucleus, either jumps to a different orbit or lets the treatment end. I felt tremendous agitation, as if every particle of me were being heated under pressure, preparing to vaporize or explode. Finally one night, after a particularly exasperating session, *I had Lydia's dream.* Do you recall it, the one at the theatre in Venice with the lecture on time? It was exactly her dream in every detail except that, when I awoke, I knew instantly that I was the lecturer. The mechanism of the clock, gone haywire, was killing *me*.

The reorganization of perspective that followed this dream was not primarily cognitive, so I doubt I can reproduce the muddled and anxiety-filled state in which I found myself. Looking back now, through the distorting lens of time, I find myself paradoxically trying to make sense of the experience while having largely lost faith in the value of making sense, not to mention lacking any certainty about what "making sense" means. Even so, it seems to me that my efforts with Lydia blasted me into a different developmental stage and one that had to do also with the realization of my true character.

As I see it now, the effort to understand life rationally and scientifically belongs primarily to youth. At some point one must come to the realization that this project is not achievable or, rather, that it is all too achievable but not worth the effort. In one of her stories—I think it is "The Roads around Pisa"— Isak Dinesen puts these words into the mouth of an old academician: "You may ask me to paint a rose in the Chinese, the Dutch, or the French manner, but do not ask me to paint a rose as it is." The effort to understand can never result in anything but a certain slant on reality. And even if we were to achieve the ideal—to have all possible perspectives at once forming an assemblage called "The Truth about Reality," what, after all, would we have? Reality? No. Just an assemblage. And, indeed, it would be an assemblage of such monstrous complexity it would be indistinguishable from a junk heap.

Some people, perhaps as part of the denial of their mortality, never cease trying to understand, just as others never cease trying to acquire money or prestige. But a better development, I think, is to move into a different relationship with life—a relationship in which one is borne along willingly by its currents rather than climbing up to view it from a high place or clinging desperately to some object on shore for fear of drowning. At any rate, that development seemed necessary for me and represented also a recovery of that more fluid spirit my adolescent self could not support.

Time was indeed killing me, and not only in the obvious sense of my aging. I was living in a cage of time—a framework that, although entirely of human devising, had come to appear natural and absolute: the very structure of reality. For this reason the dreamer's question, "But what sort of time do you mean?" is radical and deconstructive, bringing down the edifice of time like a house of cards. I have written in more general terms (Chapter 5, "The Psychoanalysis of Time") about the invention of the clock and its psychosocial dimensions. But in those days I was myself living in a machine of time. Not Wells's delightful traveling machine, tootling back and forth between the ages like a ferry. Mine was a terrible one of windlasses and weights like the strappado on which poor Damiens was hung in the dungeons of Versailles. Lydia recalled his screams coming through the chimney and mingling there in her room with Couperin's *La Favorite* as she entertained the Comte d'_____, after what she called "a memorable night of love." That recollection can be called an *extreme* image, combining refined pleasure and high civilization with unimaginable pain and barbarism. I could not help wondering (having long since suspended disbelief) whether Damiens below—his body literally torn apart by the jailers—was similarly able to hear, even intermittently, the sounds of their lovemaking and Lydia's arpeggios at the harpsichord. Extreme and contradictory images, inducing a sustained psychic tension like the moment before orgasm, can shatter the usual sense of reality and open up a new one—one that ordinary language cannot begin to describe.

Lydia's timeless discourse, poetic and senseless, did not describe reality either. In some sense, I want to say, it was reality. The reality I mean is the one revealed by art and play. This moves us, of course, from psychoanalysis to metaphysics. The metaphysical beliefs of psychoanalysts are usually implicit, but some have wished to make them more overt. Jacques Lacan, for example, has the concept of *le réel*, a Kantian unknowable that marks the limits of experience. At the same time, Lacan (1949) tends to identify this unknowable with the unstructured experience a child is thought to have prior to the mirror stage (c. 6 months). That prelinguistic landscape has, perhaps, the look of Paradise before Adam named the animals and plants. In adulthood, it remains a world to which poets especially have access. When it comes to naming, then, the primordial words they choose are not arbitrary (Rilke [1939] writes movingly of this). That first language of children and poets has a different relationship to reality than all the later ones.

In recapturing a primal reality, poets may be said to *play* with language—to move outside its socially agreed-upon rules. Among analysts, Winnicott (1971) has best understood the value of play—and not only this but the related problematic of interpretation. Interpretation, after all, is a kind of translation. But if the "language" of play is different in kind from all other languages, it cannot be translated. Anyway, <u>Winnicott wisely argued, interpretation is not always necessary for healing</u>.

Yet the most important single contribution to our understanding of art and play comes not from an analyst but from a poet. Friedrich Schiller (1800), whose aesthetic writings have been neglected in recent years, was Goethe's protégé at Weimar. You may recall that Lydia had written me from Weimar, where she'd gone on a sort of pilgrimage to his house. According to her they'd been lovers during those lost months in 1796 when, estranged from his wife and unable to write, Schiller disappeared from the town. To this day that episode in his life remains undocumented.

Schiller's theories, taking off especially from Kant, pursued an original and illuminating direction. If the *Ding-an-sich* is inaccessible, he reasoned, then all interpretations of phenomena must have equal weight. What, then, determines the choice of a particular one of them? To answer this, Schiller developed a typology of temperaments, each guided by one of three primary impulses. Those guided by the form impulse, for example, see the world in terms of structure. Those guided by the *Stofftrieb* (material impulse) are moved especially by content. Believing these positions to represent the truth, their adherents dispute them passionately. But since they are not about the truth, no position ever triumphs. Schiller then offers a third mode of apprehension: the *Spieltrieb* or play impulse. Those guided by it—principally artists—are not persuaded of the reality of their vision. Instead they play with the appearances they themselves construct and in this way free themselves—to a degree unknown by others—of any binding dogma about the real.

Lydia, I came to believe, was a daughter of the *Spieltrieb*, and her language was the language of play. To "understand" her I had to allow myself to be transported by that same mode of apprehension.

* * * *

Do you remember the Grimm's fairy tale of the youth who eats a magic snake and so comes to understand the language of the birds? This does not mean he translated their squawks and twitterings into Swabian or Plattdeutsch. That would be a curious but ultimately minor talent. No. He came to understand their language without translation.

That is, finally, how I came to understand Lydia. When she knew this was the case—and it did not take her long—she began, for a want of a better word, to recover. She recovered because, as psychoanalysis has belatedly come to know, it is in the context of a good and true bond that an aborted development can begin again and reach fulfillment. This process, I think, is well enough understood, and I have nothing to add to it. But, given such a bond, what might recovery mean for a person like Lydia? Since I do not pathologize her language, her beliefs, or her time sense, it can only mean the recovery of her destiny.

You may remember that she spoke of God's commandment, of her failure to obey it, and of the terrible consequences that followed. Eventually, Lydia blamed herself less for that inexplicable failure and then found ways, small ways at first, to obey it. As her confidence grew, her voice got bigger. She became, for want of a better word, a prophetess . . . a sibyl. When she spoke to the crowds, although the text of her speech might seem meaningless if printed, each person felt as if she had penetrated his heart and spoken his own secret language. For a period of time in which we saw each other erratically, Lydia spoke to people in this country and abroad, in stadia and on street corners, winning converts not to any particular faith but to the sense of Immanence itself. Then, after one such speech, Lydia (it still pains me to say it) . . . Lydia had a massive heart attack and died. Either it was more difficult for her than I had ever imagined, or—in her own terms—she had finally done what she was meant to do.

Her death, as you may imagine, affected me deeply. Not only had she been a rare and great woman, but she had been for me the agent of a transformation I had not thought possible.

When, more than a year later, I found myself in Rome (the city of Freud's dreams), I'd thought my mourning was complete. But then, joining the throngs at the Sistine Chapel, just recently cleaned, and looking up at that vast, now almost gaudy vault, I caught sight of a figure I'd never noticed before. The guide tried to hurry us along, but I could not get myself to move. It was Lydia (although I could hardly believe it)—Lydia, peering down at me through the centuries, swathed in Mannerist pinks and blues. In the distance an antiphonal choir was chanting: "*Hagios ho Theos,*" sang the first group; "*Sanctus Deus,*" answered the other. "*Hagios athanatos . . . Sanctus et immortalis.*" I stood there transfixed at what some have called the apex of the Western world, held by Lydia's gaze for a time I could not measure. In some sense, I am held there still.

Silence

8

The Analyst's Silence

Tempus loquendi
tempus tacendi

—Ecclesiastes 3:7

The analyst offers his silence as a sanctuary for all the elements of the hour. Within it, whatever occurs between the first and the fiftieth minutes finds an integral place. Thus his silence includes not only the words and gestures of each participant, but also the routine sounds of neighborhoods, the heat, the lingering traces of cigars and perfume.

Even the analyst speaks against the background of his silence.

This ground—which gives meaning not only to words but to passages of inflected silence—is never neutral; it is filled with intention. Moreover, it has a history in the analyst's sacrifice of speech, which is sacrifice in a very literal sense—an offering of something valuable for a still more valued purpose. Some may have a talent for silence. Others are possessed by it. "I did not enter into silence," said Ezra Pound (Heymann 1976), "silence captured me." But for most analysts, the capacity for silence is acquired through discipline.

In this way, the analyst is heir to an ancient ascetic tradition. Concerning silence, the Rule of St. Benedict and the sayings of the Desert Fathers already assume a Biblical history. So Benedict (c. 530), quoting Proverbs and the Psalms, counsels that "frequent leave to talk not be granted those advanced in perfection, even though the subject be good, holy, and edifying" (p. 300).

This wisdom recognizes that the experience of silence may reveal to the practitioner what even the best words cannot. And the experience includes not merely wordlessness, but the active suppression of speech.

In renouncing speech, even in this circumscribed way, we yield up something fundamentally human—a central means for declaring and expressing our existence. It is a kind of annihilation. Viewed this way, silence is easily equated with death. To discover that our lives are "rooted in a silence that is not death but life" (Merton 1955), one must first keep quiet. And keeping quiet entails anxiety.

Because silence is a learned technique, the analyst who has not yet made it his own can feel himself gagged—silenced against his will. To capture the feeling of *forced* silence would require the testimony of children forbidden to speak, or of criminals before the Enlightenment whose lips and tongues were amputated for blaspheming. We would need the witness of those—censored poets and prophets—who, in the very midst of their fellow men, were placed under bans of silence. In this way Aleksandr Solzhenitsyn committed reams of writing to memory in the camp of Ekibastuz. Behind the cell door of his forced silence he was building a universe—his refuge—never knowing if anyone would share it. In acquiring the art of silence the analyst can raise childhood ghosts of home and school when, no matter how urgent his need to speak, silence was imposed upon him.

Sometimes silence may be self-imposed. At least since Rimbaud, the artist's renunciation of his art for silence has been offered as a black ideal of avant-garde aesthetics. Rimbaud, of course, left poetry for slave trading. Duchamp exchanged his complex visual art for chess. And in philosophy (as an art form), Wittgenstein abandoned the project of an ideal language for the analysis of ordinary usage. The purposes of silence in psychoanalysis are distinct from aesthetic goals. Nevertheless, the artist's *experience* of silencing himself can illuminate the analyst's experience of this form of abnegation.

Take Duchamp. After abandoning work on the *Large Glass* in 1923, he applied himself, with isolated exceptions, almost exclusively to chess. But his devotion to chess was not an easy rechanneling of the energies he had devoted to object making. It demanded intense study and submission to the rigors of competition. Thus his "silence" was no less effortful than his "speech." And he did not consider it different in kind. "Why isn't my chess playing an art activity?" Duchamp asked Truman Capote. Indeed, he dared to assert, "All chess players are artists" (Schwarz 1969). So, we may say, the analyst's silence, acquired with similar effort, is part of his artistry.

To many, Duchamp's silence has seemed different from Rimbaud's. There is a tendency to condemn the poet's negation of his work and his plunge into the darkest activities of his society while viewing Duchamp's silence as a purification through which "he affirms that art is one of the highest forms of existence" (Paz 1970). But they are not so dissimilar. Both gave up art work, conventionally defined, either for the pure pursuit of play (Duchamp) or the pure pursuit of money (Rimbaud). For both there must have been a profound awareness of the cultural implications of their silences.

Silence breaks a basic social code. For this reason it contains the possibility of unexpected insight and freedom. But at a price. There is guilt for not speaking. Since the patient is paying for words, the analyst cheats and deprives him with his silence. Because of this he can experience himself as cruel and ungenerous. Moreover, by breaking this code a landmark is lost and we step into an uncharted world. If responses are not required, what *can* we count on? This disorientation is shared by both analyst and patient.

The process of reduction is the asymptote that approaches silence. In modern painting, the elimination of a referential third dimension liberated color, pattern, line, and atmospheric field. In poetry, the elimination of description and syntax liberated connotation and sound.

One has only to look at Kandinsky's great watercolors of 1910–1914 (considered the first abstractions) to experience the lyrical energy and the heightened sensuality achieved through this *via negativa*. So the analyst's reduction of speech heightens his sensitivity to all the events of the hour—and especially to the flow of his own associations evoked by those of the patient.

But renunciation has its darker side. Some rare and passionate lovers of words have chosen silence at a critical juncture of their lives. And their silence retains the ferocity and grandeur of their former speech. Following his hideous confinement at St. Elizabeth's, Ezra Pound fell into the great silence that lasted until his death. From its depths, his occasional words acquired great poignancy. In 1963 he told Grazia Livi: "I have lived all my life believing that I knew something. And then a strange day came and I realized that I knew nothing, that I knew nothing at all. And so words have become empty of meaning . . .'Everything that I touch, I spoil' " (Heymann 1976, p. 276).

Pound's bitter silence contained the discovery of language's capacity for evil. "In much talk you shall not avoid sin," says the proverb. Grasping this, he lost the naive use of words, and the resulting self-consciousness left him tongue-tied.

Something like this can befall the analyst early in his career. Language that once flowed easily, like the babbling of an infant, suddenly becomes the object of scrutiny. Poets and copy writers also use language self-consciously, but the analyst's speech cannot be rewritten. He works with the living word.

We cannot doubt the power of the living word. In times of trouble, multitudes are captivated by messiahs and demagogues. And it is precisely in times of trouble that the analyst's help is sought. The new awareness of his power can be intimidating. Silence demands an apprenticeship.

The master can create a total universe of silence—a perfectly self-contained world in which silence, like an amniotic fluid, is the medium that nourishes and binds. The apprentice's painfully self-conscious silences are broken by gratuitous words. Rembrandt and Gainsborough create *atmospheres* in which par-

ticular forms breathe. Amateurs make patchworks in which bits
of "background" jostle bits of "thing."

Very gradually, the analyst achieves technical mastery.
The choice of speaking or not speaking comes within his conscious control. Now, having become capable of virtuosity, his
silence can also be plainly cruel. Or it can assume a romantic
cast: the rigorous, delicately nuanced beauty of silence—his
creation—draws him into its vortex.

From a popular point of view, the power of the analyst's
silence is more accessible than its aesthetics. Indeed, the analyst
sitting in stony silence behind the couch has become a stock
figure of our age. Functionally, this silence mirrors the speech of
another archetypal figure—Dr. Baloardo of the Italian Comedy.
The purpose of the stock analyst's silence and of Baloardo's
cascade of Latin jargon is the same: to preserve the difference in
status between doctor and patient. Both caricatures also reveal a
sadistic element: the good doctor must practice his cure even at
the cost of his patient's life. And the analyst must preserve his
technique even if his patient suffers.

There is more than a kernel of truth in these caricatures. If
the process is viewed as a power struggle, then as Jay Haley
(1958) observes, "The most powerful weapon in the analyst's
arsenal is the use of silence. The problem posed for the patient is
this: how can I get one-up on a man who won't respond and
compete with me for the superior position in fair and open
encounter?" (p. 15).

The psychoanalytic literature details few power struggles in
which silence is the chief weapon between analyst and patient.
But theatre and film offer several. Ibsen's acid sketch, "The
Stronger," evokes the potency of silence in a duel of this sort. He
portrays two women, former competitors for the same man, who
meet by chance in a café. The "winner" who has married him
harangues and struts before her old rival, who remains impla-

cably silent. Drawn out by that silence, she reveals, little by little, the unhappiness of her marriage and the hollowness of her victory.

But the perfect contemporary crystallization of the struggle between silence and speech is in Ingmar Bergman's film *Persona*. Elizabeth, an actress, is playing the part of Electra, when she suddenly and inexplicably stops speaking. After a brief hospitalization she is sent to the seaside in the care of a young nurse, Alma. At first, Alma's chatter is innocent and giving. But in the perfect vacuum of Elizabeth's silence she ultimately weakens and implodes. With increasing desperation Alma attempts first through cajolery and later through force to get Elizabeth to say something, *anything*. But Elizabeth never relents. In this way Alma's sense of reality, little by little, falls into pieces.

Otto Kernberg (1975) discusses the interaction between Alma and Elizabeth as exemplary of an important dynamic between the analyst and the severely narcissistic patient. He sees Elizabeth's silence as "cold, unscrupulous exploitation" by someone who is "completely unable to acknowledge any loving or human feeling expressed toward her. The sick woman seems to be able to live only if and when she can destroy what is valuable in other persons." When Alma turns on Elizabeth, "it is as if all the hatred within the sick woman had been transferred into the helping one, destroying the helping person from the inside" (p. 245). He notes that this confrontation reproduces the essential transference–countertransference situation in the analysis of the severely narcissistic personality. Kernberg is convinced that Elizabeth's silence is within her control. Moreover, he condemns her for it (calling her silence "cold, unscrupulous exploitation") and exonerates Alma for her reaction (her hate is not her own; it is Elizabeth's transferred).

The diagnosis of fictional characters is necessarily controversial. What is incontrovertible is the power of silence to engender impotence and rage. Inadvertently, Kernberg reveals these feelings himself in the examination—even at this theoretical level—of a fictional relationship. He seems to identify himself with Alma as the spurned and frustrated helper and evidences little empathy with the silent Elizabeth. Of course Alma's, and the analyst's, narcissism are deeply wounded by the patient's unreachability—as Kernberg himself has helped to clarify. It is a tribute to Bergman's art that Elizabeth's silence can provoke such feelings in an analyst of Kernberg's authority.

In fact, Bergman gives us too few fragments—and those few highly ambiguous—of Elizabeth's history and state of mind to speculate effectively on the reasons for her silence. Her silence is thus as inscrutable as the analyst's. And Alma's reaction is remarkably like that of the patient to the silent analyst. At first she is grateful for what seems like compassionate interest. A positive transference develops, and she confesses things that increasingly crumble her defensive persona. When her narcissism is wounded—by reading in Elizabeth's unsealed letter that she is merely an object of interest—the transference becomes rageful, even murderous. Later, merging fantasies develop that assume psychotic proportions. In this confrontation with an implacable silence, Alma's self-concept—as a warm, giving person with conventional aspirations toward marriage and motherhood—is called radically into question.

The analyst who has tamed silence has daily proof of its power. Like a master of marionettes, his silence enables or provokes a multitude of responses in his patients that reveal everything about them—leaving him perfectly castled in anonymity. Little by little his silence erodes their defenses, rendering them infant-like and hungry. Then, with one word, he can feed them and earn that measure of gratitude only children can offer.

Descriptions of the exercise of power and of the pleasure

taken in it may have an evil ring, evoking images of domination. But the use of power is not necessarily ruthless. Unless he is sadistic, the analyst's powerful use of silence (and the satisfaction he takes in his skill) enables the patient to be safely, and subjectively, powerless. And in that condition he can recover a stratum of infantile feeling immured in defenses that limit his dimensions as an adult.

The stage of the analyst's development in which he takes self-conscious pleasure in the power of silence is a necessary one. Any artist who acquires proficiency in a technique revels for a while in its exercise. To this stage of development, for example, belongs Bach's D minor Toccata and its breathtaking Fugue. They may lack the depth of his later work, when a fully integrated technique became the perfect expression of his being. But on this level below the sublime we are moved in very human ways. Equally self-conscious is the journeyman analyst's sense of the aesthetic value of his silence. It is, to a degree, an art-for-art's-sake aesthetic, divorced from the function of therapy. Moreover, it is not a mature aesthetic of process that appreciates the necessity of fragmentation. Rather it seeks completion. Silence begins the hour and ends the hour, and in its embrace a perfectly formed universe is conceived, gestated, and born. The events of the hour unfold with an elegant necessity. Nothing extraneous; no loose ends left untied.

This aesthetic sense of a "good hour" understates process and is to be distinguished from the technical concept. There are nodal moments (hours, weeks) when the long work seems to distill itself in crystalline form. One drop and the cloudy liquid turns a limpid green. At such times it is as if the analyst holds in his hands a globe of thin glass in which the primal world takes shape. Thus power, indeed omnipotence, is also part of this experience.

The convention of putting "good hour" in quotes reveals

the love tinged with shame the analyst bears such episodes. He feels them to be beautiful and precious, but his pride is inseparable from his shame. For he also senses the condescension in treating patient and process as his creations. If he fails to transcend this view, they will become truly inert or else will leave him diminished and alone.

The silence of the "perfect" hour is not the analyst's only aesthetic response. Sometimes, centered at the heart of his silence, he appreciates the perfection of things as they are. From this inclusive position, the syncopated unfolding in advances and retreats, the arrhythmic progress and regress of the hour, appear sufficient. This silence imposes no demands.

Such moments foreshadow the masterly silence of the analyst's maturity. Now he has become his silence, which is nothing less than the expression of his particular way of being. Because his silence has ceased to be a technique (necessarily distinct from the user) but has grown to be a manifestation, it is no longer manipulative and controlling. It does not force an order upon the hour—it contains it.

John Cage (1959), whose own work (especially 4′ 31″) exemplifies this principle, writes of Morton Feldman that he has "changed the responsibility of the composer from making to accepting. To accept whatever comes regardless of the consequences is to be unafraid or to be full of that love which comes from a sense of at-one-ness with whatever" (pp. 129–130).

Cage links acceptance with "no-continuity":

> No-continuity simply means accepting that continuity that happens. Continuity means the opposite: making that particular continuity that excludes all others. This is, of course, possible but not any longer nourishing for we have found that by excluding we grow thin inside though we may have an enormous bank account outside. [p. 132]

The analyst's growth in silence is precisely a growth in acceptance.

Within this context, interpretations, questions, comments, inflected silences, all continue to occur. But not as organizers of a "well-formed" hour. They are areas of organization that develop within the silence, knots of condensed energy in the field.

Some of the analyst's interventions help build the strength with which to appreciate his silence.

One principal thrust of interpretations, constructions, and the like is to impart faith in the intelligibility of experience and to increase the capacity (and faith in the capacity) to assess reality and to act effectively. However, since the data of experience are not known to be structured in themselves, these formulations are fictions. For this reason, their truth value is less important than their believability. Strengthened by these beliefs, the patient may come to tolerate—even to appreciate—the no-continuity of reality represented by the analyst's silence.

This formulation begs profound epistemological and ontological questions. Is the world an orderly place and perceived as such, or are the data of experience seen as structured because perceived through organizing agencies? At very least, ordinary perception is greatly informed by tacit causal expectations and explanatory systems. When these cognitive/perceptual functions are suspended (through drugs, thought disorders, or spiritual exercise), we are given a glimpse of relatively uncooked experience. I associate this experience with Cage's concept of "no-continuity."

Analysis is conducted in the intersection of the cooked and the raw. These two modes also give rise to alternative views of the analyst's function: as reinterpreter/teacher (a cognitive/emotive function) or as container/presence (an existential function).

But in the analytic process, the cognitive is inseparable from the existential. This concept is perfectly expressed in Jesus's startling assertion: "I am the resurrection, and the life." We take in the teaching while incorporating (adoring) the man. In this way the analytic relationship belongs to the family of human relations that includes guru:novice and parent:child.

It also belongs to the family of spiritual paths explicitly or implicitly outlined by various religious systems. Schematically, one progresses from a condition in which perception is well but mistakenly organized to a breakdown and restructuring of perception in better accord with some socially acknowledged reality. If the process does not end here, the analysand moves to a stage where the structuredness of experience itself is understood as apparent and there is a greater capacity to accept and value a more aleatoric world.

All along the way, the analyst's uninflected silence stands for the noumenal order, different in kind from *any* system of organized experience. In this sense, inflected and uninflected silence cannot be compared. The former is part of language, often no less precise than verbal communication. The latter, as Wittgenstein suggested, *points to* what cannot be said. Thus it is not a failure of language that it cannot express uncooked experience. Because language is an organizer, anything it expresses is necessarily organized.

"No-continuity" is pure endless process. Analysis is also, in that it postulates no product—a sane, thing-like personality, a "cure." The "cure" proposed by the silent treatment is just this: a heightened sense of the moment where the "painful structural contradictions inherent in the human situation" (Sontag 1969) are resolved from the perspective of transcendence.

9

The Patient's Response

Patients react to inflected silences much as they would to verbalizations. Nevertheless, writers on the phenomena of silence tend to speak of the "uncanny" clarity some people exhibit in discerning their analysts' unspoken feelings. This use of "uncanny" may merely express the belief that silence effectively guards the analyst's privacy. Is the anonymity of the analyst a fiction that patients conspire to support, or do most, consciously or otherwise, discern the character behind the professional mask? It may be that "uncanny" is used for those who, like Alice among the playing cards, dare to break this implicit contract.

What the patient discerns of the analyst's attitude toward him ranges anywhere from benevolence to contempt. The value of an empathic, attentive silence has been noted by virtually every writer on the subject, as has the destructiveness of a hateful silence. Needless to say, while attitudes cannot be legislated, they must be monitored. This is especially crucial in the context of silence. Because it is a mandated technique (and was more exaggeratedly so in earlier years), malice can easily hide in its shadows. Hateful confrontations of silence with silence, when not irreparably damaging, can prolong or reinforce the use of silence as a resistance.

David, an only child, had been raised by the maxim that children should not speak unless spoken to. He had found this humiliating and enraging since, in fact, the rule contained the message that any spontaneous act was of no value. The adults in the household, and particularly his father, held themselves aloof and spoke little. David's silence on the couch recreated the environment of his childhood and also manifested an identification both with his father and with myself. But these silences were not all the same. Those which were a reaction to my silence had an agitated, expectant quality—like an angry Adam waiting for God to give him life. Sometimes my silences were indeed hostile—induced by the undertone of rage in his silences and functioning to maintain them. In one session, when I understood the dynamics of his silence more fully, I kept silent about my understanding. When I subsequently became aware that my silence contributed to a joint acting out, this aspect of the transference could be worked on and the silence was broken.

The analyst's uninflected silence is the *cantus firmus* against which the patient's motives unfold. Although this is central to the process, Theodor Reik's (1926) lecture on "The Psychological Meaning of Silence" remains one of the only discussions of the patient's developing interpretations of the analyst's silence in the course of treatment. Reik observed that this silence is experienced in the beginning as benevolent interest. But little by little it changes its meaning. The patient wishes to avoid something difficult, at first substituting other things, but ultimately growing silent—like the analyst himself.

Then, as the first serious resistance becomes manifest, the analyst's silence takes on the quality of a refusal to speak. The patient's effort now becomes directed at breaking the analyst's silence by giving more and more of what he believes the analyst wants to hear. But no matter what and how much he produces, the silence continues. Now it begins to feel like outright denial. This is a period of intense anxiety in which silence is experienced as a loss of love accompanied by intense guilt and castration fears.

Inexorably the silence goes on. Now the patient may begin to wish the analyst dead or to entertain the thought that he may actually be dead. The feeling that the analyst is at a great distance can express this fantasy.

Reik concludes that this development traces "a return of feeling which played an important role in the patient's relationship to an old love object—from the original tenderness to the embitterment over an imagined or actual denial. The transition from one interpretation of silence to another is by no means as obvious as it may seem at first glance" (p. 181).

Reik's unique discussion traces the patient's reaction to an *implacably* silent analyst. To the extent that this reproduces a childhood experience of denial, it does so especially for those with severely depressed or sadistic parents who could or would not respond to them. And it does this by means of a relationship that is potentially noxious in itself. The *relative* silence of the more usual analyst does undergo changes in meaning for the patient as the treatment unfolds, but I would trace this evolution differently. First, the initial perception of the analyst's silence as benevolent interest is never lost. Although it can only be apprehended in the beginning when the patient is too defended to integrate the analyst as a caring object, that apprehension is at the core of the working alliance. It is against this ground that the patient struggles both to maintain and to dismantle his defenses. Reik treats the evolution of treatment as an unfolding of resistance. But, as Kris (1956) reminds us, if integrative drives were not at least equally strong, the project would fail.[1]

In the eighth month of treatment one patient said, "Even though you're not saying anything, I sense you are there for me. If I didn't know that, I couldn't go on. But at the same time, I can't believe you really care." Silence at this stage contains the *possibility* of being loved.

The extended work of analyzing and working through resistances and the transference can be seen as clearing a space for admission of a new object: the analyst. Because of the turmoil and complexity inherent in this period, perceptions of silence vary greatly. After all, a battle is being waged between an awareness of current reality and a skewed vision of it programmed by the past. The analytic relationship develops in the tension between the two. Therefore the analyst's silence is alternately a dark closet into which the patient's worst fears are projected ("You find me boring; you've gone away.") and a clear space in which he is seen as listening with care while the patient struggles toward a new sense of himself and the world.

---

[1]In discussing the "good hour," Kris distinguishes between those produced in consequence of the patient's integrative drives and those produced either in compliance or defensively, to obviate the analyst's function. These distinctions are apparent phenomenologically and result, theoretically, from the degree to which the energies involved are neutralized.

Melissa, a woman in her mid-20s, was particularly sensitive to my silences, which, from the earliest sessions, she experienced as my "leaving" her. She had in fact been left in the care of an aunt from the age of two when her mother, a concert artist, went on tour. The child's personality, formerly outgoing and energetic, was so obviously altered after this episode that the mother abandoned her career for several years to be with her. The mother's narcissism, however, created a discrepancy beween her attentions and the child's actual needs, so that Melissa felt equally threatened—although in different ways—by her mother's presence and absence. After two and a half years Melissa said, "When you say nothing, I feel terribly alone and I begin to withdraw into myself. But when you speak, I feel controlled and angry, especially if I think you're not understanding me and are just pleasing yourself. But I have another way of feeling now which is newer and more tentative where I'm neither abandoned nor over-whelmed—just with you. You're silent but you're there, or you're speaking and I'm not overpowered. I would like to be there more but I can't be sure of it yet."

As the capacity to trust grows and the patient can relax into a state that approximates infantile receptivity, the ground is prepared for a new introjection. The patient's vulnerability at this stage of treatment is a great achievement. Handled respect-fully, the analyst's silence will continue to be experienced as benevolent interest—but with a fullness that would not have been possible in the beginning.

After nearly four years, Sylvia began to drop her protective chattiness and grew increasingly silent in a way that expressed her openness. During one such mutual silence I had the feeling of being pregnant with her. Later, she reported her own fantasy. She imagined a bucolic setting with a large tree by a river bank. We were sitting under the tree, she nestled in my arm as I held a balloon. Then she saw herself *inside* the balloon, which I was holding by a long, tubelike string. So long as we were connected, she knew she would be safe.

This deep sense of connection with the analyst marks an existential change; the analyst has been included alongside the original objects and is thus able to influence the balance of internal forces in an ongoing way. The patient's core sense of himself has been fundamentally altered. The working-through process must continue, but now it has the quality of a coda—solidifying and elaborating an undeniable achievement.

In the evolution I have traced, the patient's reactions to the analyst's silence (as well as the patient's own silences) reveal the workings of integrative drives as well as of resistances. But for Reik and others of his generation, silence could only be perceived negatively. The temptation to split the unified object into good and bad is universal. Reik and other pioneering analysts yield to it when they identify silence with resistance and death, and speech with life. So, for Reik, the expression "dead silent" is redundant: "If we here are only 'on leave from death,' " he noted, "then all speech is only a fleeting interruption of the eternal silence" (p. 185).

Reik's poetic insight is misleading. The tension is not, as he would have it, between silence and speech, but between life and death, either of which may modify these and other categories of experience.

The patient's experience of one aspect of silence—silence-as-death—can be like Christ's harrowing of Hell, literally the passage between death and resurrection. If the analyst can transcend technique, as well as the particularities of his own silence, then he can *enter into* this experience with his patient. The purpose of that mythical foray into Limbo, after all, was to liberate the souls held captive since the death of Adam. And liberation is the purpose of this descent as well. It becomes a liberating possibility because, unlike the death-silence of the patient's infancy, this expedition is made jointly. The patient is not alone.

SILENCE AS DEATH

When silence becomes the vehicle of death, we must discern which form it carries. Is the patient's silence a fuming *suppression* of rage? Is he actively torturing himself with guilt? Is he deadening himself to avoid his anger? Or does his lifeless look protect and conceal a deeper life within?

Most of the earlier papers on silence, beginning with Ferenczi's (1916), speak of it as a resistance phenomenon.[2] Since, in the most obvious way, the patient's silence breaks the fundamental rule by denying verbal access to the unconscious (in the limited sense of primary process), it is resistance par excellence. Later, more complex views of silence do not alter the value of these earlier insights.

If silence is, among other things, an expression of resistance, who is resisting what? Although Freud's (1895) earliest thoughts on resistance are ambiguous with respect to whether the force emanates from the repressed or from the ego, in "Analysis Terminable and Interminable" (Freud 1937) resistances were seen more clearly as manifestations in treatment of defense mechanisms the ego had already employed elsewhere. But Freud found inadequate this account of resistance as exclu-

---

[2]Freud, of course, recognized that keeping silent does not by itself deny access to the unconscious. In the "Fragment of an Analysis of a Case of Hysteria" (1905), he noted that "he that has eyes to see and ears to hear may convince himself that no mortal can keep a secret. If his lips are silent, he chatters with his fingertips; betrayal oozes out of him at every pore. And thus the task of making conscious the most hidden recesses of the mind is one which it is quite possible to accomplish" (pp. 77–78).

sively an operation of the ego. Some instances of resistance could be explained only as deriving from the id itself—particularly as the source of the repetition compulsion. A third resistance, discussed in terms of the negative therapeutic reaction (Freud 1923), would derive from the superego's imposition of guilt and the demand for retribution (Freud 1926).

If we define resistance not only as behavior that obstructs verbal access to the unconscious but, more generally, as a reaction against forces in the therapy that would alter the personality, Freud offers a tentative classification of resistance as deriving from one of the three psychic structures. On this definition, resistance is conceived of negatively as in opposition to the curative goals of treatment. We are justified, therefore, in linking it—at least poetically—with death. But more specifically, Freud viewed the death instinct as the ultimate source of certain obdurate resistances—particularly those of the superego.

This view of resistance is embedded in a particular theory of psychopathology and treatment technique. When, in a particular developmental context, an instinctual impulse is overwhelming, the ego experiences anxiety and deploys some mechanism of defense. In analysis, the conflict appears again as resistance to the reemergence of the impulse. If it were to emerge, however, it could at last be integrated into the now more mature ego, and the person's picture of reality would become less distorted. The analyst helps its emergence by analyzing the resistance to it. Silence, on this view, is an attempt *first* to counter the reappearance of a once dangerous instinctual demand and *second* to counter forces that would disrupt the now stable system that developed in reaction to it.

But silence can also resist the emergence of a hidden self. If the cohesive self of a certain stage of development (Kohut's grandiose–exhibitionistic self; Winnicott's True Self) does not meet with the maternal response it requires to confirm its subjective reality, it may split off and continue—hidden and embryonic. Since the vitality associated with this split-off self is unavailable, its emergence and integration would animate the now depleted and distorted personality. The analyst's task is to enable its emergence by empathically understanding the patient's situation and offering this highly vulnerable hidden self safe haven and the chance to continue growth. Silence, in this case, is an attempt to protect a precious core of authentic existence from destruction.

In both cases silence-as-resistance is used to separate one part of the personality from another and to separate the patient from the analyst. It is because he links silence-as-resistance with separation, and then separation with death, that Reik is obliged to interpret the expression "dead silent" as a redundancy. It follows too that "at the deepest level the anxiety of silence is death . . . anxiety."

A further consequence is that speech, taken as the opposite of silence, becomes a connector and thus a manifestation of the life instincts. A more complex view (discussed in the next section) would acknowledge the separating function of some speech acts and the profound communion experienced in certain silent meetings. No less importantly, the divisive purpose of particular silences may be understood as in the service of preserving life.

Finally, should the concept of the death instincts be accepted along with Freud's assertion that they are found almost exclusively in fusion with the life instincts, we have the added difficulty of discerning, in any silence, the relative strength of destructive and conjunctive forces.

These issues may be illuminated by examining some instances of silence in the hour.

Marilyn, a woman in her early 40s, was frequently silent at the beginning of the hour and acknowledged that this was a habitual way of handling anger. Her mother too had been a silent figure throughout Marilyn's childhood, and this had at times provoked intensely angry, even murderous feelings. But her mother treated even her rage with silence. Now Marilyn's silence contained a challenge: "Can I force you to talk if I don't?" Stubbornly she waited for me to prod her into speech. Then, just as she had hated her mother's silence, she expected me to hate her for not talking.

As a resistance, this angry silence derives principally from the defense of identification with the aggressor. The aggression, in this case, was the mother's silence. Whether that silence was indeed hostile or was interpreted as such by the daughter we do not know. But since patients who have identified with silently depressed mothers retain a sad, lonely quality in their own silences, it appears that children can make these distinctions. Thus the patient identifies with what she perceives as the object's dominant affect in the context of a relationship's particular dynamics. Here the dynamics have a markedly sadomasochistic quality. The two-sidedness of this relationship is recreated in the analysis, since the patient's silence both punished me for my silence and invited punishment for her own. But as it invites punishment—entailed by guilt for the murderous feelings her mother's silence engendered—so it also invites communication.

No less importantly, the patient's silence *is* communication—of the most passionate and demonstrative sort. The communication is not verbal and descriptive; it *points to* her past experiences more vividly than language could possibly do. We may call her silence communication because, in the context of the session, it is meaningful. At times I felt attacked by her silence and then either fearful or enraged or both. These induced feelings enabled me to understand her situation more profoundly than could any report. She was letting me know how she had felt as a child.

But the issue of resistance as communication remains problematic. While there is no doubt that both silence and verbal resistances are communicative, it is debatable whether they are as valuable for the analytic process as the communications offered by following the fundamental rule. Greenson (1961) distinguishes between silence as a resistance and as a communication, and, within the latter, between silence in the hour as a repetition of an event in which silence was important or as an identification with a silent, sleeping, or (in the case of depressed or psychotic patients) dead object. But, according to stricter usage, what Greenson calls communication are examples of acting in, and thus instances of resistance.

While silence in the hour is—by definition—resistance, resistance may be no less communicative and illuminating than an unblocked chain of associations. As much and more may be revealed in the patient's breaking the fundamental rule as in keeping it. Moreover, breaking the rule is intrinsic to the process.

Some of these difficulties result from fundamental confusions in the concept of resistance. One such muddle can be clarified if we allow that some demonstrative nonverbal behavior cannot meaningfully be called resistance in that it neither denies access to the unconscious (understood more broadly than primary process) nor impedes the therapeutic work, even as it embodies earlier mechanisms of defense. This is especially true in the communication of experiences that were themselves nonverbal or that belonged to a preverbal stage of development.

In addition to identifying with the aggressor, Marilyn turned the impulse against herself by choking back the angry speech intended for me. These resistances certainly place her pathology within the conflict model in which silence as an aggressive expression of destructive and self-destructive impulses separates even as it communicates.

But this same patient's silence in a later phase had a quite different feeling. Her father had left when she was 2 and so her mother's parents, who lived nearby, played a larger role in her life. They were a dour couple who insisted that children be seen and not heard. Thus the silence in which she passed her childhood denied her very existence. She felt it as an emotional *gulag* and recreated this sense of it in the analysis—seeing herself as one who denies and is denied in a zero-sum exchange. Once she said: "Sometimes I am silent because I am completely alone."

This silence—this state of mind—does not readily fit the conflict model. Marilyn found herself in a wasteland where the absence of response brought her very being into question. Children are not self-sustaining. Without their sense of life being affirmed by the adults who care for them, they can die. More commonly, they can secrete the living parts of themselves in psychic hiding places where the malevolence and aridity of their environments cannot reach. While this state of affairs may be analyzed, the analysis itself cannot breach the wall that divides the living self from everything else.

In this silence, too, we can feel the presence of death. The child's life is threatened no less by emotional abandonment than by actively hostile forces. The parent's silence is deadly, and in the command to "be silent" the child is ordered to die. But she does not comply—she obeys. She seems to die while waiting secretly (and unconsciously) for the chance to live again.

When that chance comes in the analysis, the analyst has the task of encountering the patient through the medium of a language of extraordinary difficulty and subtlety. If the silence is largely a stoppage of communication—the suppressing of conflictful thoughts or feelings that are largely preconscious—a few words of interpretation will often start the flow of speech again.

Much more is required when silence is the primary mode of communication and the material is largely unconscious. Then the analyst must pay exquisite attention to his own reactions. More poignantly than any other, the encounter with a silent patient reveals the two-person nature of the analytic process. This process is powerfully evoked in a case history recorded by Masud Khan (1963).

Khan worked with an adolescent patient, Peter, who was completely mute for eleven sessions following the initial interview. By paying sedulous attention to his own fluctuations of feeling, Khan was able to offer a construction and to explain Peter's silence as the living memory of his childhood with a depressed mother who could not mirror his vitality. Peter's confirmation and detailing of this construction marked a turning point in treatment.

In the silence, Khan's reactions varied from straightforwardly "analytic" to empathic, countertransferential, and induced—distinguishable sometimes only with great subtlety. Of all, the induced reactions—the product of projective identifications—require the most delicate handling for silent patients. The analyst's vengeful feelings can lead him, as Hannah Segal (1973) cautions, to " 'shove back' into the patient automatically what he had projected" (p. 121). Thus, destructive drives are to be found not only in the patient's silence but in the analyst's reactions to it.

In my own work with silent patients I have encountered only one in whom self-destructive drives predominated. Karen was usually talkative, but periods of silence—lasting from one to four sessions—punctuated the analysis at crucial points. In each instance her silence was associated with suicidal thoughts, but only once did she actually attempt the act. This attempt followed a period of three sessions in which she said nothing. A frighteningly cool atmosphere prevailed—efficient and mechanical—like a death camp. My attempts to reach her were in vain, and I began to experience in myself an icy intellectual anger in response to the pain of being cut off from her. In this state I remained essentially alert, but *I did not care*. We had robotized ourselves.

Before I was able to connect my condition with hers, Karen attempted suicide by turning on the gas—stopping moments before she was overcome. She had taken this action without anguish or pain; it seemed, she said, "the logical thing to do." Her reporting of this in the following session broke the silence and led to the understanding that a series of cerebral interpretations had initiated the process. Karen had just begun to loosen her schizoid defenses and tentatively to permit the emergence of a very tender, molluscan self when I—perhaps fearful of her trust—reacted with a kind of intellectual brutality. But her sense of betrayal went far beyond these interpretations. After a lifetime of protecting a private core behind a very successfully constructed social persona, she had dared to risk exposure. My response made her despair of ever finding an environment in which she could be real again—a situation so terrible that death seemed preferable. Her silence was thus an expression of her deep feeling of betrayal and hopelessness—and a preparation for death.

Although overdetermined like all human actions, the thrust of Karen's attempt was ultimately life-preserving—if by "living" we understand the maintenance of a True Self rather than of the organism as a totality (Winnicott 1958). Later suicidal thoughts, related again to several silent sessions, were less equivocally self-destructive. Karen realized increasingly the degree to which her mother fostered a split in her being and behavior—encouraging a compliant personality and identifying her spontaneity and normal aggression as bad. After she had written her mother a denunciatory letter—the first such confrontation she had dared since childhood—she fell into a silence that was deeply depressed. This time her suicidal thoughts were more violent—with the idea of atomizing herself and not merely fading imperceptibly into oblivion. Karen's suicidal impulses gathered force from the partial identification of her True Self as bad. It was as if she harbored an evil homunculus that drew to it all the thoughts and actions she felt to be wrong. Since she would habitually blame herself rather than evince anger—a tendency that originated in protecting the image of her alcoholic and abusive mother—this inner picture grew increasingly malignant. Now the thought of suicide meant eradicating her evil self.

One might argue that this too was ultimately self-protective, since in erasing her bad self she would be preserving the good from infection. But we must remember that this bad self was profoundly associated with Karen's sense of being an alive, authentic person. Consequently, to kill it would be profoundly self-destructive—as unalloyed an embodiment of the death instincts as I can identify. Since, however, they are largely expressed through the agency of the superego—the structure that is most clearly the product of introjecting an object in its judgmental and punitive aspects—the primacy of the self-destructive drive remains in question. But not its reality. In the silence Karen's rage against herself was palpable. I felt a terrifying, murderous force in the room that moved chaotically and at jet speeds.

At other times—and especially at later stages of treatment—Karen silently raged against herself rather than directing it at someone in her life who had angered her. How do we distinguish between anger turned against the self and the phenomenon just described? Although difficult to discern in any instance, the distinction can be made. The action Karen actually took—writing the letter—evoked guilt and the wish to destroy not her total self but rather a well-developed internal object experienced as bad and potentially infectious. Simple anger turned against the self defends against an action *not yet taken* by a process of deflection. The self becomes the object of rage less because of any belief in its badness than to avoid the destruction of the object.

These differences were present in the silence. When Karen was angry at me and deflecting it to herself, I experienced her silent suffering as hostile. However fleetingly, I feared for myself and not for her. Moreover, I often did not need to break my silence for Karen to interpret her own feelings. And if I chose to make an interpretation, it would be quickly accepted and effective. But when she would be swept by storms of guilt, I experienced her terror empathically, fearing for her and not for myself. Moreover, her self-destructive impulses evoked protective ones in me; the child she saw as a bad seed was the child I loved and wanted to restore. At such times an interpretation had to be made, yet finding the right words was neither easy nor assuredly effective.

In certain of Karen's silences I was able to discover a further meaning: a true yearning for death. Not the death that obliterates a painful life, or sacrifices one's self in place of another or— still less—offers a chance for renewal. She yearned for a final death that contained the possibility of eternal union. Karen's father had died when she was 3. A normal idealizing process was heightened by this death and further reinforced by her mother's remarriage to a man Karen felt as brutal and rejecting. In fantasy her dead father became an infinitely tender figure, merging with childhood images of Jesus the Comforter and of Death, the refuge and giver of peace. In her father's arms at last she would find rest.

In these silences I experienced myself completely at ease. Like a sobbing child held close, I felt the tension drain from my body. I buried my face in an envelope of warmth and knew how much I too had lost. This silence of Karen's lasted for two sessions. During them and in between, these feelings stayed with me. Thoughts of my own death would appear quite without anxiety, and the idea of heaven—normally remote—seemed perfectly accessible. It was only with effort that I returned to the demands of ordinary life and work.

In the wish to rejoin her father, Karen—herself a writer—consciously identified with Sylvia Plath, many of whose poems reveal implicitly the sensible quality of silence as death. For her, and more rarely for Karen, images of death and silence were cut from the bone by an intellect sharp as a fillet knife. This nirvana is not redemptive. It is an operating room paneled in steel and defined by thin lines of blood. Within it, despair ends speciously, to be revived again and again.

SILENCE AS CONNECTION

Longing for a state of union does not itself entail death. Many shared silences between analyst and patient, between lovers and friends, are concentrated moments of communion. Well-individuated people can share times of deep appreciation—a sentiment I associate with the ability to love without blurring one's boundaries. Sometimes they are birth moments of incorporation—the patient takes the analyst in as a new object and an indestructible resource. Or there can be a joyful mingling of feelings that is not threatening but revitalizing. These are *healing* passages in a relationship. Perhaps for that reason the psycho-analytic literature, with its inevitable focus on the knottier moments in the process, offers little technical and even less clinical material on the subject. But, increasingly in the last twenty-five years, there has been a willingness to question the conventional view of silence as simple resistance and to explore its integrative values.

For example, silence can both express and guard a developmental achievement. Gertrude Blanck (1966) treated an anally fixated patient who experienced free association as a loss of control and was typically silent. Her mother had administered enemas throughout latency so that sphincter control had been forcibly taken from her. Now she figuratively reasserted that control in the analysis with someone who appreciated its value. "The patient by silence fought for the integrity of her ego in the analysis just as she fought the onslaught of the enemas." Thus she used her silence "to maintain and restore the ego's original achievement of withholding" (p. 10).

It is an important revision in the concept of resistance to understand silence of this sort as an achievement. However, Blanck, like all those who followed in Ferenczi's path, overestimates the control of verbalization as a displacement of other instinctual controls. Indeed this led Robert Fliess (1949) to formulate a rather ridiculous dictionary relating "forms of silence as the equivalent of the closure of a particular sphincter" (p. 23).

Speech control is a development in its own right and can be seen as an avenue for asserting the distinction between public and private, inside and outside, *paralleling* the avenue of sphincter control. Using it, the child guards his integrity not only by realizing his capacity to keep mum, but also by learning to lie. Parents violate their children's boundaries differently, but as violently, whether they're worming the truth out of them or administering enemas. And the sort of invasive parent who is likely to do the one is also likely to do the other.

In this way, lying and misleading and evasive speech join silence as ways of achieving position and integrity in relationships with the powerful.

A 27-year-old man suffered from chronic feelings of unreality origi-
nating in his relationship with a narcissistic mother who demanded
that he exist for her. Because of his ability to discern the unspoken
needs of others and his need to please, the authenticity of the working
alliance was questionable. Consequently, this statement, made after a
largely silent session in his third year of treatment, marked an
important achievement: "I sensed your discomfort because I was
saying nothing and I wanted to ease things for you. But then I said
'Fuck it!' I'm here for myself, and I just don't feel like talking."

   In his silence the patient may be reworking problems in still
earlier stages of development—particularly those of the practicing subphase of separation–individuation. Without using
these terms (his discussion preceded their coining by several
years), Winnicott (1958) illuminates this aspect of a patient's
silence in "The Capacity to Be Alone." This capacity may be
represented in treatment "by a silent phase or a silent session,
and this silence, far from being evidence of resistance, turns
out to be an achievement on the part of the patient" (p. 29).
Winnicott traces the origin of the mature capacity to be alone to
the infant's experiences of being alone *in the presence of the
mother*. "Being alone in the presence of someone can take place
at a very early stage, when the ego immaturity is naturally
balanced by ego-support from the mother. In the course of time
the individual introjects the ego-supportive mother and in this
way becomes able to be alone without frequent reference to the
mother or mother symbol (p. 32).[3] This state, which has been
referred to as the establishment of an "internal environment," "is
more primitive than the phenomenon which deserves the term
'introjected mother' " (p. 34).

---

[3]Winnicott notes: "If conditions (that will allow the True Self to flourish) cannot be found,
then there must be reorganized a new defense against exploitation of the True Self, and if there
be doubt then the clinical result is suicide. Suicide in this context is the destruction of the total
self in avoidance of annihilation of the True Self" (p. 143).

In the practicing subphase, the infant begins an independent life *as if* his mother were not there. But it can only be negotiated successfully if the mother is in fact available—not as an assertive object but, so to speak, as part of the furniture. Since the end of symbiosis is a difficult time for mothers, some degree of trauma is virtually inevitable and will be reawakened in the transference.

Alice, a 31-year-old woman at the time I began seeing her, talked incessantly from the couch, eliciting responses so well that we were connected by an endless tissue of words. At some point I found myself responding less and less. Through this I came to understand that she was beginning to let me drift into the background where my presence alone was sufficient. Finally she began one session by saying, "I have nothing to talk about." In the half hour of silence that followed, I allowed my own thoughts to drift, reassuring myself at intervals with a glance in her direction. I had the feeling that she was "playing by herself" and that I could attend to other things so long as some deep but nonspecific connection remained unbroken. When she began speaking, she confirmed this trend in her own associations. Later we were able to reconstruct that her mother, whose husband was a soldier throughout Alice's infancy, had in her loneliness overextended a symbiotic connection that altered suddenly on her father's return. Now, with me, Alice regulated both the symbiotic tie and its loosening *in accord with her own rhythms*. My task was only to let her come and go as her impulses dictated and to be there for her calmly and responsively, in the wings.

Silence can be the medium in which many subtle issues of identity formation belonging to the earliest developmental phases are played out. In this silence, the patient may experience himself being held in a deep symbiotic union. How else but in silence could this primitive nonverbal state be revived? This, too, is an achievement, since it represents a state of profound trust that is the result of successfully laying aside outmoded defenses. And having done so, a deep inner peace becomes possible. Patient and analyst transcend the working alliance to share in a state of communion. This is the silence celebrated by Valéry (1971, p. 320)—the core of authentic existence from which one soul, wordlessly, grasps the reality of another:

> L'on se comprend sans vaines paroles
> Et sans dissiper par le bruit des voix
> Le charme divin des idées folles[4]. . . .

For most patients—indeed for most adults—the experience of intimacy is an achievement because of the great difficulty of submitting to a trustful, dependent relationship. But the situation of the psychotic is otherwise and therefore affects the quality and meaning of a shared silence. Franco Bassaglia (1965) writes: "The psychotic, whose boundaries, sense of integrity, self, etc., have been broken, must reestablish, in the silence of the two, a silence-interval in which he can master himself and reach out to the other, and in which he will be able to distinguish that the other has invaded him" (p. 101). Silence between the analyst and the psychotic patient offers the chance to rebuild walls that have been ruptured catastrophically. It is a precondition of a true object relationship—as opposed to a relationship with a narcissistically conceived object—that each person be independently defined. Silence offers the space in which that definition can develop. When each person's limits are unspecified, language undergoes corresponding distortions. Whose voice is speaking and to whom? Even to hear a voice in such a situation can be terrifying, exacerbating the sense of

---

[4]English translation: "There we are understood without useless words/Without breaking the spell/Of wild, unbridled thoughts/Through the clatter and bang of our voices. . . ."

invasion by persecutory entities babbling in confusion. Silence
offers respite. Martin Buber (1958) reminds us:

> Only silence before the *Thou*—
> silence of *all* tongues, silent
> patience in the individual word
> that precedes the formed and vocal
> response—leaves the *Thou* free . . .

The catastrophic collapse of a personality or the gradual
relaxation of one can lead to similar alterations of perception.
Thus the patient who has *achieved* a state of symbiotic union and
the psychotic who is plunged into fragmentation can both be
open to a deeply creative level of experience. Michael Balint
(1958) sees this as a state in which the person, quite without
relation to an external object, creates "out of his self" (p. 337). To
this creative level belongs the capacity to envisage new and
universal connections sometimes associated with the early stages
of psychotic episodes—and with spontaneous recovery.

Sometimes the silent patient has retreated to this Precam-
brian stratum when the connections possible in his current
language cannot solve the dilemma that torments him. In the
safe haven of his silence he is solving riddles that words cannot
comprehend. Painters and poets are familiar with these fertile
intervals. One thinks of Rilke's (1939) watchful silence between
beginning the *Duino Elegies* in 1912 and completing them in a
great burst of power ten years later. The words that ultimately
emerge from this silence can have reborn, primal meaning. They
form "a language of word-kernels, a language that's not gathered,
up above, on stalks, but grasped in the speech seed" (p. 18).

Words can be heard as well as formed in this way. In a state
of reverie, the poem can be read *as if the reader were creating it.*
The words penetrate to where, simultaneously, they sound the

depths of the reader's being and produce multitudes of ripples—waves of association that spread out over its surface. From a creative silence, the analysand's experience is similar, and so, in describing it, it is perhaps not so remarkable that Seymour Nacht (1964) shares Rilke's imagery: "Words sow seeds; just as seeds germinate and sprout first in peaceful silence of the earth, so now in silence and in peace the self grows and develops." Further: ". . . if the patient listens . . . from his peaceful inner silence, the [analyst's] words will form *roots* in his deepest being and will bear fruit . . . " (p. 302).

This kind of creative listening has affinities with the infant's hallucinating the breast, which, if all goes well, appears regularly in response to his need. So it is as if the words were *almost* there, were just forming themselves in the patient's mind when they are spoken by the analyst precisely as the patient himself would have said them. Or it may be that words already spoken—found objects—are created anew in a unique act of taking possession. Winnicott (1952) traces the primary source of all creativity to the infantile relation to the transitional object. At a crucial moment the child takes an entity—a doll, blanket, even a song—presented in fact by the world, and treats it as his own creation, endowing it with attributes that alter it phenomenologically. Thus the transitional object is the essential cult object and the essential work of art. Heard from a deeply creative silence, the analyst's words can assume this primal function in a process essential to the capacity for independence.

But the ultimate requirement of the capacity for independence is the internalization of a good object. Unless this happens in infancy or in the analytic process, the person will remain a shell. The necessary analysis of resistances and of defenses and of repetitive patterns will produce only superficial changes if the patient fails to take the analyst into his heart.

The preparation for "taking in" is a slow, incremental

process. But the actual moment of internalization can be quite specific.

After nearly a full session of silence, a patient in his mid-30s who had been very spiky and argumentative during four years of treatment, described this fantasy: "I was sitting in a rocking chair giving my son his bottle. I felt so close to him, so full. Tears welled up. Then I had the sense that you were holding me as I was holding him, very lovingly. The three of us were nested like a set of Chinese boxes, like a sort of Trinity. I knew that I could never lose you, just as my son can never lose me."

Because he could never lose me, I knew that the end of the analysis was in sight. The poignancy of such moments can, of course, be talked about. But in some sense it cannot be shared. We were both, after a long and intense experience of interpenetration, once again on our own, and *that* sense is quite private. To translate it would not merely betray it—it would falsify it. Silence is the only truthful response.

The Art of
Psychoanalysis

10

The Practice

of

Unknowing

Having passed psychoanalytic therapy through the prisms of space, time, and silence, we achieve nothing like a spectral graph. The appearance of a color here is no guide to the presence of an element: objectivity is simply not to be had. If psychoanalysis were to be called a science of any sort, it would be a subjective one, such as Goethe once envisioned for optics. Viewed from the perspective of wave lengths and refractive indices, Goethe's beautifully designed experiments often yielded wrong results. Yet they represent a noble effort: the last attempt before the final triumph of modern science to preserve the unity of observer and observed.

When the Newtonian conception prevailed—so that it became synonymous with science itself—that unity was lost. Freud could think of his new science in none but the Newtonian way. The analyst was made to design himself as an instrument of objectivity, constructing from his observations an *underlying* truth whose revelation would undo neurotic conflict. The problem, as Lydia put it in Chapter 7, is that the patient does not want merely to be understood; the patient wants to be loved. The distance the method demands creates a disorder of its own: the deepening of an emptiness that is the legacy of a childhood without love.

Perhaps psychoanalysis could reconstitute itself, in line with Goethe's model, as a phenomenological science. Yet even that effort may be misguided, revealing in its wish to stay a science at all costs an overevaluation of "science"—indeed of rationality itself. Might we instead take psychoanalysis to be not a science, but an art?

That we should recoil from this question—if that is what we do—owes something to the decline in status of aesthetics since its apogee in the early nineteenth century. For Schiller (1800) and, later, Hegel (1830), art was pivotal: the point where the highest level of mind manifests itself sensually. Freedom is the essence of mind, as Hegel saw it, so that art is a manifestation of mind's freedom in a particular realm. How can psychoanalysis fit such a picture?

Although one can show its scientific claims to be weak, as I believe Adolf Grünbaum (1984) has done, the underpinnings of psychoanalysis remain scientific. That is to say, within its conceptual framework is the belief that mind follows lawlike patterns, making behavior, at least in principle, predictable. The task has been to discern the regular connections between configurations of childhood experience and adult psychopathology, so that curative interventions can be made with precision and effectiveness. In such a framework, there is no place for freedom, in analyst or patient. What may look like freedom results from the practical impossibility of formulating statements with too many and complex causal lines. The purpose of a psychoanalysis is to free the patient from blind obedience to the past. But this freedom is quite relative and circumscribed. The notion of absolute freedom—behavior that is not *in principle* predictable— makes no sense in psychoanalysis *qua* science. Yet, at the same time that our faith in capturing a law-abiding mind in law-like formulae has grown, our appreciation of art as spontaneous creation has grown with it. Isn't it poignant that, in art, we value the appearance of a freedom we no longer believe possible?

The realms of science and art are not mutually exclusive, of course. The cult of the avant-garde, especially in the United States, has accustomed us to thinking that skill, knowledge, and convention are alien to art; that freedom—working at the shimmering edge of madness and formal invention—is the exclusive business of creativity. But there is an older tradition, never entirely lost, that would ground the artist's inspiration in a context of craft and cultivation. That model, to my mind, fits psychoanalysis.

There is a tension between these visions. At one extreme is a dead, academic art, which risks nothing and leaves us cold. Alternatively we have the art of, say, abstract expressionist painting, which risks everything and moves us through its courage. Yet, lacking cultural markers, the emotions it evokes can remain inchoate, simple, or too idiosyncratic to be named.

In Jackson Pollock's earlier *Pasiphäe*[1] (1943), by contrast, a delirium of violent sexuality is held by the associations of the title and the painting's just-recognizable images. Our reactions can be complex without losing depth.

Craft, knowledge, cultivation, and rules are all containers of the psychoanalytic experience. Loosely gathered under the heading of "science," they have been emphasized at the expense of the irrational. There are many reasons for this, of which Freud's subscription to a scientific ideal is perhaps not the most basic. Temperament is more fundamental. For the most part, the analyst has been the sort of person who prefers predictability and formal structure to anarchy and chance. He lives his life, after all, by the clock: forty-five minutes per session, one session per hour. He sees his patients at the same times each week and takes his vacation in August (see Chapter 5, "The Psychoanalysis of Time").

The attempt to characterize psychoanalysis as science manifests this temperament. Freud's (1933) famous dictum, "Where Id was, Ego shall be," is the scientist's credo as well: chthonic nature summarized in laws—her dark forces not so much borrowed through magic as harnessed through machinery.

Religion, too, can be said to attempt to control mystery. Yet there is a difference. The forms of religion—liturgies, theologies, sacred texts—do not substitute for God, who remains, despite them, wholly Other.

The hubris in the scientific project lies especially in the wish to substitute knowledge for nature. In psychoanalysis that grandiosity is most visible in the original German of Freud's assertion, *"Wo Es war, soll Ich werden"*—literally, "Where It was, shall I come to be." I shall take the place of It. And the I that takes It's

---

[1]The painting captures the moment of consummation between a bull, for whom Pasiphäe (mother of the Minotaur) has conceived an "unnatural" passion, and the queen, who has, for this purpose, shut herself up in a bronze cow.

place is precisely the I that knows—knows through scientific procedures or Aristotelian syllogisms. The I is reduced to a knower and reality to the knowable.

Let me borrow Primo Levi's[2] imagination. The It arrives as a truckload of ore. The I subjects it to a conversion process that results in some amount of pure metal and throws away the rest as slag. There is a devaluation of the *materia prima* and of the slag that renders them both less than real. With the metal, then, a world is created—an I-made world—one that is experienced, however, as the world *tout court*. The mines from which the ore is taken and the steaming slag heaps at the city's edge are somehow *not there*.

I am interested in what is not there. If it is acknowledged— if its reality is given back—it seems to me that the distortions of the scientific project cannot go forward and that a new wholeness can happen.

There are many directions such a project might take. Among them is a revaluation of the primal stuff to which psychoanalysis was originally addressed. Then, a reexamination and redirection of the analytic process itself. And, finally, a look at what has been excluded or explained away. Although I recognize that these issues cannot be absolutely separated, I shall begin, more or less, with It.

* * * *

Freud, focusing on mental phenomena, looked for the It especially in dreams, in free associations, in parapraxes, and, generally speaking, in what he took to be the manifestations of instinct. But he might equally have sought it in the Viennese zoo, in ethnographic museums, Gothic novels, and Renaissance

---

[2]This Italian-Jewish writer who died in April of 1987 was a professional chemist who drew on his work for powerful and arresting metaphors.

Revival drawing rooms. He might have found it in pictures of harems or of tempests and cataracts. Also in penal colonies, garbage dumps, tenements, and whorehouses. The list could be greatly lengthened, especially to include the repulsive, the exotic, and combinations of the two.

To a great extent, I am identifying the It with the Other — with whatever, from the viewpoint of the I, is seen as alien. The experience of otherness is, no doubt, a part of the human condition. But the extent of its range, its special contents, and the particular quality of the I's experience of it vary historically and between cultures. That is because, to a great extent, it is the I that determines the It, and the shape of the I itself, following Lacan (1949), is largely determined by culture. Therefore, in speaking of I except at the most general levels, one ought to specify a context.

The relationship between I and It is complex and delicate. In its grandiosity, the I does not recognize its dependency on the It. Therefore, as it enlarges its own domain, apparently at the It's expense, it also destroys its own sources. For example, at a social/environmental scale, it is the I that clears the Brazilian jungles to create more arable land. Here the jungle is an It — typically repulsive and exotic in its otherness but, most importantly, something to be tamed, something for which I must be substituted. The raw It is an affront to the grandiosity of the I. (Was it for this reason that Louis XIV chose for Versailles the most inhospitable spot in France?) Indigenous animals, plants, and people are destroyed whose subtle linkages look like chaos in the I's simplistic rational/utilitarian view. At the same time the I knows — ironically through its own efforts — that the jungle is the earth's chief oxygen maker. In its compulsion to extend its own domain, however, it denies this knowledge and asphyxiates itself. Could it be that the I — not the It — is the chief source and carrier of the Death Instincts?

A parallel dynamic operates individually when the imperialism of the I subjugates body, imagination, sentiment, and spirituality. It can do this through simple suppression—wiping out whole realms of experience. More insidiously, it can do it through cooptation. So, for example, in professional athletics or on health-club Nautilus circuits the body's capacities are not so much enjoyed as molded to the I's own program and standards. The process involves pain, labor, and the substitution of relatively distant goals for the pleasures in immediate experience. Indeed, pleasure becomes largely redefined as pride in the capacity to indefinitely postpone achievement.

* * * *

What is the It at which the I's imperialism is directed? Here we encounter the insuperable problem of the inarticulateness of the It. Language, leastways the language of ordinary discourse, is the language of I. The It's own language, from the viewpoint of the I, is incomprehensible when taken at face value. When I listens to It, it tries to figure It out. In the process of explicating It's text, an interpretation-cum-translation is produced—and, as we know, any translation is necessarily a different text.

The only way to interact with the It without translating is to listen with the It.

In its grandiosity the I regards the It as a wayward child, a savage, a madman, or an object for scientific investigation. Alternatively, the It can be endowed with a Romantic appreciation in the manner of Rousseau or R. D. Laing. Negative, positive, or ostentatiously neutral, these terms reveal the same spirit.

To itself, of course, the It is not the It: "It" is a designation of I. The cat's own name for herself, as T. S. Eliot reminds us, is an "effanineffable" secret. How can we penetrate this secret to say something about the It that is not merely a reduction?

Put this way, the problem is similar to the critic's. In

criticism (of whatever art) the play, film, painting, or poem is weighed and interpreted by the critic's I. Taking art as an It, the critic subjects it to a process that ends by substituting I. What else can he do?

Perhaps he can dream.

Early in our relationship, the writer A. N. (see Chapter 1) — a person with access to a remarkable and powerful It — gave me the following poem (quoted with permission):

Archaeology

Exhumation,
Excavation.
Down to the bones of an old . . .
Machine-gun it! No fire,
Earth, no . . .
Sign of a dustbowl, Anaximenes said,
"Sound of a motor becomes part of the book."
A surface, stirred by whatever
Lands there — banks of scent,
Shit,
Your stone lips on my
Cheek.

After reading it many times, "I" could make nothing of it. Then, in the middle of the night, I woke up crying. I had dreamt my son was dead. He'd actually died long before, but I'd forgotten. I was thinking (in my dream), "What if he died?" and then suddenly remembered that he had. In the morning my first thoughts were of this poem. I then told my dream to the poet.

There is a great deal that could be said *about* both the poem and the dream, but my interest lies especially in the dream as an answer to the poem — an answer complete in itself.

Most importantly, it is an answer *in kind*. Because of this there is no attempt to substitute for the poem or, through interpretation, to impose a meaning on it. The poem's primary and fertile ambiguity is not foreclosed. Instead of interpretation there is appreciation. For the usual hermeneutics, as Susan Sontag (1964) suggests, an erotics has been offered.

And that is precisely how A. N. understood my response: as an attunement that still left him free.

I want to say that both the poem and the dream are It. Yet both reveal the presence of I. The poem, after all, is a language phenomenon, and even if its words were used in quite eccentric, private ways, words remain cultural artifacts.

We arrive at a basic metaphysical distinction: noumenal/ phenomenal; appearance/reality; thing-in-itself/datum of perception, and so forth. Since the I is deeply linked with the sensorium (Freud 1923), the It can be experienced and expressed only in I terms. That ought not to be taken to mean that the distinction is invalid—that a continuum cannot be established with I-dominated expressions at one end and It-dominated ones at the other.

Yet, how can any particular item (poem, dream, etc.) be located on this continuum? We have all dreamt or been presented dreams so seemingly transparent one wonders why they could not have been simply stated as propositions. On the other hand, we have dreams so opaque they can seem arbitrary, if not intentionally obscure. In fact, the ambiguity is pervasive; all dreams are equally indecipherable. No chains of association can illuminate them—not only because such chains are endless, but because the dream itself is a link in such a chain. We can *respond* to a dream (poem, image, etc.), but we must not imagine that in responding we are giving its meaning.

So, for example, in the case of the poem I cited, I do not think we can say that my dream is an *interpretation* of the poem. It was just a response that happened to be the sort of response the poet valued. Indeed, we are not even entitled to say that it

was a response, for that is already an interpretation. It remains
true that my telling him the dream was a response to his offering
me the poem. But that, I think, is all we are actually entitled to
say.

If the truth of an interpretation cannot be demonstrated—
if, in fact, meaningfulness (which is logically prior to truth)
cannot be predicated of dreams and poems—then the It is truly
impenetrable to the I. Like Russia in pre-ICBM days, the It can
afford to be invaded. Its vastness and the primal power of its
elements must ultimately prevail. The primacy of the It is such
that we are even entitled to ask whether the I is perhaps a dream
of the It?

Because so much of psychoanalysis—classical and Jungian
too—has attempted to decipher expressions of the It one way or
another, the idea that the It may be inherently indecipherable
can seem radical and appalling. Yet, meaningfulness has to do
with a community of usage. This applies not only to language
but to any cultural artifact. Let me take the once-notorious
example of Marcel Duchamp's 1917 urinal. Now, a urinal is an
object whose meaning depends on its recognition by a group—a
recognition that centers on use. Appearance is a part of recognition, and a urinal can indeed have only a certain range of
shapes and features without losing recognizability. It does not
have to *function* to remain identifiable, since we have the concept of "out of order." Neither must it be used exclusively for
urinating, since we have, in relation to many objects, the notion
of "misuse." Objects can even be *reused* quite originally without
losing their first meaning—as, for example, when an old
chamber pot gets reframed as a jardinière. Duchamp, however,
did something *categorically* different. He took a urinal, turned it
upside down, signed it with the name R. Mutt, and hung it in an
art gallery. Through these manipulations he shoved it through
the wall of I into the realm of It.

We can never recapture the eye with which this object was seen in 1917 when—dumbfounded and scandalized—the jurors of the Society of Independent Artists refused to display it. Such is the I's capacity for cooptation that it now evokes, at best, a wry smile. Volumes have been written on its place in art history—in particular as a precursor of dada—and on its place in Duchamp's development and the development of modernism. Needless to say, at Christie's or Sotheby's it would fetch a high price. Through locating it historically, philosophically, and economically, the It is tamed. Duchamp, determined to remain free, gave up making art and became a chess master.

The urinal, signed and hung on a gallery wall, is an enigma—an enigma that is not cleared up by calling it art or writing about it. Diagnostically, those are good indications of It-status: that we are initially nonplussed or awed, that we are then compelled through our discomfort to figure out, and that— if we are intellectually scrupulous—our efforts are ultimately recognized as futile.

But that kind of rigor is uncommon. I's anxiety in the face of It impels it not only to construct systems for understanding, but to believe in them.

Not that the effort to understand is entirely without value. But, if it becomes an end in itself, independent of any function and cancerously self-consuming, we are entitled to call it a disease. I-domination is a widespread disease. It is particularly insidious because, being perfectly in sync with an I-dominated culture, it is called health.

What is often approvingly called a thirst or hunger for knowledge is actually—as we might guess from these oral metaphors—an addiction. A satisfied person does not want to know more than he needs to know, any more than he wants to eat or drink beyond satiation. The addictive pursuit of knowledge or understanding signifies an inner emptiness whose true source is hidden. For this same reason it is unsatisfiable and endless. The scientific project can be seen as an addict's attempt to eat the world.

I am identifying the I to a great extent with intellect—intellect allied to a pathological grandiosity that is ravenous and, perhaps by definition, "off the ground." The intellectual I *can* turn on itself (one thinks of Zen kōans, and in the West of the writings of E. M. Cioran) in an effort to explode its own illusions, but such efforts are uncommon. Mostly, the I promotes its illusions individually and collectively, builds them, takes up residence in them, and calls them reality. To my mind, Hitler's final solution was paradigmatic. We live in the ethos of the final solution; only the Jews are missing.

If what I have identified is indeed a pathology, what is the cure?

* * * *

When we address ourselves to the questions of cure, we must try to discern whether the disease is primarily congenital or else rooted in a history that might have been otherwise. But in the present instance we have an additional and subtle problem. What I am calling a disease is also integral to the culture's conceptual framework. Consequently, we have the further difficulty of discerning whether any curative effort might itself be an instance of the disease.

With respect to history, Kohut (1977) suggests that disorders of the self are especially post-Freudian and the result of altered patterns in family life. In his reverence for the founder of psychoanalysis Kohut may, of course, have preferred to say that the times had changed rather than that Freud was wrong. Yet, if we read old correspondences and biographies of historical figures, we see that long before psychoanalysis, much less self psychology, people's lives reveal pervasive narcissistic damage. At the same time, historical frames of mind—like those of alien contemporary cultures—are arguably impossible to grasp.

To take just one example, the sense of being an individual— that almost palpable experience of oneself as a unique person living in the boundaries of one's skin—may turn out to be quite modern, linked, among other things, to the possession of a personal space. Such "rooms of one's own," as Yi-Fu Tuan (1982) notes, were unknown in medieval times and remained rare until our own. Yet, without the famous stove to which he retired in 1628, Descartes might never have arrived at a notion of existence grounded in a thinking I. What might it be like not to feel like an individual? That is something we simply cannot know.

Because of the inaccessibility of historical frames of mind, our capacity to say what is part and parcel and what is accidental to human experience is necessarily limited. Although I shall offer some speculations, it seems to me impossible to ground them factually. What we would like to determine first is whether narcissistic damage is universal, with I-domination being merely a strategy used to counteract it. If that were the case, then I-domination could be expected to dissipate like any other by-product as the result of a self psychological cure or, at a social scale, as the result of different patterns of family interaction. If, on the other hand, I-domination is part of being human, then a self psychology cure can have no effect on it, and we must turn to other systems that treat the I itself: Zen Buddhism, perhaps, or Lacanian analysis.

I would like to sketch my own thoughts about this question without, for the present, offering very much in the way of defense. It seems to me first that the long childhood and high sensitivity of human beings make narcissistic damage inevitable. The specific sort of damage, its extent and depth, and the strategies used to deal with it must vary enormously—but, because of it, we shall not find a golden age or a people that does not suffer. No less a part of the human condition is an I that, again following Lacan (1949), tends, after some developmental turning point, to create narratives or *Gestalten*, eventually fitted to cultural templates. This I takes pleasurable control over what was primally experienced as a more aleatoric, moment-to-moment reality. Lacan calls that turning point the mirror stage, when, with a sense of triumph (sometimes heightened by the illusory power of a baby walker), the child correlates his own movements with the corresponding ones in a mirror and begins to experience his body as having the wholeness of the image he perceives there. Although Lacan would have said that the Real is ultimately ungraspable, the pre-mirror-stage experience is somehow closer to it. The task of psychoanalysis, therefore, would be to deconstruct the fictive wholes created aggressively by the I, beginning during the mirror stage, in an effort to approach the Real. To the extent that the I is an imperialistic agent colonizing the It, the analyst becomes, in this context, a kind of armchair guerrilla fighter. That this role has a certain appeal can be seen from the way Lacan was taken up by French students during the events of 1968.

The self psychologist attempts to attune himself empathi-cally to the patient, not only to promote a certain kind of transference but also because the attunement itself is seen as curative. In accord with Winnicott (1971) and Christopher Bollas (1978), among others, many self psychologists would agree that interpretation—which is addressed primarily to the I—is often not necessary and may even obstruct the curative process. The analyst does not attune himself to the patient's I. Rather, both I's are bypassed to establish a more fundamental bond. The Lacanian analyst actively disattunes himself to the patient's I, not only to make himself "other"—the object of desire—but to establish a base camp from which to undermine the I. These very different notions of therapy are allied in their devaluing of the I and also, as one might expect, in their attitudes toward ego psychology.

It seems to me that the two views are complementary. Self psychologists may be horrified, however, by some Lacanian tactics—such as the short session—seen as crude and wounding. But the object of the analyst's attack in abruptly ending a session is not supposed to be, say, the patient's emerging grandiose–exhibitionistic self, but rather his I. It is the grandiose–imperialistic I—trying to establish its control over the It of the hour—that the analyst seeks to foil. In abruptly standing up in the middle of the patient's sentence he does what the Zen master does, when, in the midst of meditation, he suddenly raps an acolyte on the head.

If they are complementary—and it is not yet clear that they are—there is also an undeniable tension between the two. I am tempted to say that an effective assault on the I cannot be launched unless a strong, cohesive self is already present. If not, I would imagine, there is the likelihood of continuing fragmentation with a redoubling of the strategies used to counter it—not the least of which arise from the I's own gestalt-making tendencies.

At the same time, how can we discount the 2500-year experience of Buddhist spiritual practice, which suggests no prior need to repair the damage of each practitioner's childhood? Buddhist method works to cultivate an inner observer. Not an observing *ego*, for the I is itself an object of observation. Not a superego, either, for there is nothing parental, moralistic, or even containing in its stance. The observer simply observes *everything*: the body, thoughts, feelings . . . everything. Through this discipline, as I understand it, the sense of identity comes increasingly to reside in the observer until a certain critical moment when an explosion takes place. That explosion—and the altered sense of reality that follows it—are not I experiences. Consequently, ordinary language, based in the I, can neither describe nor account for them. Perhaps all that can be said— without it being clear that one is communicating anything by saying it—is that these experiences are not of fragmentation, entailing emptiness, joylessness, and loss of function. What people report is that nothing is lost—including the capacities for pleasure and accomplishment—but that everything is profoundly and permanently different.

Yet, not everyone who believes in the value of this path sets out on it, and not everyone who sets out becomes enlightened. The Buddha himself is described as a nobleman, married and the father of a son. When he left everything to become a wandering ascetic, he was motivated to do this by "*sannyāsin*"— an aversion or repugnance for the so-called good things of the world. This giving up has been described (David-Neel 1936) as a "joyous liberation," comparable to "throwing off dirty and ragged clothing" (p. 17). It is not a sacrifice, still less the sour-grapes gesture of someone who has not been *able* to make it in conventional terms. Rather it is a step taken from the realization that the satisfactions of the I are relatively trivial and, in the end, entail more pain than they are worth. In a world where death and destructability are inevitable, every gain—in objects, relationships or social position—necessitates eventual loss or at least the threat of it. Seeing this, the *sannyāsin* takes himself off the path of gain and loss. He is not yet enlightened, but at least he is not an active participant in illusion.

If the Buddha is the paradigm *sannyāsin*, it is clear that he had something to give up.

People who are drawn to asceticism (as was L. in the case discussed in Chapter 6), often reveal the bitter grandiosity of the deprived—"If I can't have everything, then I'll have nothing." "Nothing" takes on the same value as "everything." Of course, there is a certain poetic truth in this. The person who has detached himself from desire is equal, if not superior in power, to the person who can fulfill all desires at will. The difference is in motive. The *sannyāsin* is not motivated by a rageful sense of deprivation. On the contrary, having acquired a great deal, he comes to see that it does not and never will yield the happiness he'd expected. He sloughs off a dead-end existence with relief.

To my mind, a self psychology analysis can provide that grounding in fullness—that sense of having—with which the Buddha allegedly began. But can it take the patient further, toward the destructuring of an I-dominated sense of the real?

The answer, I think, depends greatly on the condition of the analyst's I. To say, as I did earlier, that the self psychologist works by attuning himself empathically puts the process perhaps too actively. To the extent that the attunement is an action—something one tries for—it will fail. The process works only when it is effortless. It works through us—one might almost say despite us. Because of this, we have all had the bittersweet experience of seeing patients go further than we ourselves have gone.

But there are limits to how much further they *can* go.

What would an enlightened psychoanalyst look like? To return to the Buddhist model, the *sannyāsin* is described (David-Neel 1936) as "freed from social and religious laws; freed from all bonds, he walks on the path which is known to him alone, and is responsible only to himself. He is, par excellence, an 'outsider' " (p. 17). In many ways this describes the life and character of Jacques Lacan, to which I shall return. But first, a Buddhist example.

Ikkyū was a fifteenth-century Zen poet-monk—the illegitimate and unacknowledged son of an Emperor (Arntzen 1986). He first studied with the monk Ken'ō, a man of such modesty that he had refused a seal of enlightenment (equivalent to analytic certification) and so could not pass one on. When this monk died, Ikkyū studied with another, no less austere master and attained enlightenment. He himself was then presented with a certificate, but destroyed it. At a time when the Zen monasteries were politically powerful, rich, and dissolute, Ikkyū's behavior, in this and other ways, was unheard of. Nevertheless, despite his iconoclasm, his authenticity was indisputable and he was made abbot of a subtemple in the great Daitoku-ji compound. Soon after, he sent his superior this outrageous poem:

> Ten days as abbot and my mind is churning.
> Under my feet, the red thread of passion is long.
> If you come another day and ask for me,
> Try a fish shop, tavern, or else a whorehouse. [p. 73]

Ikkyū is the only Zen monk to have written poems about sex in a religious context—vividly erotic poems on his own amorous exploits. He moved sex from a common but illicit activity to an integral part of spiritual training and even an aid to enlightenment. Sonja Arntzen (1986), a commentator, writes that for Ikkyū, sex was "a kind of touchstone for his realization of the dynamic concept of non-duality that pivots upon the essential unity of the realm of desire and the realm of enlightenment" (p. 33). The authenticity of Ikkyū's vision was manifested in many ways, but among them in his rejection both of conventional piety and of conventional secularism. In all of this, he meets the definition of a sannyāsin.

Such a concept resists cross-cultural translation. Yet there are interesting affinities between Ikkyū and Lacan.

Lacan's character and career were equally iconoclastic and independent. Because he had also a brilliant mind and a charismatic style, he became the center of psychoanalysis in France. Compared to Ikkyū, however, Lacan was less fortunate in his mentors. His analyst was Rudolph Loewenstein, who later became a pillar of the New York society and one of the founders of ego psychology. At that time, however, Loewenstein had come from Germany to Paris, where the society was dominated by Marie Bonaparte. On his rise to eminence, Loewenstein became her lover as well as the analyst of her son. Lacan must have learned something from his work with Loewenstein, because he managed to secure membership in the society before completing his analysis, then broke off. Loewenstein blamed Lacan's heterodoxy—which ultimately led to his expulsion from the International—on this failure to complete his analysis.

From the points of view of Marie Bonaparte and Anna Freud—in accord with the Americans who then controlled the International—what was Lacan's sin? The ostensive issue was the ethics of the short session. Politically, of course, short sessions enabled Lacan to do many more training analyses than others and therefore to produce more disciples (Turkle 1978). But perhaps neither ethics nor politics was ultimately decisive. Equally crucial was Lacan's heretical distrust of the ego—his view of it as pathological. In "The Ego and the Id," Freud (1923) had said, "By interposing the process of thinking, [the Ego] secures a postponement of motor discharge and controls access to motility." Stuart Schneiderman (1983) suggests that Lacan probably understood this to mean that "the longer the postponement, the stronger the ego." The ego, then, can only delay things and, indeed, "makes postponement something pathological" (p. 150). What can break this cycle of delay to make action possible? Only the desire of the Other. For this reason, Lacan distrusted thought that proceeded from the Ego. What makes authentic action possible are thoughts that do not come from the I, that "come to me when I do not think to think"

(Schneiderman, p. 150). As with Ikkyū, the realm of desire – of which sex is emblematic – and the non-I, thought-free state of enlightenment are linked.

If we take Lacan and Ikkyū as models for the enlightened analyst, we can see in both an affinity with the dada–surrealist sensibility – with, for example, the creativity of Duchamp. The notion of psychoanalysis as a science would be quite alien to them. Yet, these men were certainly not know-nothings. Ikkyū's poetry is so steeped in allusions to classical Chinese literature that it cannot now be approached without extensive explanatory notes. Lacan similarly draws on the linguistic theory of Saussure, on a formidably extensive reading of classical and modern literature, and on a scholarly knowledge of Freud.

But they were not scientists. Their use of knowledge is unsystematic because the kind of truth they were after is outside systems. Even the sense in which they were scholars is not academic, for they were not explicators of other thinkers' quasi-sacred texts. Indeed, following the Rinzai Zen tradition,[3] an enlightened analyst might say that Freud's *Traumdeutung*, Lacan's *Écrits*, and Kohut's *Analysis of the Self* are all so much toilet paper.

To return to my original question – whether we might take psychoanalysis to be not a science but an art – I want to say that it is an art precisely as that notion is understood in the dada--surrealist–Zen tradition. That concept can present more difficulties in a country where the scientific/ego psychology ideals are strong and the philosophical tradition of conceptual analysis

---

[3]Rinzai, "The Twelve Fold Teachings of the Three Vehicles are all old paper for wiping filth," quoted in Arntzen (1986, p. 91).

has overthrown the once-central place of aesthetics. There was an easier integration of art and psychoanalysis in France, largely because it was a group of artists and writers—Gide and his circle at the *Nouvelle Revue Française*—who first took it up in a serious way long before the French psychiatric establishment. Although Freud himself was uncomfortable with the connection, the notion of the unconscious he introduced is central to surrealism. Through his 1907 article on Jensen's *Gradiva*, for example, that strange image of the stone woman becoming flesh became a favorite surrealist motif—the subject of paintings by Masson, Dali, and Ernst, and even the name of Breton's gallery. René Allendy (Anaïs Nin's Paris analyst) was the chief supporter of Antonin Artaud's primal theatre—arguably the most It-centered events ever staged. To bypass the I and work directly from the It is central to the surrealist ideal. That Lacan—who was close to surrealist circles—should draw on this ethos and return it to the psychoanalytic process becomes, in this light, entirely comprehensible.

But that is history. The ongoing essence of art, understood in this way, is openness to It. Yet, because of the coopting power of the I, one generation's radical vision of It becomes the next one's I-centered orthodoxy. Kohut's heroically achieved insights are now being codified, rationalized, and glossed. In this way, they suffer the fate of Freud's, Jung's, and Lacan's visions. Explicating the texts of these visionaries quickly becomes an industry. To the extent that those texts embody It, the I goes to work on them, digesting them until they too become I. Through this process, the disciple—at the same time that he expresses his idolization—castrates his mentor. Instead of assuming his own It, paralleling his master's, he achieves that power in an illusory way through the bond of discipleship and through the intellectual caging of the mentor's wild It.

The "proof" of analytic mastery is usually the final case

presentation before an institute committee. Because this process is I-centered, based on the I's illusory construct of reality, passing or not passing can have very little to do with the candidate's actual condition. The proof of a Zen student's enlightenment, by contrast, is not I-centered. Ideological good behavior and political astuteness are, therefore, of no help. Since it is It-based, the evidence is as palpable to the master as a slap in the face. And, indeed, the Zen tradition is full of stories about enlightened students slapping their masters and the latters' pleasure in a gesture whose irreverence establishes the student's authenticity.

Lacan's *École freudienne* had been perhaps the only institute to deeply question the I-centeredness of psychoanalytic training. Without arriving at a solution, it at least recognized that the process ought to be something different in kind from acquiring competence in, say, auto mechanics or law. Accession to the title took two directions. The first has been summarized this way: "A person is a psychoanalyst who authorizes himself to be considered as such" (Barande and Barande 1975). Like Napoleon, one snatches the crown from the Pope's hands and places it on one's head. Of course, it is possible to be mistaken in this, but no more so than for one's judges to be. The alternative course was "the pass"—a rite so Byzantine (for example, the candidate had to convince two representatives—peers and therefore rivals—to present his case effectively for him) it is hard not to see it as a send-up of the usual process. At any rate, through these means the nature of psychoanalytic knowledge, how it can be passed on, and how the practitioner's authenticity can be recognized, were questioned by Lacan with an unparalleled seriousness. Indeed, they become the central problem of the psychoanalytic project (Turkle 1979).

To return to the main issue of cure, then, it seems to me that I-domination is not a condition to which most psychoanalytic systems, as they now stand, can respond. They may provide a foundation for addressing it, but are too I-centered themselves to move beyond.

* * * *

If analysis has largely centered itself in the I, what parts of the self have been lost to both theory and practice? Those parts of which the I cannot make sense or, alternatively, of which it can make only a specious sense.

In the Zen tradition, the correct response to a kōan appears to be a non sequitur. But it is not merely a non sequitur, suggesting a kind of gimcrack idiocy. Nor is it intelligent nonsense full of will. If authentic, it is inspired—nonsense that neither cleverness nor stupidity could have produced.

In the analytic situation, a relative spontaneity is cultivated through the parallel processes of free association and evenly hovering attention. This flow of associations in both participants is monitored by the analyst's observing I, which may actively intervene when a pattern is noticed. Two difficulties immediately arise: first, how free are each person's associations? and, second, are the observed patterns present or imposed?

Since the analytic procedure is heavily aimed at character problems—the unhappy ramifications of programming by certain, in a sense, stylized interactions between parent and child—I want to say (despite the still-unresolved epistemological problems) that patterns *are* present that appear in the associations. Indeed, because of the programming, patterns are inevitable, and the associations are free in only the most restricted sense.

At the same time, it is no less clear that what is observed by the analyst is screened through the mesh of his theoretical outlook. To some extent, no doubt, the material will be forced to fit this mesh, so that the patterns to which he is predisposed are put there whether present or not. More benignly, the screen admits only certain shapes and thus renders others invisible. We know this retrospectively when someone formulates fresh views that spotlight seemingly new phenomena. Kohut, to my mind, did this. Those classically trained analysts who found his insights valuable (and true) now perceive their patients differently. Was what they see now always there? More importantly, I think, these changes reveal the limitations of any view and the fact that—latent or expressed—multiplicities of perspectives exist focusing on an endlessly receding reality. Is it possible to see not just one perspective (or even numbers of them) but, rather, *what is there?*

The classical controversies of knowledge theory revolve around this question. Naive realism takes the objects of perception at face value: what we see is what is there. Plato's idealism locates the real in a realm of forms, accessible perhaps only to disembodied souls. What we perceive is just a shadow of that realm. A skeptical epistemology suggests we know only phenomena; things in themselves are out of reach. In a more hopeful version, reality can be known as a theoretical construct (analogous to knowledge of atomic particles) postulated to explain the regular behavior of appearances. I realize these are caricatures of complex positions, but I think a fuller presentation would make no difference here.

Only naive realism asserts the unobstructed availability of the real. This position must capture some truth, since if large-scale stabilities did not prevail, life would not be possible. Yet we know how profoundly culture qualifies perception. Jorge-Luis Borges puts this question in a historical mode through his now-classic story of "Pierre Menard" (1939). This man sets out in the twentieth century to write the novel, *Don Quixote*, never having read Cervantes. He succeeds in producing the ninth and thirty-eighth chapters of the first part and a fragment of chapter twenty-two. Borges compares the following passage from the

Cervantes work with a seemingly identical one by Menard: ". . . truth whose mother is history, rival of time, depository of deeds, witness of the past, exemplar and adviser to the present, and the future's counselor." For Cervantes this was just conventional rhetoric, but Menard, Borges demonstrates, has taken a serious philosophical position contra his contemporary, William James. History, in Menard's view, is the origin of reality—not merely an enquiry into it. Truth in history is pragmatically based; it is what we judge to have happened. The styles are different, too—Cervantes writing with ease the Spanish of his time and Menard affecting a certain archaism. "There is no exercise of the intellect," Borges concludes, "which is not, in the final analysis, useless. A philosophical doctrine begins as a plausible description of the universe; with the passage of the years it becomes a mere chapter—if not a paragraph or a name—in the history of philosophy" (p.43).

Borges's surrealism delights in the cadacity of all our grand illusions. It is surprising, therefore, that he did not pursue Zen with a more personal urgency.[4] Zen alone claims the possibility of seeing through illusion into reality itself. Plato's forms are not reserved for the large but still exclusive club of the unborn. Living night soil carriers may see things as they are, along with certain emperors and psychoanalysts. There is no descriptive word for what they see, but there are exclamations: *Katsu!* and *Nyoze!*

An analyst who sees his patients not from a Freudian, Jungian, or Kuhutian perspective (much less an eclectic one), but rather sees them as they are, will never intervene predictably. And, in a sense, his perceptions can be neither true nor false. Such judgments apply only to checkable statements about

---

[4]In his lecture on "Buddhism" (1980), however, Borges says, "What does it mean to reach Nirvana? Simply that our acts no longer cast shadows" (p. 75).

reality, and he makes only OUTBURSTS. He does not know what to say: he exclaims.

This lack of a perspective (a perspective, after all, is just an angle on reality) begins to return to the patient the missing portions of the world—the world that is not there. As a single example, let me focus on a classic psychoanalytic concern.

Because we cannot penetrate historical minds, sex may have sometimes held meanings we can no longer fathom. But if we think of sex as an encounter with It, it seems clear that the I soon moved to hedge it round. It did this collectively through religious law and ritual, prescribing with whom and under what circumstances sex would be permissible. It did it through prostitution, making this It a commodity like any other. It did it through the use of sex for procreation or the equally purposive use of it for recreation. Vividly in pornographic works (the artistic expression of perversion), and less so in ordinary bedroom scenes, sex becomes a *mise-en-scène* for early childhood interactions: parent–infant, brother–sister, controller–controlled. Whether repetitions or reversals, the links with childhood, as Georges Bataille (1928) has shown, reveal these behaviors to be anything but free.

What would sex be if it were not appropriated by the I—if it were not, for instance, a language by means of which *something else* got expressed? Arntzen (1986) quotes Ikkyū:

> The rain drops of Wu-shan fall into a new song;
> Passionate fūryū, in poems and passion too.
> The whole wide world and Tu-ling's tears;
> At Fu-chou tonight, the moon sinks. [p. 174]

I shall comment only on the second line of Ikkyū's erotic poem—one of a group entitled "Chronicle of the Dream Chamber." Introducing them, Ikkyū claims that, unlike other, more virtuous masters who dream of higher things, he dreams only of the bedchamber. It is his Way. In sex, no less than in poetry, he finds the real in a passionate burst.

The key word is *"fūryū"*—untranslatable. Fūryū has many connotations, but even when only one is intended strongly, the others are there residually. Sonja Arntzen (1986, pp. 66–67) picks out three in Ikkyū's work, noting first that the component characters of the word itself are *fū* ("wind") and *ryū* ("to flow").

The first meaning refers to the quality of an unfragmented rustic life, which, free of artifice, flows on in attunement with the natural world.

The second meaning is erotic, sometimes specifically sexual but also including nonbody experience. One can see the connection with the first meaning: an erotic life that is not I-dominated flows mindlessly.

The third meaning—which can be linked intuitively with the others—is a kind of slang expression showing appreciation for an inspired gesture. Or it can be said of the gesture itself that it is *fūryū*. Finally, there is the implication that to appreciate a *fūryū* gesture, one must be *fūryū* oneself. Here is a classic example (from the *Blue Cliff Record*, kōans 63 and 64, quoted in Arntzen, 1986):

> One day, the monks of the East and West were fighting over a cat. When Nan-ch'üan saw them he raised up the cat and said, "If someone can speak, I will not kill it." (Taking a life being forbidden.) When no one answered, Nan-ch'üan cut the cat in two. Later he recounted this incident to Chao-chou and asked what he would have done. Chao-chou took off his sandals, put them on his head, and walked away. "If you had been there," Nan-ch'uän said, "the cat would have been saved." Chao-chou's gesture was *fūryū*. [p. 81]

There are affinities between *"fūryū,"* the concept of "duende" from flamenco cante jondo, and the jazz exclamation, "far out" (mentioned too by Arntzen). "Far out" arose in the 1940s describing and responding to the qualities of bop and cool. In an idiom that centers on inspired improvisation, the word acclaims the musician's risk in moving through uncharted space—as well as indicating the otherness of that space. To play a far-out riff is to both to confront the It and reveal it to the listener. "Duende" similarly belongs to an improvisational music bound, like jazz, by complex rules. It similarly values the courage to explore new depths of feeling ("cante jondo" means "deep song") that take the listener into them.

What, in psychoanalysis, would count as *fūryū*? Here is a possibility.

Once I worked with a painter as restricted in sex as she was in her work. R.'s superficially ravishing canvases—each a feminine paradise—streamed with veils of red and gold. Like them, she wore her history of victimization on the surface, almost sexily. In Richard, her husband, she found a handsome if clumsy bedmate who bruised her white skin, but always by accident. With her lover, Victor, she explored a sensual Eden of fingertip sensuality—dreamy and blind.

As our work advanced, an angel with a sword appeared. R.'s paintings became electric torture rooms—blue-black and shocking to the casual visitor. She herself wore a pendant of a cock-and-balls bound with wire. If a curious person fingered it, the thing made a hideous buzz. During these months, R. was nearly celibate.

One day R. flounced in wearing a blond wig. The transformation announced what she would later call her "cunt period"— not those romanticized lesbian vaginas of Georgia O'Keeffe: these flowers ate flesh. They managed to be rosy-pink and inviting and at the same time stinking holes. R. called the entire show, "For Dick" (she hadn't yet divorced) and titled the paintings, for example, "Too Hot Twat," "Pussy LaGore," and "Baby Lips." These names belied R.'s prudery, but the show sold out.

Not long after this success, R. showed up without the wig. Because she was beautiful, she remained so. But, for the first time, she seemed not to care about her looks. Abandoning painting, she turned to photography, producing abstract prints in subtle *grisailles*. Without containing a single objective referent, they seemed deeply concerned with the real.

Against this neutral-looking ground, R.'s dreams flared. At first they were complex, mythologically dense images of heroes and their goddess lovers—dressed in Venetian velvets, rubies, and pearls. Eventually all this richness resolved itself into a single frame: a phallus.

In a panic of frantic I-work, R. tried to capture this image in thought: "male power"; "penis envy"; "generativity"; "castration anxiety." It was the only truly boring phase of treatment.

As I listened to her thinking week after week, I grew increasingly exasperated—overtaken by a desperate and impotent violence. Finally, something snapped. A noise came out of me—a sound that felt, from the inside, like a deep twanging drone, growing louder and louder without losing its snarl and roll. The noise filled me until I was aware of nothing else. I felt (or perhaps I say this only retrospectively) as if the noise/I were filling the room, emanating from a glowing point source, rather than from "me."

Much later, R. revealed that while this was happening, the image of me in my chair and the phosphorescent phallus of her dreams had merged. More immediately, when the noise eventually stopped, we both stared at one another, silenced and dumbfounded. After a while a smile flickered on her face. Soon we were both grinning, then laughing like kids with the giggles. The session ended without comment.

I shall mention only two developments that followed this event and which I take to be outcomes of it. Until then, all the

men in R.'s life, and indeed R. herself, had been full of character—sparkling, sullen, brilliant . . . there was no end to the
vivid adjectives that fit them. Now R. took up with B.—a quite
nondescript man; she could hardly find the words to talk about
him. Yet she began to love him and, from her reports, he loved
her. It was certainly not an operatic love, but it was not prosaic
either. To describe it, I must borrow an image from painting.
Their relationship reminds me of a picture by Chardin. In an age
that alternated between courtly heroics and decorative banality,
Chardin chose the real. His domestic interiors and even more
his still lifes capture the luminous mystery of the ordinary. R.
similarly saw a god in this quite undistinguished mortal. The
dream phallus, paved with sapphires and radiating light, came to
rest between B.'s thighs. Not that it turned into a penis; rather,
the two dimensions came to coexist. A parallel process took
place in R.'s feeling about herself, and eventually this showed up
in her work. Her earlier paintings, intentionally weird, created
only a momentary notoriety. Her new ones gave common,
twentieth-century objects an inexplicably luminous presence.
That they also made her famous was a surprising and not
entirely welcome outcome.

* * * *

Although the capacity to heal is a gift arising from an alien
part of the self, the analyst takes responsibility for cultivating it,
largely through the spoken word. Analysis remains, after all, the
talking cure—the idea with which this book began. That idea
has led, as any discussion of language must, to questions of
meaning as the basis for knowledge. Such questions present
particular difficulties in a field that claims its knowledge to be
scientific, yet depends for its raw data on material whose meanings are necessarily multiple. If such materials—dreams and
freely associated thoughts especially—indeed form the knowl-

edge base of analytic therapy, then ours is a structure built on shifting sand. I have tried to rethink these difficulties by focusing on analysis as a practice—one that depends for its success on the analyst's openness. I have called this openness "unknowing."

Knowing, understood as a state of mind, is a condition of reasoned assuredness: a state of closure that structures further experience. Unknowing, by contrast, is a state of openness that does not foreclose experience through predetermined structure. Reaching for that openness and maintaining it are the analyst's chief and lifelong work.

Ironically, had Freud been right in viewing analysis as a science analogous to physics, applying it to individuals would give the analyst the role of handyman—one who fixes faulty structures. That trade, however useful it may be, requires ingenuity and skill rather than creativity. As an art, however, analysis requires of its practitioners that they be unendingly creative. And, as with other artists, they become voyagers on a path that is as healing for themselves as it is for those who travel with them.

References

Abraham, R. (1979). Freud and "Mater". (Doctoral dissertation, University of California, Davis). University Microfilms International No. 8003489.

Anthony, E. (1975). Between yes and no: the potentially neutral area where the adolescent and his therapist can meet. In *Adolescent Psychiatry*, vol. 4, ed. S. Feinstein and P. Giovacchini, pp. 323–344. Northvale, NJ: Jason Aronson.

Ariès, P. (1960). *Centuries of Childhood*. Trans. R. Baldick. New York: Vintage Books.

Arlow, J. (1984). Disturbances of the sense of time. *Psychoanalytic Quarterly* 53:13–37.

Arnaud, N. (1950). *L'état d'ébauche*. Paris: Les Messagers Boiteau.

Arntzen, S. (1986). *Ikkyū and the Crazy Cloud Anthology: A Zen Poet of Medieval Japan*. Tokyo: University of Tokyo Press.

Artaud, A. (1938). *The Theatre and Its Double*. Trans. M. C. Richards, p. 46. New York: Grove Press, 1958. Quoted in B. Knapp (1969), *Antonin Artaud*, pp. 98–99. New York: David Lewis.

—— (1946). *Antonin Artaud: 4 Texts*. Trans. C. Eshleman and N. Glass, p. 10. Los Angeles: Panjandrum, 1982.

Augustine, Saint (c. 400). *Confessions*, Book 11. In *Problems of Space and Time*, ed. J. J. C. Smart, pp. 58–72. New York: Macmillan, 1964.

Bachelard, G. (1958). *The Poetics of Space*. Trans. M. Jolas. Boston: Beacon Press, 1969.

Balint, M. (1958). The three areas of the mind. *International Journal of Psycho-Analysis* 39:328–340.

Barande, R., and Barande, I. (1975). *Histoire de la Psychoanalyse en France*, p. 11. Toulouse : Edouard Privat.

Bassaglia, F. (1965). Silence in the dialogue with the psychotic. *Journal of Existentialism* 6:99–102

Bataille, G. (1928). *Story of the Eye*. Trans. J. Neugroschel. New York: Berkley Publishing Group, 1982.

Becker, E. (1973). *The Denial of Death*. New York: The Free Press.

Benedict, Saint (c. 530). *The Rule of St. Benedict*. In *Western Asceticism*, trans. O. Chadwick. Philadelphia: Westminster Press, 1958.

Bion, W. R. (1965). *Transformations: Change from Learning to Growth*. New York: Basic Books.

Blanck, G. (1966). Some technical implications of ego psychology. *International Journal of Psycho-Analysis* 47:6–13.

Bléger, J. (1967). Psycho-analysis of the psychoanalytic frame. In *Classics in Psychoanalytic Technique*, ed. R. Langs, pp. 459–467. Northvale, NJ: Jason Aronson, 1981.

Bollas, C. (1978). The transformational object. *International Journal of Psycho-Analysis* 60: 97–107.

Borges, J-L. (1939). Pierre Menard, author of the Quixote. In *Labyrinths: Selected Stories and Other Writings*, trans. J. Irby. New York: New Directions, 1964.

_____ (1952). The modesty of history. In *Other Inquisitions*, trans. R. L. C. Simmons. New York: Washington Square Press.

_____ (1980). Buddhism. In *Seven Nights*, trans. E. Weinberger. New York: New Directions, 1984.

Breuer, J., and Freud, S. (1895). Studies on hysteria. *Standard Edition* 2.

Buber, M. (1958). *I and Thou*. 2nd ed., trans R. Smith, p. 39. New York: Scribner's.

Cage, J. (1959). Lecture on something. In *Silence*, pp. 129–130. Middletown, CT: Wesleyan University Press, 1961.

Choisy, M. (1955). Memories of my visits with Freud. In *Freud As We Knew Him*, ed. H. Ruitenbeek, pp. 291–295. Detroit: Wayne State University Press, 1973.

Cioran, E. M. (1964). *The Fall Into Time*. Trans. R. Howard. Chicago: Quadrangle, 1970. Quoted in the introduction by C. Newman, p. 18.

David-Neel, A. (1936). *Buddhism: Its Doctrines and Its Methods*. Trans. H. Hardy and B. Miall. New York: Avon/Discus, 1979.

Edel, L. (1982). Abulia and the journey to Lausanne. In *Stuff of Sleep and Dreams: Experiments in Literary Psychology*, pp. 164–191. New York: Harper & Row.

Eigen, M. (1981). The area of faith in Winnicott, Lacan, and Bion. *International Journal of Psycho-Analysis* 62: 413–433.

Eliot, T. S. (1917). The Love Song of J. Alfred Prufrock. In *Collected Poems 1909–1962*, pp. 3–7. New York: Harcourt Brace Jovanovich, 1970.

_____ (1920). Gerontion. In *Collected Poems 1909–1962*, pp. 29–31. New York: Harcourt Brace Jovanovich, 1970.

_____ (1922). The Waste Land. In *Collected Poems 1909–1962*, pp. 51–76. New York: Harcourt Brace Jovanovich, 1970.

_____ (1927). Shakespeare and the stoicism of Seneca. In *Elizabethan Essays*, pp. 33–54. New York: Haskell House, 1964.

_____ (1935). Burnt Norton. In *Collected Poems 1909–1962*, pp. 175–181. New York: Harcourt Brace Jovanovich, 1970.

_____ (1935–1942). Four Quartets. In *Collected Poems 1909–1962*, pp. 175–209. New York: Harcourt Brace Jovanovich, 1970.

_____ (1940). East Coker. In *Collected Poems 1909–1962*, pp. 182–190. New York: Harcourt Brace Jovanovich, 1970.

_____ (1941). The Dry Salvages. In *Collected Poems 1909–1962*, pp. 191–199. New York: Harcourt Brace Jovanovich, 1970.

_____ (1939). The Family Reunion. In *The Complete Plays of T. S. Eliot*, pp. 55–122. New York: Harcourt Brace Jovanovich, 1967.

_____ (1950). *The Cocktail Party*. New York: Harcourt Brace Jovanovich.

Engelman, E. (1976). *Berggasse 19*. New York: Basic Books.

Erikson, E. H. (1950). *Childhood and Society*. New York: W. W. Norton.

Ferenczi, S. (1916). Silence is golden. In *Further Contributions to the Theory and Technique of Psychoanalysis*. London: Hogarth, 1926.

Fliess, R. (1949). Silence and verbalizations: a supplement to the theory of the "analytical rule." *International Journal of Psycho-Analysis* 30:21–30.

Freud, S. (1885). In *Letters of Sigmund Freud*, ed. E. L. Freud, p. 141. New York: Basic Books, 1961.

_____ (1900). The interpretation of dreams. *Standard Edition* 5:583.

_____ (1905). Fragment of an analysis of a case of hysteria. *Standard Edition* 5:77–78.

_____ (1910). Leonardo da Vinci and a memory of his childhood. *Standard Edition* 11:117.

_____ (1910a). In *Psychoanalysis and Faith: The Letters of Sigmund Freud and Oskar Pfister*, ed. H. Meng and E. L. Freud, pp. 34–35. London: Hogarth Press, 1963.

_____ (1914). Remembering, repeating and working through. *Standard Edition* 12:154.

_____ (1914). On narcissism: an introduction. *Standard Edition* 14:73–81.

_____ (1923). The ego and the id. *Standard Edition* 19.

_____ (1924). The economic problem of masochism. *Standard Edition* 19:160.

_____ (1926). Inhibitions, symptoms and anxiety. *Standard Edition* 20:160.

_____ (1933). New introductory lectures on psychoanalysis. *Standard Edition* 22.

_____ (1935). An autobiographical study, postscript. *Standard Edition* 20:71.

_____ (1937). Analysis terminable and interminable. *Standard Edition* 23:238.

Gay, P. (1976). Introduction: Freud/for the marble tablet. In E. Engelman, *Berggasse 19*, pp. 13–54. New York: Basic Books.

Greenson, R. (1961). On the silence and sounds of the analytic hour. *Journal of the American Psychoanalytic Association* 9:79–84.

Grünbaum, A. (1984). *The Foundations of Psychoanalysis*. Berkeley: University of California Press.

Haley, J. (1958). The art of psychoanalysis. In *The Power Tactics of Jesus Christ*, p. 15. New York: Avon Books, 1969.

Hartocollis, P. (1983). *Time and Timelessness*. New York: International Universities Press.

Hegel, G. W. F. (1830). *Encyclopedia*. 3rd ed. Heidelberg: Osswald (C. F. Winter). Entry no. 385.

Heymann, C. (1976). *Ezra Pound: The Last Rower*. New York: Viking.

Jones, E. (1953). *The Life and Work of Sigmund Freud*, vol. I. New York: Basic Books.

_____ (1955). *The Life and Work of Sigmund Freud*, vol. II, pp. 408–409. New York: Basic Books.

Kernberg, O. (1975). *Borderline Conditions and Pathological Narcissism*. Northvale, NJ: Jason Aronson.

Khan, M. M. R. (1963). Silence as communication. *Bulletin of the Menninger Clinic* 27:300–313.

_____ (1979). *Alienation in Perversions*. New York: International Universities Press.

Kleist, H. von (1810). Puppets and dancers. Trans. B. de Zoete of *Über das Marionettentheater*. *Ballet* 2:1 (June 1946), 42–49.

Kohut, H. (1971). *The Analysis of the Self*. New York: International Universities Press.

_____ (1977). *The Restoration of the Self*. New York: International Universities Press.

_____ (1979). The two analyses of Mr. Z. *International Journal of Psycho-Analysis* 60:3–27.

Kris, E. (1956). On some vicissitudes of insight in psychoanalysis. *International Journal Psycho-Analysis*, 37:445–455.

Lacan, J. (1949). The mirror stage as formative of the function of the I as revealed in psychoanalytic experience. In *Écrits: A Selection*, trans. A. Sheridan, pp. 1–7. New York: W. W. Norton, 1977.

Landes, D. (1983). *Revolution in Time*. Cambridge, MA: Belknap Press of Harvard University Press.

Langs, R. (1982). *Psychotherapy: A Basic Text*, p. 364. Northvale, NJ: Jason Aronson.

Merton, T. (1955). No man is an island. In *A Thomas Merton Reader*, pp. 490–491. New York: Harcourt Brace Jovanovich, 1962.

Miller, A. (1981). *Prisoners of Childhood*. New York: Basic Books.

Milosz, O. V. de (1910). *Oeuvres Complètes*, vol. 2, *L'amoureuse initiation*. Fribourg: Egloff, 1944.

Nabokov, V. (1966). *Speak, Memory*. New York: Perigee Books.

Nacht, S. (1964). Silence as an integrative factor. *International Journal of Psycho-Analysis* 45:299–303.

Paz, O. (1970). *Marcel Duchamp or The Castle of Purity.* Trans. D. Gardner. London: Cape Golliard Press: Unpaginated.

Recouly, R. (1923). A visit to Freud. In *Freud As We Knew Him,* ed. H. Ruitenbeek, pp. 58–62. Detroit: Wayne State University Press, 1973.

Reik, T. (1926). The psychological meaning of silence. English translation in *Psychoanalytic Review* 55:172–186, 1968.

Rilke, R. M. (1910). *The Notebooks of Malte Laurids Brigge.* Quoted in G. Bachelard, *The Poetics of Space,* trans. M. Jolas, p. 57, Boston: Beacon Press, 1969.

——— (1939). *Duino Elegies.* Trans. J. Leishman and S. Spender. New York: W. W. Norton.

Roustang, F. (1980). *Psychoanalysis Never Lets Go,* p. 97. Trans. N. Lukacher. Baltimore: Johns Hopkins University Press, 1983.

Schachtel, E. (1959). *Metamorphosis.* New York: Basic Books.

Schiller, J. C. F. (1800). *On the Naive and Sentimental in Literature.* Trans. H. Watanabe-O'Kelly. Manchester, England: Carcanet, 1981.

Schneiderman, S. (1983). *Jacques Lacan: The Death of an Intellectual Hero.* Cambridge, MA: Harvard University Press.

Schur, M. (1972). *Freud: Living and Dying,* p. 247. New York: International Universities Press.

Schwarz, A. (1969). *The Complete Works of Marcel Duchamp.* London: Thames and Hudson.

Searles, H. (1975). The patient as therapist to his analyst. In *Tactics and Techniques in Psychoanalytic Theory,* ed. P. Giovacchini, pp. 95–151. Northvale, NJ: Jason Aronson.

Segal, H. (1973). *Introduction to the Work of Melanie Klein.* New York: Basic Books.

Socaridis, D., and Stolorow, R. (1984). Affects and selfobjects. In *Annual of Psychoanalysis,* vols. 12 and 13, ed. Chicago Institute of Psychoanalysis. New York: International Universities Press.

Sontag, S. (1964). Against interpretation. In *Against Interpretation and Other Essays,* p. 14. New York: Delta, 1966.

———— (1967). The pornographic imagination. In *Styles of Radical Will*, p. 60. New York: Delta, 1978.

———— (1969). The aesthetics of silence. In *Styles of Radical Will*, p. 3. New York: Delta, 1978.

Stevens, W. (1947). "Someone Puts a Pineapple Together." In *The Palm at the End of the Mind*, ed. H. Stevens, p. 298. New York: Vintage, 1972.

Stolorow, R., and Atwood, G. (1978). *Faces in a Cloud*. Northvale, NJ: Jason Aronson.

Stolorow, R., et al. (1983). Intersubjectivity in psychoanalytic treatment. *Bulletin of the Menninger Clinic* 47:2, 117–128.

Stolorow, R. (1987). *Psychoanalytic Treatment: An Intersubjective Approach*. New York: Analytic Press.

Sulloway, F. (1979). *Freud, Biologist of the Mind*. New York: Basic Books.

Tournier, M. (1969). *Friday*. Trans. N. Denny. New York: Doubleday.

Tuan, Y-F. (1982). *Segmented Worlds and Self: Group Life and Individual Consciousness*. Minneapolis: University of Minnesota Press.

Turkle, S. (1978). *Psychoanalytic Politics: Freud's French Revolution*, pp. 106–108. New York: Basic Books.

Unger, L. (1966). *T. S. Eliot: Moments and Patterns*. Minneapolis: University of Minnesota Press.

Valéry, P. (1971). La Voix des Choses. In *Poems*. Princeton, NJ: Princeton University Press.

Viderman, S. (1979). The analytic space: meaning and problems. *Psychoanalytic Quarterly* 48: 257–291.

White, M., and Weiner, M. (1986). *The Theory and Practice of Self Psychology*. New York: Brunner/Mazel.

Winnicott, D. W. (1952). Anxiety associated with insecurity. In *Through Pediatrics to Psycho-Analysis*. London: Hogarth, 1975.

———— (1953). Transitional objects and transitional phenomena. In *Collected Papers: Through Pediatrics to Psycho-analysis*, pp. 229–242. London: Tavistock, 1958.

_____ (1958). The capacity to be alone. In *The Maturational Processes and the Facilitating Environment*. New York: International Universities Press, 1965.

_____ (1968). Playing: its theoretical status in the clinical situation. *International Journal of Psycho-Analysis* 49:4, 591–599.

_____ (1971). *Playing and Reality*. New York: Basic Books.

_____ (1977). The squiggle technique. In *The Psychiatric Treatment of the Child*, ed. J. F. McDermott, Jr., and S. I. Harrison, pp. 35–74. Northvale, NJ: Jason Aronson.

Wittgenstein, L. (1960). *The Blue and Brown Books*. New York: Harper Colophon.

Woolf, V. (1919). *The Diary of Virginia Woolf*, vol. 1, p. 262. London: Hogarth, 1977.

Wortis, J. (1954). Fragments of an analysis. In *Freud As We Knew Him*, ed. H. Ruitenbeek, pp. 283–289. Detroit: Wayne State University Press., 1973.

Index